A COMPLETE SOMERSAULT INTO THE ORCHESTRA

COMIC AND CURIOUS CLIPPINGS FROM THE LEGENDARY THEATRICAL PAPER

THE ERA
1870 – 1880

COMPILED BY

JULIA D ATKINSON

Copyright © 2018 Julia D Atkinson

All rights reserved.

ISBN: 978-1-9997610-9-7
ISBN-13:1-9997610-9-X

THE audience at the Surrey Theatre on Thursday (11th inst.) were thrown into a state of considerable alarm by an incident that occurred which might have been attended with serious, if not fatal, consequences, but which, happily, passed off without any mischief whatsoever. During the performance of the farce of *The Doctor's Boy*, while Mary (Miss Nellie Russell) and Tom Gabb (Mr Harry Taylor) were in front of the stage, close to the orchestra, Miss Russell appeared to slip; one of her feet caught the guard of the footlights, and she fell forward, and made a complete somersault into the orchestra. The event was so sudden that everyone present was completely astounded for the moment, and it was feared that the young lady must have been seriously injured, particularly as a piercing scream was heard immediately after the fall. Happily, however, she was unhurt, and in a minute or two reappeared on the stage, and the performance proceeded.

The Era, 21st January 1877

CONTENTS

ACKNOWLEDGEMENTS.....i

1 – 1870: IT WAS NOT LIKE MISS HAMILTON'S NOSE.....3

2 – 1871: EACH CAT WAS PROVIDED WITH A SPITTOON.....9

3 – 1872: WHY SHOULD WE THRUST MORE TREATS UPON THEM?.....17

4 – 1873: THE BAND STOPPED THEIR SOMBRE PRISON MUSIC.....24

5 – 1874: A D-----M S-----, A B-----D T-----F, AND A B-----Y LIAR.....30

6 – 1875: FIVE MURDERS, SEVEN SUICIDES, AND EIGHT GHOSTS.....44

7 – 1876: A GLASS OF STOUT IN HER BONNET.....58

8 – 1877: ENLARGED PHOTOGRAPHS OF LOVELY YOUNG MEN.....71

9 – 1878: A TARGET FOR FLORA'S ARROWS.....82

10 – 1879: DON'T CHOKE THE BALLET.....96

11 – 1880: THROWN WITH GREAT VIOLENCE INTO A CHINA SHOP.....107

INDEX.....115

ABOUT THE AUTHOR.....119

ACKNOWLEDGEMENTS

Many thanks to the British Newspaper Archive for making *The Era*, and many other fascinating vintage newspapers, available online.

The cover was designed by Maduranga Sampath of MSN Art Studio.

The back cover image is of the 1878 poster and playbill for *H.M.S. Pinafore* at the Opera Comique, London. This image, the author of which is unknown, is in the public domain because it is an artistic work other than a photograph which was made available to the public more than 70 years ago (before 1 January 1948). It is in the public domain in the United States of America because it was published (or registered with the U.S. Copyright Office) before 1 January 1923.

INTRODUCTION

First published in 1838, *The Era* started out as a journal owned by, and dedicated to the interests of, members of the public-house business. After a shaky start the paper passed into the ownership of Frederick Ledger, who edited *The Era* for three decades and expanded its coverage to include Freemasonry, sport, and – above all – the theatre, music hall and popular entertainment in general. Between the 1850s and the beginning of the First Word War *The Era* was required reading for actors, music hall artistes, musicians, and indeed everyone connected with the theatrical profession (the paper lingered on until 1939 as a shadow of its former self). Performers used its columns to find work and companies to find theatres; reviews and gossip columns helped members of the public to find sources of entertainment and keep abreast of the doings of their favourite stars.

1
1870
IT WAS NOT LIKE MISS HAMILTON'S NOSE

DREADFUL CATASTROPHE AT THE BRISTOL THEATRE.
One of the most tragic and terrible catastrophes it has ever fallen to our lot to chronicle, and by which eighteen poor creatures were, at a few moments' warning, hurried into eternity, took place on Monday night at the New Theatre in Park Row. Mr Chute having issued an attractive programme, thousands flocked, as usual, to witness the performance. The entrance to the pit and gallery is down a passage about twenty feet wide, leading from Park Row. There is a steep gradient from the level of the road, and at the bottom of the passage there is a sharp turning, leading, at right angles, to the gallery on the left. The door to the pit is situated also on the left-hand side, but about two feet higher up, and consequently nearer the roadway.

It is, of course, impossible to compute the exact number of persons in the passage; but it is stated by several policemen, who were near the spot, that nearly 2,000 persons were were endeavouring to gain admission either to the pit or the gallery, the crowd extending some distance into the roadway. Directly the doors were opened those behind pushed forward, heedless of the cries of those in front of them. Women and children were screaming for help, and even strong men seemed powerless to act. The tide behind was too strong to be resisted. Those behind called "Forward!" but in vain those in front called "Back!" They might as well have appealed to the waves to stay their progress. The momentarily gathering crowd outside – ignorant, of course, of the imminent danger of those packed in the passage – pressed on with all their energy.

Things at this juncture looked ugly enough, when a new alarm arose. Some one, desirous of restraining the impetuous advance of those behind, called out "Fire!" A panic was the result. Men, women, and children immediately made a frantic effort to drive back those coming in. In consequence of this movement a woman about fifty years of age fell down, and others fell upon her. The crowd began to sway backwards and forwards, and those who were down were trampled upon. The scene was now a most terrible one. Screams and moans rent the air. Cries for assistance were made in vain. People were pushed down and trampled underfoot, and when once down it was almost impossible to recover their footing.

As soon as the crowd had to some extent cleared away a sad spectacle met the view. Bodies were lying about the passage in various spots. A boy named Charles Talbot, living at South Green Street, Hotwell Road, was the first rescued, and he was found to be very seriously injured. Police-constable 95 took him to the shop of Mr Saunders, chemist, at the top of Park Street, who considered him in a dangerous condition, and advised his immediate removal to the infirmary. He was taken to that institution, but died soon after his admission. In the meantime other bodies were picked up, and sixty or seventy policemen were soon in attendance, and they at once drew a cordon round the entrance to the passage, thus preventing any one from getting admission. Meanwhile a number of bodies had been removed, and it was found that fourteen were quite dead. The bodies of all these were laid out in the lower refreshment-room of the Theatre, and no one except the representatives of the Press were allowed to see them. Eight persons whose condition appeared to be very precarious were taken instantly to the infirmary, where every attention was paid them. Three, however, did not yield to the treatment, and died after they had only been a short time in the institution. […] An inquest was opened on the bodies on Tuesday afternoon, before the City Coroner, Mr H.S. Wasborough, at the Griffin Inn, Griffin Street. The Jury proceeded to view the bodies, and evidence of identity having being given, the inquiry was adjourned. On Thursday the inquest was resumed, when the Jury, after fifteen minutes' consultation, returned a verdict of Accidental Death, fully exonerating the Proprietor of the Theatre from all blame. (From the *Western Daily Press.*) The *Bristol Daily Post* says, and our own correspondent attests the accuracy of the statement: –

It may be worth mentioning that the catastrophe remained all but entirely unknown in the inside of the house until the performance closed and the audience came out. A sudden stoppage of the receipts drew the pit money and check takers to the matter at once, and we believe that they joined the efforts employed to get out the sufferers. The Manager, treasurer and officials in attendance on the boxes were likewise necessarily informed of the sad event. Beyond them, however, scarcely any one before the curtain was aware of it, and on the stage the secret was confined to the Stage Manager, the head carpenter, and one or two others. We are assured by a member of the orchestra that he played through the night without the smallest suspicion that anything was amiss, and that when he heard the mournful tidings on quitting the house he was as much pained and astonished as ever he had been in his life. It was a most fortunate thing that this ignorance so widely prevailed, for, as had been already remarked, a panic within the Theatre might have proved even more disastrous than that which ended so tragically without.

ON Wednesday evening, during the Transformation Scene at Astley's Theatre, a ballet girl named Hunterini was strapped to an iron support attached to a trap, in order to be raised to her position in the scene. After the machinery had been set in motion it was found that the person in charge of the trap had neglected to open it, and in an instant the poor girl's head came in contact with the flooring of the stage. Before she could be liberated from her perilous position she was very much crushed and bruised, and will, in all probability, be prevented from resuming her employment for some time to come.

WANTED, the Address of AN ACTRESS, by one who promised to meet her in the Exchange, December 16th, but was prevented. Age, Twenty-five; 5ft. 5½in.; fair; full bust; near sighted. Uses gold eye-glass. Spoke of having an appointment this Christmas, Theatre Royal, Jersey. Pity poor Bogle. Address, Mr KETTLE, in care Jos. Pitt, Chelmsford.
2/1/1870

A SCENE AT ST GEORGE'S HALL, BRADFORD.
An unrehearsed scene of a most unpleasant character was enacted at St George's Hall, on Saturday evening, at the usual entertainment. A gentleman named Albert Jones, whose advent was heralded with glowing announcements as the "greatest mimic and ventriloquist of the age," was to give an entertainment entitled *A Night in London*, he was to display "that consummate mastery over the expression of the features, instantly moulded to the character he is representing, accompanied by an electric change of voice, as to appear almost supernatural, and render it the most brilliant entertainment of the day." Fresh with the recollections of Maccabe's recent pleasant visit, the public of Bradford were raised to the tiptoe of expectation by these flourishing platitudes, the result being that the hall was filled by probably 3,000 persons.

Mr Jones introduced his entertainment by some complimentary remarks, and, unfortunately for himself, his first venture was a supposed imitation of Maccabe, but it was a long way after that genuine artist. Next came John Parry's "Gloomy Party," then an attempt at ventriloquism, and a portraiture of Southern as Lord Dundreary, said to be "universally admitted by the Press of the United Kingdom as unparalleled in the annals of mimicry," the "Christy Minstrels" concluding the first part. With the exception, perhaps, of "Dundreary", none of the imitations came up to what had been expected, and the delineation of the "Minstrels" was simple buffoonery. A few ominous hisses, mingled with clapping, informed Mr Jones that his audience was not pleased. At the close of the first part he said he had a cold, promised more satisfactory results to follow, and was rewarded with applause.

The second part, however, was less relished than the first. Mr Jones gave "The Wandering Minstrel", again a long way after Maccabe, a "Stump Speech," then imitations of well-known actors, and as a conclusion "The Peepshow Man." The auditory sat patiently for some time, in the expectation apparently of something clever turning up, but, nothing coming up to satisfy them, their temper at length gave way, the most discordant sounds arose – yells, hisses, hooting, clapping, whistling, and uncomplimentary epithets being freely used; some one threw an orange at Mr Jones, and a lad in the gallery, more daring than the rest, thrust his legs over the gallery, and holding on by the iron bar, drummed with his feet. In the midst of this uproar Mr Jones made his exit, and the band followed. A portion of the audience had left, but as it was barely nine o'clock others remained, expressing their dissatisfaction.

Mr C. Ollivier, Manager of the entertainment, at length came forward, and said Mr Jones was so overcome by the immense auditory that his nerves had given way, and he was lying prostrated in the ante-room, totally unable to continue his performance. Under these circumstances Mr Ollivier trusted the audience would extend to him their kind liberality, and promised that in future the frequenters of the Saturday evening entertainment should have nothing to complain of. The audience then peaceably departed – *The Leeds Mercury*, February 8th
20/2/1870

MR EDITOR. – Sir, I have just read in a cheap evening paper "Elopement of an *Actress*." Allow me to say the person referred to was never on the stage, therefore is no more an actress than I King of Bohemia. If the paper had said "Elopement of the *Wife* of a Pantomimist," it would have stated the truth; as it is, they have stated the reverse. Why do the Press invariably drag in the name of actor and actress without the slightest ground or knowledge that they are either one or the other. They might as well call the gasman or stage carpenter's wife, who, perhaps, are engaged to wash the stage, an *actress*. It is done because they think it sells their papers? – I am, dear Sir, yours, A PROFESSIONAL.
10/4/1870

AT the Westminster Police Court a youth was convicted and fined 5s. for riding a velocipede recklessly and furiously through the public streets, "to the common danger." This is said to have been the first conviction for an offence which, in many parts of the Metropolis, has now become extensively prevalent and a perfect nuisance.
17/4/1870

ON Thursday evening, April 21st, a serious accident happened to Miss Davis, the principal dancer of the company performing at the Northampton theatre. Miss Davis was dancing near the footlights, when the high heel of one of her boots caught, it is supposed, in some irregularity on the flooring, and she was thrown forward on the footlights, and her light dress was instantly in a blaze. Her struggles threw her over the orchestra into the pit, where some gentlemen instantly wrapped her in their coats and extinguished the fire, but not before she had been terribly burnt about the arms and body. Dr Bryan was instantly sent for, and, with his son, attended immediately, and remained with the sufferer till midnight. Under the efficient medical care she will, there is good reason to hope, recover, but at the best her restoration to her Profession must be very remote. During the excitement which the accident occasioned in the house, a lad jumped from the gallery to assist in her rescue, happily without injury. We are happy to state that the sufferer is going on very favourably.
1/5/1870

TED LAURI, the Little Lump of Fun, will soon arrive from San Francisco, and will be happy to engage with Managers for Clown at Christmas. All letters addressed 6½, Oxford Street, London.
5/6/1870

A DISPUTE CONCERNING AN ACTRESS'S NOSE.
Court of Queen's Bench, Guildhall, July 1st (before Mr Justice HANNEN and a Common Jury).
A'BECKETT v. GIOVANELLI. – This was an action to recover the sum of £37 10s., for advertising, &c. The defendant pleaded never indebted.

Mr Sergeant Parry and Mr Joyce appeared for the plaintiff; Mr Philbrick for the defendant.

The plaintiff was the Proprietor of the *Tomahawk*, and the defendant was the Proprietor of Highbury Barn Tavern and Gardens. The defendant had also a Theatre on the premises, at which two popular actresses performed, Miss Hamilton and Miss Seymour, and the action was brought to recover £25, for an advertisement in the shape of a cartoon that filled the back page of the Derby number of the periodical, and £12 10s. for 2,000 copies, which the defendant intended for distribution on the Derby Day. The cartoon was described as Giovanelli's "tip" for the Derby, and the drawing represented in caricature the defendant and the two ladies riding the Derby race on Macgregor, Camel, and Sunshine, the three horses being placed in that order. The heads of the three riders were to be large and portraits, and the block was to become the defendant's property after the publication of the Derby number of the *Tomahawk* had finished on the Monday. The plaintiff's case was that he had complied with the terms of the contract, and that the defendant refused to pay.

The defendant's case was that the drawing was to be subject to his approval, and that, in order that the faces should be portraits and the figures correct, he and the ladies were separately photographed sitting on chairs, holding reins that had been fastened to a door. The drawing on the block was submitted, and approved of by the defendant, and also the engraver's proof of the faces, but either in finishing of the engraving or working the block in printing the copies Miss Hamilton's nose was so much disfigured that the defendant refused to accept the first 500 copies that were sent to him on the Saturday morning.

Mr Justice Blackburn said he was quite ready to believe that the nose in the engraving was not like the nose of any human being that ever lived, and that it was not like Miss Hamilton's nose (laughter).

The defendant having sent the first lot back on that ground, the block was altered, but with no great success, and instead of receiving all the 2,000 copies on the Monday, he only received part on that day and the remainder on Tuesday, and the consequence was he did not get the block, which he thought more of than the publication in the *Tomahawk*, in time to get his bills printed for the Derby night's performance. He contended the plaintiff had not fulfilled his contract, and he returned the whole of the copies, and now refused to pay the plaintiff's claim.

The Jury ultimately returned a verdict for the plaintiff – damages, £25.

To Equestrians or Others. WANTED, to Place a Smart AFRICAN BOY, who is an Orphan, as an APPRENTICE to a competent master. Address, M.S., King's Arms, Westminster Road, London.
3/7/1870

MR ARTHUR LLOYD has accomplished a feat never attempted by any other vocalist or public performer. He sang on Saturday last at the Canterbury Hall, Pavilion, and Sun, at Knightsbridge. On Monday night he appeared at the Theatre Royal, Edinburgh, for the benefit of his father, Mr Lloyd (the celebrated comedian, who has been for so long connected with the Edinburgh and Glasgow Theatre). He was on the stage at Edinburgh at half-past nine o'clock Monday night, and on Tuesday evening he was doing his turns at the various halls, as usual, in London, thus appearing in Edinburgh and London within twenty-four hours, and travelling a distance of over eight hundred miles, not having rested in a bed from the Saturday till the Tuesday night. Mr Arthur Lloyd felt that it was "something attempted, something done," and he had earned a night's repose.

BOW STREET. – A young man, named Charles Bailey, a medical student, and said to be very respectably connected, was yesterday charged with stealing two gold watches, a chain, &c.

It appeared that the prisoner, mistaking his ambition for the stage for the capacity of acting, had obtained a trial as a "super" at the Olympic Theatre. One evening, soon after his advent to the theatre, a gold watch and chain, belonging to Miss Nelly Joy, an actress in the company, was stolen from a tray in one of the dressing-rooms. The matter was placed in the hands of Sergeant Dowdell, of the detective force, and eventually the prisoner was taken into custody on the charge. He then confessed that he had pawned the watch, at the same time mentioning that he had buried the chain and etceteras on Barnes Common, near his residence. He stated that he had been rash enough to engage in betting transactions, and had become involved, and not getting a remittance from abroad when he expected it, was tempted to take the watch, fully expecting to return it. The watch was identified by Mr Vaughan, in the absence of the owner, as the property of Miss Joy, and the prisoner was remanded.

When the prisoner was taken into custody on this charge a pawn-broker's duplicate relating to another watch was found in his possession. This turned out to be the property of another medical student, a friend of the prisoner's, and had been pawned for £5.

The prosecutor in this case, a young gentleman at Guy's, named Hughes, stated that on the night of the 17th June last he went with the prisoner to St James's Hall to hear the Christy Minstrels. At about ten minutes to nine o'clock the prisoner said "he wanted to call on a friend in Oxford Street, and should be only gone about ten minutes." He asked witness to lend him his watch, as he did not like his friend to see him without one, as he (the friend) knew that he had got one. Witness consented, and waited at the Hall till the performance was over, and some time afterwards, but he never returned with the watch, and witness never saw it again. He knew where the prisoner lived, and applied to him for it afterwards; but he pretended he had dropped it, while in the act of winding it up, and had taken it to a goldsmith's to be repaired. The watch was worth £20.

The prisoner, in reference to both charges, stated that he was in temporary difficulty through rashly gambling, and hoped to have received his remittance in time to redeem the watches.

The Sergeant said that the prisoner had given every information required as to the disposal of the property.

The prisoner begged for leniency, not on his own behalf, but in consideration of an aged father and an afflicted mother, who were living abroad.

Mr Vaughan said that he should have thought of them before. He had committed the felonies, and there was but one course open to him as a Magistrate, and that was to commit him for trial.*

The prosecutors and witnesses were then bound over in the usual way.

The prisoner, a married man whose name is elsewhere given as Clement Bayley, was sentenced to six months' imprisonment. Halfway through his sentence he died of fever at the age of twenty.
17/7/1870

FROM THE CONVENT TO THE STAGE. – A young lady who was mixed up in the Hull convent case, "Saurin v. Starr," is now fulfilling an engagement at the Alhambra Music Hall, Nottingham. It may be remembered that while at Hull Miss Saurin had the supervision of the convent school, in which a Miss Bessie Armytage was a teacher. One of the "sins" of insubordination laid to the charge of Miss Saurin was that on one occasion she put back the school clock. Miss Saurin denied the accusation, and a subpoena was issued for the attendance of Miss Armytage, who in the witness-box confessed that she committed the "sinful" act. On leaving Hull Miss Armytage joined Madame Tonneller's Opera Company, and for the last two or three years she had been singing at Music Halls. She is a young lady of prepossessing appearance, and has a fine contralto voice. At the Alhambra, on Monday night, she sang

the popular old ballad "I cannot mind my wheel, mother," and the merry laughing song "I'll be no submissive wife."
21/8/1870

MODEST assurance is an essential qualification for every actor, and, when not overstepped, materially assists to ensure success. That the members of the Marlborough Dramatic Club, hailing from Derby, as our Scotch friends would say, are not devoid of that qualification is shown by the following characteristic letter, lately addressed to Mr Sefton, the Secretary of Mr Sothern, who conducts that gentleman's business arrangements during his Provincial tour. Were such requests as those of the Derby amateurs generally made and complied with, we should have more of the amateur nuisance than already exists, and the actor would be doubly robbed of his bread, first by the would-be performers occupying the stage on which only properly educated actors should appear, and secondly by their claiming admission to all places of amusement at reduced prices. Amateurs are very well in their proper places, but when they want to learn how to deport themselves on the stage they should not begrudge the necessary fee: –

THE MARLBOROUGH AMATEUR DRAMATIC CLUB.
Derby, September 10th, 1870.
Dear Sir, – The acting members of this Club (twelve in number) desire me to convey to you their compliments, and to ask whether, upon the approaching visit of Mr Sothern to this town, they may be permitted free admission upon presenting their card of membership (as enclosed, which please return), and a lady friend (or wife), at half-price?
Yours faithfully, HENRY G. CHURCHILL, Secretary and Treasurer.
25/9/1870

A VERY serious accident befel Miss Julia Leicester, the leading actress at the Stockton-on-Tees Theatre on Friday week. During the performance of the burlesque of *Cinderella* Mr Sidney, Jr., and Miss Leicester, as Prince Poppetti, were performing the swing dance, and whilst revolving with clasped hands at great speed Mr Sidney suddenly and without warning loosed his hold from his partner, and they being at the moment in front of the footlights the lady fell with terrible force backwards into the orchestra, and was picked up insensible. Although no bones were broken Miss Leicester is severely bruised, and likely to be confined to her bed for some time.
13/11/1870

CHARLEY. – You are earnestly entreated to Write home at once, to your Aunt in the North, to your Uncle at Taunton, your Cousin in Harley Street, or to your FATHER, Brook Street, Hanover Square, London. Matters may possibly not be so serious as you fancy.
27/11/1870

2
1871
EACH CAT WAS PROVIDED WITH A SPITTOON

"WHITTINGTON AND HIS CAT," at the Theatre Royal, Bradford, appears to have created a *furore*, hundreds being turned away on many occasions, but on Saturday last the excitement reached a climax somewhat alarming. Nearly two hours before the time for opening many hundreds were clamouring at the "extra doors," which were opened very early; still the multitudes increased as train after train arrived from surrounding towns (one train alone consisting of twenty-six carriages). This continued until the band was heard by those struggling outside, who then became furious, and with a sudden rush burst open the other doors, only to find the place crammed, while those outside vented their rage by smashing the windows. It was only on the Manager's haranguing them that they could be dispersed.
29/1/1871

DEATH OF A JUVENILE PANTOMIMIC ACTOR. – On Tuesday evening Dr Hardwicke, Deputy Coroner, held an inquest at the Belvedere Tavern, Pentonville Hill, on the body of Frederick Robert Herbert, aged eleven years, who was engaged to appear in the character of a frog at the Opening of the Pantomime at Covent Garden Theatre. Dr Sheehy said the post-mortem examination revealed no marks of violence externally, but the congested state of the head led him to attribute the cause of death to congestion of the brain, from external violence – either a blow or fall.
    Samuel William Thorn, a dresser engaged at the theatre, said he had twenty boys under his control from the ages of seven to fifteen years. He remembered on the night of the 10th inst. being told that a lad had thrown a stick and struck deceased on the head. He took him out of the room, which was underneath the stage, to the bar, and there placed a quart pot to his head, and afterwards bathed it with vinegar. There was a large swelling on his forehead. He did not hear him complain after night, and he came to his business as usual. The lad who was accused of throwing the stick gave his version of the affair. He said they were playing together when the stick slipped out of his hand. He disclaimed any intention of injuring the deceased. Thorn said the boys waited, as they were not allowed about the stage until it actually came to their turn to go on; but the boys were very unruly, and in addition to himself and assistant there were two policemen to look after them and keep them in order. The Jury returned a verdict of Accidental Death.
5/2/1871

COUNT BISMARCK. – That prince of entertainers and comic writers, the late Artemus Ward, in referring to Bismarck, speaks of him as that gifted but bald-headed "Prooshun:" but curiously enough, as though actuated by a spirit of prophecy, hopes that when the time comes he will be moderate and gentle in his hour of "triump." That hour has at length arrived; stern, and but little open to persuasive influences, the great German statesman will, no doubt, follow out the dictates of his own iron will. Gifted he will most assuredly be found, but bald-headed he would not remain if he could be induced to listen to friendly counsel and avail himself of the inestimable reproductive powers possessed by "ROWLAND'S MACASSAR OIL." – (ADVT)

DIED at St Petersburg, Russia, on January 8th, 1871, from cramp, through the intensity of the climate, Mr William Gilbert, for many years cornet player at the Exchange Music Hall, West Bromwich. A widow and three children are left to mourn the loss of a kind husband and father.
19/2/1871

DURING last week the celebrated Wizard of the North had been performing in the Athenaeum, Sunderland, to large audiences. On Friday evening, the 10th inst., the performance terminated amidst a scene of disorder not often witnessed.

During the evening Mr Anderson had made continual references to the Continental war, to Bismarck, Germany, and Germans, in anything but complimentary terms. In the front seats were the German Consul, his wife, and a party of friends. Another gentleman, the head of a German firm in the town, gave a denial to the statements of the Wizard, and this seemed only the more to irritate him. Just before the close of the performance, Mr Anderson stepping forward, and, claiming to be independent of any party, and to hold opinions of his own, stated that his agent (Mr Hodges) had told him that he ought not to have spoken as he did in the presence of the German Consul, and his daughter then (pointing to Miss Anderson at the pianoforte) had declined to play "The Marseillaise" because of the presence of the German Consul. "Who," Mr Anderson asked, "was the German Consul? What was he?" He thanked him for his patronage, but no more; and then went on to say that if the German Consul had been in his place he would have been at the Lyceum Theatre, where Mr Davis had one of the most crowded houses of the season for the French Distress Fund – a statement that was met with a prompt rejoinder from a gentleman who had just left the Theatre. Mr Anderson went on to say that the Germans should have been fighting for their country, and proceeded in a most offensive strain, which called up the German merchant previously mentioned, who protested that they had come there to see the Professor's tricks, not to hear his politics.

A scene of indescribable confusion followed; the audience at the back part of the hall got on to the seats, some hissing the German merchant and others the Professor; the occupants of the front seats rose and took their departure, including the German Consul and his friend. The Professor, excited, was declaiming from the stage, the German merchant was on his feet appealing for a hearing, when the Wizard fired a pistol, a lot of ducks scrambled out of a tub of water, and the performance broke up amidst much disorder.
19/2/1871

HOAX AT THE YORK THEATRE. – Mr Henry Corri's Opera Company was announced to appear at this theatre, for six nights only, commencing on Monday last with *Il Trovatore*. A very large multitude of people assembled, St Leonard's Place being lined with cabs and private carriages, and the Theatre was lit up, but the doors kept closed. About half-past eight Mr Hawkins, Mr Coleman's deputy, announced outside the Theatre that the company had not arrived, but could not give any reason why they had not come. At this the "roughs" began to be very excited, and would, no doubt, have done great damage to the Theatre had it not been for the interference of the police. On Tuesday evening *Lucrezia Borgia* was announced, when a large number of people again assembled, no notice being issued by the Lessee of the Theatre whether the company would appear or not. Threats of all kinds were uttered on this occasion, but the mob was quietly got away. All sorts of rumours are afloat as to the reason the company did not appear.

MR EDITOR. – Sir, in last week's *Era* I saw an advertisement in which a Mr Harry Sefton styles himself the "original Dancing Spider." Now, as I have been known for some years as the Dancing Spider (in consequence of my peculiar style of dancing in black tights), I should like to know from him who is the original Dancing Spider. If he can give me proof that he performed under that title prior to October 26th, 1866, I will most willingly crawl out of the web; otherwise I shall continue to subscribe myself ZIPO, the original Dancing Spider, Bones, and Comedian, of Dwight's Maryland Minstrels.
5/3/1871

PAINFUL DEATH OF A VOCALIST AT MANCHESTER. – An inquest was held last Wednesday, by Mr Herford, in reference to the death of William Percival, late of 20, Roe Street, Livesey Street. The deceased was a professional singer, and was thirty-seven years of age.

Mary Makin, a servant at Mr Barratt's, Victoria Music Hall, Victoria Bridge, said that the deceased sometimes sang there. On Tuesday morning, between eleven and twelve, he came down to the Hall and went to the water-closet. About one o'clock Mrs Barratt said she thought she heard somebody snoring in the water-closet. Snoring was heard again, but no one could get in. Mr Barratt came home about four o'clock, and he had the door burst open. The deceased was lying on the floor, and he thought he was drunk. He left him lying there for about twenty minutes. They all thought he was drunk, although he was perfectly sober when he came down in the morning. At five o'clock he was taken out of the closet, and placed for about half an hour before the fire. A cab was then sent for, and he was taken home. A doctor attended him, who said he was suffering from apoplexy, and the man died at ten o'clock at night. After other evidence confirmatory of their statements had been given, the Jury returned a verdict that the deceased had died from apoplexy, aggravated by want of proper medical aid. They censured Mr and Mrs Barratt for their conduct.
9/4/1871

RYE V. LAMB. – This was a singular action, tried before the County Court Judge of Sandwich (W.C. Scott, Esq.)

The facts of the case were these: The plaintiff was an organist at Canterbury and a teacher of music, and he had made arrangements for giving a concert at Sandwich some weeks ago, and he had engaged Messrs Rhodes and Plant, and Mr Henry Collard, a former pupil of his own. This latter, it seemed, was a little gentleman, who, it was expected, would prove a great attraction, inasmuch as he is smaller than Tom Thumb, and known, from his superior vocalisation, as the "Pocket Sims Reeves." This diminutive gentleman arrived at Sandwich at half-past six, and partook of tea with the other *artistes*. Shortly afterwards the plaintiff was surprised to hear the town crier announcing the concert was not likely to take place, because Mr Collard was obliged to be in London that night to perform at Drury Lane Theatre. This was the grievance complained of, and it was alleged that the defendant had sent round the crier, and the consequence was that many persons did not attend the concert, and that plaintiff suffered seriously through it. The plaintiff said that he had spoken to the crier, but he refused to give up the name of the person employing him. He considered that he had lost nearly 100 customers through this announcement.

The crier himself was called, and said that he was appointed by the Magistrates. He did not know who the announcement was written by, but it was to the following effect: – "The inhabitants of Sandwich will be pleased to take notice that Mr H. Collard, the Pocket Sims Reeves, who is advertised to take part in the concert this evening at the Bell Hotel, is also announced in the morning papers to appear at ten o'clock at the Drury Lane Theatre, London."

It was submitted on the part of the defendant that the action was a trumpery one, and if brought at all it should have been for slander.

The Judge, without calling witnesses, said the plaintiff had not made out his case, and found for defendant with costs. *16/4/1871*

AN interesting discussion is going on concerning the disputed point whether Mrs Rousby, or rather Joan of Arc, ought to be burned or not at the Queen's Theatre. Hitherto the critics have had it all their own way. They are decidedly of the opinion that the burning of Joan of Arc is a disgusting sight. But Mr Ryder steps forward to say that the fair heroine is, after all, only burned a very little, and another correspondent goes so far as to say that there is nothing he delights in so much as burned women, and that had Joan of Arc not been burned he would have considered the whole thing a do and a disappointment. *Quot homines tot sententiae*. There is no accounting for tastes.

HOLBORN THEATRE, LONDON. WANTED, SYMMETRICAL YOUNG LADIES, for the Ballet of the above Theatre. Apply on Monday, at Twelve o'clock, to Madame COLLIER, 33, Ravensdon Street, Kennington Cross.
23/4/1871

PABLO FANQUE (William Darby)* died on the 14th inst., at the Britannia Inn, Stockport, aged sixty-seven. He was well known in the Equestrian Profession as an experienced Circus Proprietor, possessing a kind, benevolent heart, and always behaving liberally to everyone he employed. His wife, son (Edward), Mrs Birkett (mother-in-law), Alec Cooper, and Mr H. Montague were present at his decease. The latter had been his Manager for many years, and sincerely regrets his loss, as well as will numerous friends, and a great number of his old pupils will long remember their good-natured and clever tutor.
Pablo Fanque (born William Darby) was Britain's only black circus proprietor. His name was immortalised by the Beatles in Being For the Benefit of Mr. Kite!
7/5/1871

ONE of our Liverpool correspondents who was accidentally in the Theatre Royal, Manchester, last Saturday night, says: – "One of the most amusing yet unexpected sensation scenes ever witnessed in a Theatre occurred at the Theatre Royal, Manchester, on Saturday night last. The curtain drew up for Mr Toole to address the court in *Bardell v. Pickwick*, when the whole of the jury mysteriously disappeared, their 'box' suddenly giving way and engulfing the 'good men and true.' At first the vast audience who crowded every part of the Theatre were silent, fearing some dreadful accident had occurred; but as the unlucky jurymen rapidly reappeared unhurt, although looking very foolish, they broke out into a perfect hurricane of laughter, which lasted several minutes. The curtain had to be dropped to allow the jury to be 'boxed' again, and when Mr Toole began his address he provoked another burst of risibility by alluding to the jury as 'that worthy body of steadfast and immovable men.' A particularly amusing feature of this novel scene was the fact that the majority of the 'jury' were stage carpenters, and they suffered in this case from their own carelessness."
28/5/1871

CAT SHOW AT THE CRYSTAL PALACE.
[...]THE show was held in the Northern Nave, and here we found a large number of entries admirably arranged, under the care of Mr Wilson, of the Natural History Department of the Crystal Palace. Every cat had its cage furnished with straw and a handsome cushion in the centre. [...]
With catalogue in hand we wandered through the Show, misquoting Pope with the query, "Pray tell me, Miss, whose cat are you?" and this question we particularly applied to No. 147, in Class 25, a monstrous white animal for which a price of £50 was asked. This we learned was the property of Mrs Crundell, who can truthfully say, "What a monstrous tail our cat has got." But if Mrs Crundell's cat is worth £50, what shall we say of Mrs Maguire's French African, aged ten years, and valued at *five hundred pounds*? Imagine "mice, and rats, and such small deer," being kept down with an outlay of £500. But most probably Mrs Maguire's magnificent creature is never permitted to condescend to such ignoble pursuits as the destruction of vermin. So aristocratic a cat would never be a ratcatcher, and her

days are probably passed in placid ease and comfort. A great attraction in the Show was the Scotch wild cat, exhibited by his Grace the Duke of Sunderland; but in our presence the little tiger was as tame as our own domestic mouser, and neither spit nor scratched nor dashed itself against the bars of its cage, as we were led to expect. Mr S. Carleigh, well known in the Music Hall world, exhibited a cat with twenty-six claws, and this *lusus naturae** excited not a little curiosity. Then there was the Refreshment Department cat, the envy of all other cats in the Show, by reason of the good things in the power of Messrs Bertram and Roberts to supply. There were some splendid specimens of the Persian cat, and No. 50, a huge black animal, originally belonging to the late Lord Palmerston, and now shown by Mr Tanner, of Hanwell, was an object of much remark. No. 63, a Persian cat, it was stated, was *brought to this country on the shoulders of an Arab*; but the force of meaning of this we failed to comprehend. In Class 19 Miss Hales exhibited a beautiful spotted tabby and three kittens, the said kittens being valued at ten shillings each. The heaviest cat in the Show was No. 118, Class 25, shown by Mr Amos, and weighing 21¾lbs. Each cat was curiously enough provided *with a spittoon*, and although we know that Puss is addicted to late hours, we have yet to learn that smoking is to be numbered among her bad habits.

The cats, for once, behaved with great propriety, and during the whole of the day we heard not so much as a single mew. "Care will kill a cat," says an old writer, but the Crystal Palace cats evidently had no care, and in the majority of cases they passed the day in peaceful repose, doubtless congratulating themselves on the fact that, in common with babies and barmaids and horses and dogs, they have been thought worthy of public exhibition.

*Sport of nature.
This was the first British cat show, and was attended by twenty thousand people.
16/7/1871

WANTED, August 9th, a Good LADEY ZINGER, to Zing Zum Funney Zongs at a Foresters' Fete in Zummerzetshire. Lowest Terms. Mr EDGAR KING, Adcroft Villa, Trowbridge, Wilts.
30/7/1871

SUICIDE OF AN ACROBAT IN THE HOUSE OF CORRECTIONS. – Last Tuesday evening Dr Lankester, the Coroner for Central Middlesex, held an inquiry at the House of Corrections, Coldbath Fields, respecting the death of a prisoner, named Joseph Smith, aged forty-two years, an acrobat. James Ford, a warder in the prison, said that the deceased was brought into the prison on the 5th inst. On Saturday morning last he had charge of the deceased, and was conducting him to his cell. Upon reaching the top gallery of the left wing of the prison, deceased ran a few paces before the witness, and after turning round and laughing, suddenly leapt over the railings, and fell a distance of thirty-four feet. Deceased was at once taken to the infirmary, where he expired ten minutes after the occurrence. William Smith, of 5, Shepherd's Place, Homerton, said that the deceased was his brother. He used to perform in circuses and music halls. There was insanity in the family, his father having been confined for fifteen months in an unsound state of mind. Witness did not know until after the occurrence had taken place that his brother was in gaol for theft. The Jury, after a short deliberation, returned a verdict, "That deceased destroyed his life while in a state of temporary insanity."

DISGRACEFUL ATTACK UPON HERR BANDMAN AND HIS WIFE IN VIRGINIA CITY.
The following disgraceful scene which occurred on the 2nd of May, upon the occasion of Herr Bandman's farewell benefit, is given by the *Gold Hill News*: –

There were only nine ladies in the dress circle, and about twice as many gentlemen; the parquet contained merely a few dozen men and boys. The third act of *Hamlet* was given by way of a commencement, with Mr Bandman as the Danish Prince and Mrs Bandman as Ophelia. At the close of the act loud applause, from the parquet principally, called for him to appear before the curtain, but he did not respond, evidently thinking the audience was "guying" him. This act was followed by the fourth act of *Romeo and Juliet*, Mrs Bandman appearing as Juliet, in the rendition of which character she was very justly applauded.

Don Caesar de Bazan was the concluding piece, but it was interrupted and totally closed out in a most outrageous and and summary manner not contemplated in the bills. Mrs Bandman as Maritana, Mr Hurdie as Don Jose, and Colton as the King of Spain, duly made their appearance on the stage, and commenced playing their parts all right. When Mr Bandman in his personation of Don Caesar at the proper time came out upon the stage and faced the audience, a crowd of rude boys and men who had evidently gathered for the purpose at the rear portion of the parquet, beneath the dress circle, saluted him with a fearful blast from numerous tin horns and trumpets, accompanied by the infernal clangour of cow-bells. Mr Bandman advanced to the footlights amid the terrific din, bowing low, smiling, and kissing his hands to the audience as though in the magnanimous acknowledgment of a pleasing and merited compliment. His anger, however, got the better of him, and there he stood, loudly vociferating, with fierce gestures, for some minutes, apparently telling his rude insulters what he thought of them, yet no one could hear a word he was saying.

Mrs Bandman came to him, and at length succeeded in leading him off the stage. She came back directly, and the noise having subsided as the drop curtain went down, she addressed a few words to the audience, being evidently much excited, and taking the insult to herself. She sarcastically thanked the perpetrators of the insult, and said that in all her professional travels throughout the world she had never been so cruelly and wrongfully insulted as on this present occasion.

She retired with applause, and soon afterwards Stage Manager Hardie came before the curtain, and said a few words to the still waiting and expectant audience. He deprecated the uncourteous and insulting treatment of Mr Bandman, and stated that as there were ladies and gentlemen who had paid for admission, now all was orderly and quiet once more, with their permission the play might go on. His remarks were received with applause, and the play might probably have proceeded without any further interruption.

Mrs Bandman now came out again, still naturally much excited and affected, and made another short and appropriate address to the audience. She said: – "It is impossible for the play to go on under the circumstances. I dare not have my husband come out again, for he is very indignant. It is impossible to proceed with this play. When my husband married me in England, he promised me a kind welcome and warm friendly reception in his adopted country, America, wherever we might go; and this is the way the people of Washoe treat us. This is the first time we were ever so insulted, and the curtain obliged to come down on one of our plays. If you did not like him, and would insult him, you might, at least, have been gentlemen enough not to have insulted a woman. When American actors come to England, no matter how poor they are – and we have had some very poor ones appear there – we have always treated them courteously, and see how differently you treat me. We have done here, and shall go elsewhere, but wherever we may go in this world we shall remember this night as long as we live, and never, never, never come back to Virginia City again!"

Her remarks were well spoken, and much applauded at various points, as well as at the conclusion. The play did not proceed, but the gas being turned off, the audience went home.
20/8/1871

AN inquest was held in Jersey on Monday on the body of Caroline Ellen Palmer Gee, an actress, aged nineteen, who died from drinking cyanide of potassium. Deceased, who was about to leave the island for an engagement in England, had some words with her father, a photographer, regarding the cording of her boxes. She rushed from the room where the family was sitting, and saying she was choking went to the dark-room where the chemicals were kept, poured some drinking water into a jug containing twenty grains of potassium, drank off the mixture, and died in two hours.
10/9/1871

EXTRAORDINARY SCENE AT THE THEATRE ROYAL, BIRMINGHAM.
On Saturday last Mr Barry Sullivan's first appearance this season as Richard III was the occasion of the most extraordinary scene ever witnessed, certainly, in this town. No sooner were the doors opened than an immense crowd took possession of the Theatre, and by the time the overture began, it was quite perceptible to the "knowing ones" that, even then, too many persons had already been admitted, and yet they still poured in, filling up every nook and corner of the vast building.

On Mr Barry Sullivan's first entrance as the Duke of Gloucester he was received with a welcome that made the house shake to its very foundations. From this time, indeed, the scene baffles all description, for the increasing pressure in gallery, pit and boxes led to many unseemly rows, and a continuous and deafening din, to the great discomfort of the occupants of the dress circle, and to the no small annoyance of the actors on the stage. Indeed, the first three acts were little better than dumb show, not a word being heard; and it was only after the Stage Manager appeared before the "floats," and, in a coaxing speech, implored them to be silent, that the slightest approach to order was restored; still, up to the fall of the curtain, the natural discontent of half-suffocated men and women now and again found expression in loud wailings. Such a scene of confusion and hubbub has hitherto been unknown here, even on Boxing Night. Mr Barry Sullivan may well be proud of his great popularity in Birmingham; but still we question very much whether he would, a second time, care to pass through such a terrible ordeal as that of Saturday last.
17/9/1871

Attention is Solicited to ALLISTON'S SENSATION WIG, which, at the will of the Wearer, is made to stand erect or lie smooth, producing very funny effects, and, of course, provoking roars of laughter. Price, 15s. and 20s. The higher priced Wig represents the Hair standing up all over the Head. The 15s. Wig has One Flapper and the 20s. Wig Three. The effect of either is good. ALLISTON, 422, Strand (Corner of Bedford Street). Established 1843. A Large Stock of Superior Wigs for Private Wear and Genteel Comedy always on hand.
22/10/1871

HAMLET AS POLICEMAN – LUDICROUS SCENE. – On Friday night, the 3rd inst., the large audience which assembled in the Theatre Royal, South Shields, to witness the performance of *Hamlet*, were the spectators of an amusing and at the same time time somewhat ridiculous interpolation in the middle of the play. The title role was sustained by Mr Goddard Whyatt, Lessee of the Theatre, and just as that gentleman had delivered, amidst dead silence, the famous soliloquy commencing "To be or not to be," and as he was about to address Ophelia, a drunken individual in the gallery suddenly allowed a loud volley of oaths to escape him. Mr Whyatt immediately left the stage and Ophelia, and in a minute was seen in the gallery sword in hand. With the assistance of some others he summarily ejected the noisy "god." On descending to the stage, amidst the deafening applause of the audience, he preliminarily exclaimed, "Hamlet's himself again," and proceeded with his part.
12/11/1871

The "Erratics" at St George's Hall.
[…] Amateurs surely have memories, though they are destitute of talent. But on Tuesday the gay voice of the prompter was heard carolling over the other voices, and there was the old despairing glance at the prompt wing and undesirable sticking. Words fail us to describe the shabby and woe-begone scenery which does duty on all occasions at St George's Hall. For instance, a dingy city office was represented by the well-known Gothic banqueting hall, decorated with one or two sale bills for the sake of effect. The said banqueting hall, whose acquaintance we have made on the occasion of each visit to the St George's Hall, must have an inspiration similar to that of the needy country manager, who instructed his scenic artist to paint him a good stock serviceable scene – "a scene, sir, that will do for anything, from a robbers' cave to the library scene in *The School For Scandal*."
We need hardly say that our old friend the curtain was as serviceable as ever. On the tableau of the second act of the comedy the curtain positively refused to work any more, and sternly objected to descend. The audience seized the chance of laughing at something, but the intractable curtain thoroughly disgusted the characters on the stage, who, after remaining in forced and unnatural positions until they were stiff, one by one sneaked off, even down to the old gentleman, who was lying stunned full length

on the floor. He scrambled to his feet and escaped to the wings amidst roars of laughter. It is possible that amateur scene-shifters and carpenters exist as well as amateur actors. This would seem to be implied by the inevitable fun with the curtain and the scenery at amateur performances. [...]
19/11/1871

THE grand *desideratum*, a new mode of advertising, has been invented and patented by Mr D.B. Hughes, the well known scenic artist, and is nightly exhibited in the principal street in Birmingham near the Theatre Royal. The advertisements are thrown on a blank wall in a disc of light about twenty-five feet in diameter, and follow each other in rapid succession, to the great delight of hundreds who congregate to witness the display.
26/11/1871

OUR Birmingham correspondent has witnessed a new and extraordinary feat, which, when exhibited in London, will make one of the greatest sensations ever remembered. It took place at the works of Mr Inshaw, the well-known engineer in Morley Street, Birmingham. It consisted in Herr Holtum, King of the Cannon Balls, through the assistance and scientific experiments of Mr Inshaw, performing the unexampled and apparently impossible feat of catching a 20lb. cannon ball in his hands when fired from a real field piece weighing 1,500lb., and standing at any distance, the arena of his performance permitted without any danger to himself or or the spectators. The field piece is of the ordinary construction, and will bear the most strict examination, and the loading and firing were executed without the interference of the performer.
24/12/1871

3
1872
WHY SHOULD WE THRUST MORE TREATS UPON THEM?

ON Saturday morning, the 6th inst., Mr Humphreys held an inquest at the White Hart Tavern, Hoxton Street, Shoreditch, on the body of Susannah Waldron, aged seventeen, a laundress, living in Pimlico Walk, Hoxton. The evidence of Mrs Waldron, the wife of a tobacconist, showed that on the 27th ult. she and the deceased, who was her sister-in-law, went to the Variety Theatre, Pitfield Street, Hoxton. They were waiting at the foot of the gallery stairs, and the whole staircase was one closely-packed mass of human beings. A boy clambered up the balustrade to endeavour to get nearer the top of the staircase, when he knocked over a pint pot, which was in the hand of one of the people, and and the vessel falling on the head of the deceased, she received an injury which brought on inflammation of the brain, from the effects of which she died. It did not appear that the pot had been knocked down purposely, and the boy not having been identified, a verdict of Accidental Death was recorded.
14/1/1872

ON the evening of the 13th inst., a youth named John Bell fell from the gallery of the York Theatre into the pit below, and singularly escaped with his life. Mr Charles Dillon, the eminent tragedian, was impersonating the character of Hamlet, and to witness him the gallery and pit were crowded. Bell, who is about fifteen years of age and employed at some ironworks in the city, entered the former place between the first and second acts, and was making his way from the back seat to a companion who sat on one nearer the front, when some of the audience gave him a lift, and he rolled over the heads of those below, and finally over the iron guard rail, which runs along the front of the gallery, into the pit. The distance of the fall was between twenty and thirty feet. Bell fortunately alighted in such a manner across the knees of one or two of the audience that he sustained comparatively little injury. He was, however, severely shaken, and had to be carried home. The only mark he bears as the result of the accident is a dislocation of the right leg. His escape with life at all is simply miraculous. The circumstance, it need scarcely be said, caused the utmost consternation in the Theatre, but no delay in the performance was involved.
21/2/1872

ADVENTURES OF A CIRCUS CAMEL.
AT the Cork Quarter Sessions, on Monday last, an action was brought by the plaintiff, Jeremiah Desmond, a labourer, against the defendant, Mr Thomas Batty, Circus Proprietor, to recover £15 damages alleged to be sustained by the plaintiff through a camel belonging to Mr Batty entering his house and crushing him. […]

The plaintiff was examined, and deposed that on the Friday before Christmas he was sitting at the door of his own house minding some pig's food; about half-past six in the evening a "queer thing" came up to the door; he did not know what it was; he thought it was the devil (laughter); it had a long neck, big legs, and a hump "ever so big" on its back; he screamed but could not stir, being so frightened; it put its long neck and its two forepaws in and crushed him against the side of the door with its shoulder; it got a couple of feet inside the threshold, and left the print of its paws there.

Mr Hayes – And why didn't it come in further? Witness – God Almighty, sir, the hump. (Loud laughter.) The hump was so big he could not get in the door. I got such a fright that I was not able to eat as much in three days after as I would in one day before.

Mr Hayes – How did it get out? Witness – He backed out again, sir, the way he came. I could do nothing to him.

Cross-examined by Mr O'Connell – What did you think you had when you saw it? – The devil. I believe you had been talking about him? – Maybe I vor. But were you? – I vor. (Laughter.) What put him into your head that you were talking about him? – Faith, I can't tell you. But what sort of a thing was it? – My God, sir, his neck was as far as from this over to that (pointing to the jury-box, which was about fifteen feet distant). (Roars of laughter.) Had he anything on his neck? – Oh, faith, he had a hump up on his back ever so big, and he had long legs, and eyes, and a mouth. Do you see anything in court that you could compare him to? – Faith, then, I am sure, I don't. When he came in the door I would have given all the world to get him out of my sight. Did you get up off the chair? – No; a better man than me could not do it. Did you attempt to shove him out? – I did not try to shove him out. I did nothing at all to him, for I was afraid of my life of him; if you had bayonets you could not do anything at all to him. I was not able to work for four days, for I got a pain in my heart.

Mrs Desmond, the plaintiff's wife, described the position of her husband sitting at the door. She added – All at once I heard him giving a bitter screech out of him. I looked down and I saw the animal "blow" with his neck stretched in as far as he could. "Pray to the Almighty God," says I, "for it's nothing good. Pray to the Lord to save our sowls," and then I fell in a faint. (Loud laughter.)

Did you ever see the like before? – Oh, wisha, I didn't, sir. The boys about the place took the thing away afterwards.

Cross-examined by Mr O'Connell – What is that you were talking about when the camel came to the door? – My husband was blaming me for being out too long, and he was talking about ghosts and the devil. When I looked out and saw the animal, says I, "It is the devil that is there now, surely." (Loud laughter.)

Mr Hayes – That is the defence at the other side, sir – that it was the devil who was there.

Mr Gregg – Did your husband say to you, "The Devil take you?" – Witness – He did, sir.

Mr O'Connell – Is he in the habit of talking about him? – Well, he is, sir; he is too often in his mouth, as I told him before this. (Laughter.) Don't you think it was a just judgement on him that the devil should make his appearance to see him under those circumstances? – Wisha, I suppose so, sir; he was calling on him too often, and it was serving him right. Has he been talking about the devil since? – Indeed no, sir. (Laughter.)

Mr Julian – Mr Batty has a claim for the reformation of her husband. (Loud laughter.)

His Worship considered that the plaintiff was injured on the occasion, and gave a decree for £5.

PAUPER CHILDREN AND PANTOMIMES.
AT a meeting of the Industrial Schools Committee of Kirkdale, on Tuesday last, the following extraordinary conversation took place: – "Mr Hagger (the Clerk) said that an invitation had been received from Mr De Freece, the Lessee of the Theatre Royal, Liverpool, inviting the children of the schools to the Theatre to witness a performance of the Pantomime. A Member – Another Pantomime? Another Member – It would seem almost like a conspiracy. Mr Stubbs said this was one of the results he foresaw, and one of the reasons why he opposed the children being allowed to go to the Circus. He did

not object to the Circus, but he saw that it would be opening the door for the children going to other more objectionable places, and would have the effect of exciting the feelings and disturbing the minds of the poor children. Mr Aitken – It is not opening the door; the door has been opened all along until Mr Stubbs shut it. They have been to see Pantomimes before. Mr Stubbs – The more the pity. Mr Aitken – You should have seen how they enjoyed themselves. Mr Hagger – It is due to this gentleman who had been kind enough to send the invitation to give him some answer. The Chairman – We have given them one treat. Why should we thrust more treats upon them? Mr Chapman was not opposed to the children being allowed to go and see the Pantomime, but he did not think it was necessary they should go to so many places. Mr Guilliam – It would only be unsettling the minds of the children to send them to one place of this kind and then to another. Mr Chapman moved that in the present instance Mr De Freece's invitation be respectfully declined. Mr Aitken seconded this, which was agreed to.
28/2/1872

THE performances of the French plays in King Street have been enlivened this week by more than one sensational incident, not behind, but in front, of the curtain. On the first of the occasions to which we particularly refer a chattering party in a private box became so obnoxious to the audience and to the artists on the stage that a gentleman in the stalls was compelled to rise and address the house. […]

But on the second occasion sleep was the offender, and the most remarkable power of snoring was exhibited that has probably ever come before the notice of the public. A youth – who might have been over-fed, but was certainly dreadfully tired – gave way after the first two of the *seven* (!) acts of *Le Pauvrés de Paris*, and not only slept but snored in such a stentorian manner that he almost shook the theatre. There he lay, curled in his stall, sleeping heavily and snoring awfully. At the back of the auditorium he could be heard distinctly. The folks in the gallery and boxes looked down and gaped at him. The orchestra smiled and sneered alternately, but still continued the terrible roar from the sleeper in the front row of the stalls. At last the young gentleman became a nuisance. His nose gained power as the sleep became heavier. He had long since drowned the tremulous melodramatic music, and now at last the audience caught the dialogue on stage with difficulty. The actors were annoyed and the audience irritated, but no coughs, or scrapings, or nudges would disturb the dull rapture of this noisy youth.

At last a well known dramatic critic took nobly on himself the responsibility of securing the comfort of the whole audience. He quietly retreated by a convenient door, and returned with a train of boxkeepers at his heels, prepared, for once in their lives, to be a blessing to society. It took two boxkeepers to wake the snorer; but at their polite invitation he postponed his noisy dreams for another occasion, and endeavoured faintly to revive a forgotten interest in *Les Pauvrés de Paris*. This anecdote does not speak volumes in favour of the French melodrama, but it proves that there are times when salaried servants at a Theatre may be employed beneficially to the public. If the boxkeepers who woke that man had immediately sent round the hat they would have made their fortune on the spot, and there would not have been a single grumble at the tax.
4/2/1872

MURDER AND SUICIDE IN A THEATRE.
THE Alexandra Opera House and Theatre, situated in Blonk Street, Sheffield, was on Tuesday morning the scene of a shocking tragedy. During the night it was the custom to leave the Theatre in charge of a watchman named Bradshaw, a military pensioner, who, with his wife, occupied the wardrobe as a bedroom. On Tuesday morning about seven o'clock a woman named Ross, whose duty it is to clean the hall, unable to obtain admission as usual, sought the assistance of a man named Mosley, who, by means of a ladder, climbed through one of the windows. On going into the wardrobe the woman was found lying on the floor insensible, her head and face bathed in blood. Near her were a hatchet and a poker, and her husband's boots, scarf, and other portions of his clothing, all stained with blood. The man was afterwards discovered hanging quite dead from the roof among the "flies."

From a subsequent statement of the woman it appears that he beat her, first with his fists, then with a poker, and afterwards, snatching up a hatchet, he struck her insensible, inflicting a terrible wound on the right side of her head, through which the brains protruded. Evidently supposing that he had killed her, he took off his scarf, coat, and boots, and by means of a winding staircase proceeded to the "flies" over the stage. Then he took up a rope about twenty feet in length, used for lifting the scenes, fastened an end to a piece of timber in the roof, the other end he twisted round his neck, and, having done so, he took a leap in the direction of the stage. The "drop" being some fourteen or fifteen feet, his neck was dislocated, and death must have been instantaneous. The unfortunate woman was removed to the Sheffield Infirmary, where her death is hourly looked for*. Jealousy arising from the conduct of his wife during his absence is supposed to have led Bradshaw to commit the double tragedy.

Mrs Ross died a few days later.
18/2/1872

AT Lambeth Police Court last Tuesday, Joseph Elwill, the Clown at Astley's Theatre, was summoned by Richard Manning, one of the supernumeraries at the same establishment, for an assault during the performance of the Pantomime.

The complainant said on the night of Friday week, at nearly eleven o'clock, there was a "rally" on the stage, and he, with others, had to throw carrots, turnips, &c., about. One of them struck the defendant, who was the Clown. When the carrot struck him he got the "needle." (Loud laughter.)

Mr Chance wished to know what the "needle" meant.

The complainant said it was when a person lost his temper he was considered to have the "needle." When the "rally" was over and he got off the stage, the defendant came up to him and struck him four blows, and he bled "like a pig." He did not intend to hit the defendant with a carrot.

The defendant said complainant struck him with a large fish on his head at the time of the "rally," which annoyed him, and when they got off the stage he certainly struck him two blows.

A witness named Wood said he saw defendant when struck. He lost his temper, and assaulted complainant.

Mr Pindar, the Manager, said defendant was a very clever artist, and most painstaking and enthusiastic in his profession, and no doubt felt annoyed at being struck by a supernumerary.

Mr Chance said defendant had, perhaps, felt annoyed and lost his temper, but that did not justify the assault complained of. He ordered defendant to pay a fine of £2.
10/3/1872

To be Had Immediately. A HANDSOME CHINESE MANDARIN SUIT of Silk Cloth, comprising Head-dress, Skirt, and Coat, in excellent condition; the great serpent elegantly worked in gold and various colours of silk on each side of head-dress and coat. Suitable for Waxworks, Theatrical, or Private Gentleman's Fancy Dress for Parties. Will be Sold very Cheap. Such opportunities rarely met with. Apply to ROBERT BUTTERFIELD, 37, Robert Street, Birkenhead, Cheshire.
17/3/1872

AN operatic heroine in galoshes is a novelty, yet Mdlle Colombo was compelled to appear thus on the operatic stage at Manchester, owing to a fire which took place just before the curtain drew up for *Il Barbiere*, on Monday last. Some scenery was discovered to be burning, and the hose was covered by a heap of properties. Owing to the energy of Mr Mapleson's stage manager, Mr Roper, the flames were speedily extinguished. As we have often remarked before, it is a great pity that all canvas used in Theatres is not made inflammable.

The Theatre Royal at Stratford-upon-Avon.

THIS building, which has long been an eyesore on New Place Garden, is at length doomed, Mr Halliwell having purchased it with a view to its removal; consequently, in the course of a few weeks the Theatre, which for forty-five years has been the arena for the display of histrionic talent of every grade, from the "brightest stars" to the stage-struck amateur, will no longer, in all its primitive ugliness of red brick and blue slate, offend the eye. The Theatre was erected in the year 1827, and opened by Mr Raymond with Shakespeare's *As You Like It*. An address, written by Mr Serle, of the Theatre Royal, Covent-garden, was spoken by Mr Arlan on the occasion. During Mr Raymond's management Edmund Kean, Charles Kean, Madame Vestris, Miss Foote, Mr Macready, and many other eminent actors and actresses appeared on those boards.

In 1846 the Theatre was converted into an Institute or Athenaeum, so that when not required for theatrical representations it might be made available for public dinners, lectures, readings, &c. The pit was removed, the permanent stage and proscenium taken down, the floor of the pit raised, commodious rooms formed underneath on the ground floor, and its title altered to "Royal Shakespearian Rooms." The stage and proscenium were so constructed that they could be taken down when the building was not required for dramatic performances. The Rooms were some time after let to the late Mr Jackman, of the Northampton, Banbury, and Bedford Theatres, for a theatrical season, and subsequently to his son, Mr Charles Jackman, who, with Mr Frederick Morgan, successfully catered for the Stratford public for many years. Since the retirement of Messrs Jackman and Morgan in 1862 the place has never answered as a theatrical speculation. The old Theatre will soon be one of the things of the past; but we are pleased to learn there is a prospect of a new one being erected, which will take the shape of a memorial to Shakespeare in the town of his birth.

WANTED, a PRETTY LITTLE GIRL, about Nine Years of Age, to be adopted or otherwise, as Articled Pupil to the Lady Principal of a fashionable West-end Dancing Academy. Must be of slight, graceful figure. Good home, with every comfort, and board and wardrobe all provided. No premium. An orphan preferred. Address, full particulars to M.F., care of Steel and Jones, Advertising Agents, 4, Spring Gardens.
24/3/1872

TO THE EDITOR OF THE ERA.
Sir, – Last night I was in the stalls of the Victoria Palace Theatre. Immediately in front of me were three individuals, whom, from their appearance, I assumed to be associated with the mercantile marine. One of the party had hardly taken his seat before he took to smoking, to the evident annoyance of those in his vicinity. Being anxious to avoid a disturbance I slipped out softly and complained to the stall-keeper, who made a certain show of remonstrance, but to no purpose – for five successive cautions failed even to mitigate the nuisance. At last, wearied with the ineffectual efforts of the official, I ventured, in the mildest manner, to put in a personal objection, and was forthwith assailed by an anathema, which the heaviest of heavy villains would have hesitated to hurl upon the most defenceless of stage victims; and my feeble suggestion that tobacco in general was tabooed in the stalls was met by the rejoinder of me being a "sickly" – substantive – "as couldn't stand baccy." At this crisis I took up my hat and appealed to some one in office in the lobby, who promptly and courteously came to the rescue and removed the obnoxious gentleman, followed by his compatriots, into the pit. In a few minutes, however, the whole party were relegated to their old place; but the communications interchanged amongst them and delivered in the loudest of stage whispers, were of so very caustic a nature that I deemed it the wisest course, for the credit of the establishment and the preservation of my own temper, to beat a retreat. I may add that the offender, as far as I could judge, had not the excuse of inebrity for his conduct. I am, your obedient servant,
A LOVER OF THE PLAY AND – THE PIPE IN ITS PLACE. April 11th, 1872.   *14/4/1872*

ON Monday night, during the performance of a *troupe* of Japanese known as "The Great Dragon" *troupe*, at the Gaiety Theatre, West Hartlepool, a woman who performs on the high slack wire and inclined rope was ascending the latter, which stretches from the stage at an angle of forty-five degrees to the top of the gallery front, when, only two or three strides from the top, she became so startled by a thoughtless man striking a vesuvian immediately before her eyes that she lost her balance and fell into the pit, a depth of about forty feet. A wild scream from the audience bespoke the terror caused by the accident, but marvellous to add, she was seen to rise almost unhurt, and walk to the stage to continue her performance thereon; and equally singular, as it will appear, none of the occupants of the pit, upon whom she fell, received any greater injury than a shaking and a few bruises.
28/4/1872

ALL PREVIOUS SENSATION OUTDONE. Only see CLARKSON'S New MECHANICAL MOUSTACHE. Novelty, simplicity, and grotesque combined. Change in a moment, forming three distinct moustaches, without using the hand. CLARKSON, Theatrical Wig Maker, 45, Wellington Street, Strand.
30/6/1872

ANYTHING which offers us a safeguard against the ravages of that "good servant but bad master" Fire should be welcome, and it is, therefore, with pleasure that we call attention to the patent Fire-Proof Starch of Messrs D. Nichol and Co., of 58, Paternoster Row. The stage has often presented a fearful instance for the necessity for some such commodity as this, and innumerable have been the sacrifice of both persons and property, which, with such a preventive, would have been obviated entirely. A muslin dress, or a curtain, or window blind, has often formed the little source of huge and dire calamities. Messrs Nichol's Starch recommends itself by the following qualities: – It costs little more than other kinds of starch; it does not affect the colour of any washing fabric to which it is applied; it contains no ingredient prejudicial to health; and, most important of all, it renders the fabric to which it is applied perfectly proof against flames. This last consideration should lead to its speedy adoption in all circles.

MR TOM LOVELL, a member of Fred Evan's troupe of pantomimists, was about giving his Newfoundland dog a bathe in the Thames last Sunday week, when a child about seven years of age fell into the water by Westminster Bridge, and was being carried by the ebbing tide through one of the arches. Mr Lovell immediately sent his dog in, and it succeeded in grasping the child by the clothes, and held it until a boatman rowed up and rescued it. Several gentlemen who saw the occurrence intend presenting the dog with a collar.
14/7/1872

THE PET SNAKE CASE. – Vice-chancellor Bacon had before him on Friday the pet snake case of Cockburn v. Mann. The plaintiff, Mr A. Cockburn, is a merchant, and has a private residence at 5, Cheyne Walk, Chelsea. The defendant, Mr C.P. Mann, a music-master, occupies the house No. 4, Cheyne Walk. The gardens of the two houses are separated by a wall about seven feet in height.

The plaintiff alleged that the defendant had committed, and threatened to continue to commit, a nuisance to the plaintiff by keeping in the defendant's house a number of tame snakes, of which some from time to time escaped into the plaintiff's premises and other premises in Cheyne Walk, and that the liability of the snakes at all times to escape kept the plaintiff and his servants in continual fear and uneasiness. The defendant alleged that the snakes were pets, and were harmless. The plaintiff was ignorant whether or not they were poisonous, but they could bite, and were formidable and disgusting creatures to ordinary persons. Persons accustomed to snakes might be able to distinguish by sight those snakes which were harmless from those which were venomous, but no ordinary persons were able to do so. The plaintiff instituted a suit to obtain an injunction restraining the defendant from keeping any

snakes about his house or garden, and from permitting any snakes to escape into the plaintiff's garden or premises. A motion was now made for an interlocutory injunction until the hearing of the case. […] The motion was ordered to stand over till the hearing of the cause on the defendant giving an undertaking not to permit any snakes to escape into the plaintiff's garden or house.
28/7/1872

MISS EDITH CHALLIS, a well-known actress in London and New York, whilst travelling a few months since, was very attentive to an old lady, who fell ill on the journey and subsequently died. Last week Miss Challis was greatly astonished at receiving a letter from her executors, to the effect that the kindness shown to the old lady had resulted in her being remembered in her will to the extent of a clear two thousand a year for life. In consequence of this she retires from the stage.
4/8/1872

AT the Greenwich Police Court on Monday a man complained to the Magistrate that his neighbour kept in his garden a large, old, and artful monkey, one of the prize animals at the North Woolwich Gardens, and that this monkey had pursued the applicant's wife, who was compelled to leap over a fence to get out of its way. Mr Maude said he was unable to assist the man, and referred him to a civil court.
18/8/1872

DISAPPEARED. – A YOUNG MAN, about Thirty Years of Age, of medium height, named ELLERMAN. He arrived in Bradford on Monday, September 30th, to fill a situation, and has not been seen or heard of since. In case of his having fallen ill or met with an accident, any person having any knowledge of him will confer a favour by communicating with Mr C. Rice, Theatre. In consequence of the above calamity a Scene Painter is Required. Address C. Rice, Theatre Royal, Bradford.
6/10/1872

THE officers of her Majesty's ship *Ganges*, stationed at Falmouth, gave a concert at Redruth last Wednesday night, in aid of the Foresters' funds. Mr Boynes, chief gunnery instructor, sang a humorous song in character, which was warmly applauded. He reappeared to an encore, and staggered forward upon the orchestra. His fall being taken to be intentional, the applause and laughter were renewed, but Boynes continued struggling, and the merriment was soon turned to wild alarm. Doctors were summoned, but before their arrival all motion had ceased, and in full view of the audience he had died. He leaves a widow and young family.

ONE POUND REWARD. RUNAWAY APPRENTICE. – I, SAM BAYLIS, hereby offer the above Reward to any Person who will give information of the whereabouts of my Apprentice, SAMUEL BAYLISS, who has again absconded, and legal proceedings will be taken against any one employing him after this date, October 12th, 1872. Mechanics' Hall, Scarborough.
13/10/1872

Appeal to the Musical Profession. A LADY PIANIST wishes to Bind herself for Two Years to either a Great Pianist, Organist, First-class Violinist, or Conductor of an Orchestra. If they will engage her, and enter into a contract, she will devote the whole of her time to them, and give her services for very moderate remuneration. Being utterly friendless trusts this appeal to the Profession will not be made in vain. Can play Harmonium and Organ. Can sing; sweet Contralto voice. Touch on the Piano most beautiful. Splendid execution. Wishes to have the protection and assistance in her Profession of a great Musician. Will Costa or Arditi write? Prefers to be engaged only by a perfect Gentleman and first-class Artist, on account of being a lady by birth, and highly cultured and accomplished. Address, EVA BELZONI, Professional Pianist, No. 1, Swan Street, Congleton, Cheshire.
1/12/1872

4
1873
THE BAND STOPPED THEIR SOMBRE PRISON MUSIC

A BARGAIN. TO BE SOLD, at a Sacrifice, a WOODEN-HEADED FAMILY, consisting of an Acrobat, a Bender, Flip Flap, and Risley Performers. Also, to be Sold Cheap, an India Rubber Elephant (Life size), an excellent trick for Clowns or Duettists. Apply to Fred Abrahams, 55, Waterloo Road.
26/1/1873

IN the Court of Common Pleas on Wednesday, before Mr Justice Brett and a Special Jury, the case of Perry v. East, Bart., excited considerable interest. It was an action for slander, the plaintiff being the leader of Coote and Tinney's Band, and of the Orchestra at the Lyceum Theatre, and the defendant Sir Gilbert East, Bart., of Grosvenor Gardens. In July last the defendant gave a ball on an extensive scale, the above-mentioned band being engaged to supply the music. Subsequently, when calling on Mr Coote to pay for their services, the defendant, it was alleged, accused the members of the band of playing disgracefully, of getting drunk, and of stealing his wine. This was the slander complained of. The plaintiff and several members of the band who were called emphatically denied the grave imputations made against them; and the defendant, while denying that he had accused them of stealing his wine, pleaded that what he had said was privileged. After a deliberation which occupied three-quarters of an hour, the Jury found that the words, though slanderous, were spoken in the heat of the moment, and that no dishonesty was imputed to the plaintiff.

IN the Harlequinade of the Pantomime at the Theatre Royal, Bradford, Mr E. Laurie (the Clown), has introduced a trick which is worthy of remark. We all know that in Harlequinade the poor policeman as a rule gets more kicks than halfpence. In this case the Clown seizes a huge knife and cuts off one of the legs of the "active and intelligent" officer. The amputated leg remains stationary on the stage until its owner, with the single leg he has left, commences to dance a hornpipe. A fellow feeling at once induces the amputated limb to follow suit, the effect, of course, being comical in the extreme. The mystery is explained when we state that Mr Laurie is assisted in this trick by M. Pierrot, the famous one-legged dancer.
9/2/1873

TO THE EDITOR OF THE ERA.
Sir, – Knowing that your columns are always open to fair play, I take the liberty of asking you to kindly insert the following. No actor is more willing to accept honest criticism than I am, even injustice is bearable provided it is the writer's honest conviction. But what can be said to a class of men (?) who

criticise an actor without even attending his performance? The critic (?) of a weekly contemporary, when I was playing Hamlet at the Standard Theatre a few months ago, said: –

"We do not admire Mr Bandmann's Hamlet, it has all the faults of Mr Fechler's rendering in the matter of elocution, and but few merits of any sort to recommend it. Mrs Bandmann's Ophelia, however, we can praise highly; it is intelligent, picturesque, pathetic, and at all times artistic."

Unfortunately, however, Mrs Bandmann was taken ill a few hours before the performance commenced, and could not act during the entire engagement. An apology was made after the first act, the first scenes were cut out, and in the third act a lady of the company read the part. In the fourth Miss Walreck arrived in time to act the Mad Scene.

Could that honest (?) critic have been in the theatre? In his last notice upon my performance of Hamlet he discovers that: –

"I have neither legs, head, shoulders, voice, nor intelligence, and my wife he apparently thinks it would be generous and economical to pass unnoticed."

Was this individual in the Theatre on THIS occasion?

However, he has paid no high compliment to the public who, for the past two weeks, have crowded the Princess's from floor to ceiling (which circumstance has induced the Management to prolong the engagement) to witness the performance of such as "monstrosity" as he describes.
Your humble servant, D.E. BANDMANN.
23/2/1873

WE regret to state that an accident, which might have resulted in instant death, happened the other evening to Miss Marie Courtenay, a young and promising actress, who was playing one of the principal characters in the Pantomime at Astley's Theatre. At the close of the fairy scene, and just as the curtain was descending, a piece of heavy timber, some fourteen feet in length, fell perpendicularly from the flies on to the foot of Miss Courtenay. Her shrieks were fearful. Two medical gentlemen were called, and the unfortunate lady was without delay conveyed to her residence. It was found that the piece of timber, which had cut her boot to pieces and pierced her stocking, had smashed her foot and cut the tendons, the blood from which flowed copiously. She is of course confined to her bed, and is in a very weak condition.
9/3/1873

THE following curious occurrence is said to have taken place at Brighton. The performance of *Man and Wife* at the Theatre Royal was delayed some little time on Tuesday night in consequence of it having been discovered that Mr Charles Collette, who was playing the part of Sir Patrick Lundie, was not in the Theatre. Before, however, an apology was made, Mr Collette arrived, wet to the skin, and in a state of great exhaustion, dressed hurriedly, and appeared on the stage, exhibiting no traces of the ordeal he had gone through. It appears that Mr Collette had learned the art of snake charming in India, and was explaining the process to Mr George Reeves Smith, the courteous General Manager of the Brighton Aquarium. Notwithstanding the entreaties of Mr Smith, Mr Collette insisted on exercising his science upon the octopus, and succeeded in luring the monster from its hiding place, and caused it to follow him round the tank. On bending down to the surface of the water, however, the creature seemed to shake of all control, and turning his snaky feelers round Mr Collette's neck drew him by main force into the tank. A desperate struggle ensued beneath the water, whence Sir Patrick Lundie was with difficulty extricated by Mr Smith and several bystanders. Mr Collette has since confined his powers of charming to the patrons of the Theatre, and with far greater success. We believe that Mr Smith, of the Brighton Aquarium, will vouch for the truth of this.
1/6/1873

A LAD named Edward Lawrence was charged, before Mr Ellison, at Lambeth Police Court, last Tuesday, with wilfully breaking ginger-beer bottles in the gallery of the Elephant and Castle Theatre. For some weeks past, during the performance at the Theatre, a great deal of damage and annoyance have been caused by persons in the gallery smashing ginger-beer bottles. On Monday night Millbank, an officer employed in the house, detected the prisoner smashing a bottle, and under his feet some ten or twelve others were found broken. The prisoner denied breaking any but the one bottle. Mr Ellison said such practices must be stopped. He fined the prisoner 2s. 6d.

PSEUDOPYLUM.* – CURLED CUPIDS and PAGES' WIGS, beautiful Golden and Flaxen Tints, from 18s. to 25s.; long Golden or Flaxen Stems, for Coils or Plaits, from 10s. to 20s. per set of three; other Colours in stock. Address, RICHARD ALLISTON, Wig Maker, 422, Strand, corner of Bedford Street. Established 1845. Proprietor of the Plantagenet Guard Razor, which effects the operation of shaving in an inconceivably short space of time, even by the most timid and nervous.
*A type of artificial hair invented by Alliston.
8/6/1873

MR W.S. GILBERT, the well-known dramatic author, was summoned at the Westminster Police Court, on Wednesday last, for refusing to show his season-ticket at the Victoria Station of the Metropolitan District Railway, when requested to do so by an official of the company. The offence was laid on the 28th of last month. It was stated that the defendant, although a season-ticket holder, had, on many occasions, refused to show his ticket, and handed his card instead. According to the first bye-law of the company, the penalty for not showing the ticket on demand was 40s., and, as the servants were frequently changed, regular passengers on the line could not be identified. Defendant, when asked for the ticket on the date in question, did not produce it, and said he had passed the barrier at the Mansion House unchallenged. Defendant, in general terms, contended that, as a well-known ticket holder, the production of his card as evidence of the fact that he had lost his ticket or mislaid it, was sufficient, and he complained that he had been dragged to a police-court for so trivial an offence. The Magistrate fined him 20s. and 2s. costs; and, in reply to his inquiry, he was informed that he could not appeal.

DURING the performance on the lofty wire of Fraulein Laura at the Princess's Palace, Leeds, on Saturday, the 19th inst., some villain very nearly succeeded in unfastening one of the guy ropes that tighten the wire during the lady's perilous passage on a bicycle from the gallery to the stage. He was detected just in the nick of time by one of the numerous attendants, and was speedily ejected by Mr James Ellis, the Manager, who left on the vagabond marks that he will not easily get rid of. The sympathies of the audience were entirely with the Management during this episode.
27/7/1893

A DISGRACEFUL FRACAS AT THE PLYMOUTH THEATRE.
[…] The play was Charles Reade's popular drama *It's Never Too Late to Mend*. The play is well mounted, each of the characters being sustained in a manner that is highly creditable to the company. It is pretty well known to all playgoers that the second act represents a prison carried on in a very savage manner by a jailer who is enamoured of the separate silent system – the separation and silence being for the prisoners, and the effects are such as to deeply interest, and at the same time such as to shock the humane sensibilities of the audience. As the piece progressed it exhibited the jailer (Mr Honeysett) dealing with two prisoners, Robinson (Mr Philip Day) and Joseph (Miss Amy Forrest), who were out of their cells, and were objects on whom the interest of the play at that moment concentrated. The sympathy of the Chaplain (Mr W. Bourne) in the welfare of the two prisoners who are the special subjects of the jailer's brutality awakened a corresponding sympathy in the hearts of the people.

The audience had been deeply interested in the play, and there was a general silence throughout the house, which was but rarely interrupted by applause, when something was said that awakened the listeners' sympathies. It was while this silence reigned around that the audience was disturbed by some annoying sounds that issued from the further part of the pit, known as "The Poet's Corner." The disturbance led people to cry for silence; but as the cry was not attended to, and the noise increased, there was a general burst of indignation from all parts of the pit, and loud shouts of "Turn him out." The gods were hanging over the front of their railings, shouting aloud for summary justice to be dispensed. The people in the boxes were equally anxious to know the cause of the disturbance. The occupants of the pit jumped upon their seats, crowding over to the corner, while the women either hurriedly left the house or scrambled over the partitions to reach the orchestra stalls, which were soon filled. The band stopped their sombre prison music, and the actors suspended all their performances, and looked on with concern at what had now become a great row.

Mr Newcombe, the Lessee, had got in amongst them, and was endeavouring to induce the belligerents to leave the house. He was assisted by some six or seven policemen, and there was a general scrimmage. The row was taking place amongst some naval officers, who for the time appear to have lost their heads, and forgotten altogether their position and the example which they ought to set to society. After a while there was a door burst open and a crush of men driven forward to the orchestra stairs, and in a moment one of the belligerents was seen upon the stage, where he was immediately taken possession of and handcuffed with a pair of darbies that were to have been placed on the wrists of Robinson, the felon. In these darbies the officer was walked off to the Guildhall, and the police had afterwards to send to the Theatre for the key to unlock them. Eventually the whole of the fighting force was ejected from the pit, and it would be well for them if the row had ended there, because afterwards some of the party assaulted the police, which makes an aggravation of their offence.

While the row went on the stage was left open, actors and actresses flew about in wildest alarm, representatives of convicts rushed rampant before the audience, and a most motley and curious scene presented itself. The convict Robinson at length advanced to the foot of the stage, and expressed regret that the entertainment should have been interrupted by such a shameful disturbance, and said that the curtain would be lowered for ten minutes to allow order to reign again. The curtain was accordingly lowered, and shortly afterwards Mr Arthur Newcombe advanced to the front, and stated that no such event had ever occurred before during the time that the Theatre had been under his father's management. The house soon after resumed its wonted calm; the story of the piece was taken up at the point of its suspension, and everything went well and quietly for the remainder of the evening.

The persons taken into custody and kept locked up for the night were five naval officers and a civilian, brother of one of the officers, all of whom were liberated on bail about half-past ten o'clock on Sunday morning.

The prisoners received fines of £5 or £10, plus costs.
31/8/1873

ON Wednesday, the 27th ult., Mr Richards, the Deputy-Coroner for the Eastern Division of Middlesex, held an inquiry in the inquest room of the London Hospital, respecting the decease of Emily Bevan, aged eighteen years, who expired from the effects of an injury received under the following somewhat singular circumstances. The Jury having viewed the body: –

Elizabeth Bevan, a vocalist, identified the body of the deceased as that of her daughter, who was a vocalist and dancer. On the evening of Thursday, the 24th of April last, witness was in the Hoop and Grapes Music Hall, Ratcliff Highway, where her daughter was fulfilling an engagement, when she was told she had met with an accident. Witness then saw the deceased bleeding from her left leg, and being supported by Mr Newman. While in the hospital the deceased said she was going up the staircase leading on to the stage, when a young woman named Jenny Dent, also a vocalist, tickled her leg, and she fell down. She thought that Dent was spiteful, but forgave her.

The Coroner here asked the witness whether she was positive the deceased told her that Dent was spiteful, and upon receiving a reply in the affirmative, remarked that there did not appear to be any intention to injure the deceased, and what had been done seemed to be done in a joke.

James Newman said he was a professional vocalist, and engaged at the Music Hall in question. Witness, the deceased, and Miss Jenny Dent were going into a dressing-room near the stage on the evening of the 24th of last April, when Dent tickled the deceased in the ribs. The deceased, who fell down, exclaimed, "Oh, you have broken my leg." Witness fetched some brandy, and after binding the wound which had been caused to her left leg, he procured a cab and had her conveyed to the London Hospital.

George Morgan, M.R.C.S., house surgeon at the London Hospital, said the deceased was treated as an out-patient until the 2nd May, when she was received into the wards. On the 20th ult. it was considered expedient to amputate the limb, and it was accordingly done. She was then placed under the usual treatment when amputation was performed, but she expired from exhaustion.

The Coroner, in his remarks to the Jury, alluded to the absence of any motive on the part of any person to intentionally injure the deceased, and, after a short consideration, the Jury returned a verdict of "Accidental death."

7/9/1873

MR EDITOR. – Sir, – Permit me, through the medium of your columns, to call attention to the totally inadequate supply of gas furnished to public places of amusement by the London companies. On Saturday evening last the performance at this Theatre of *Antony and Cleopatra* was seriously interfered with, and its scenic effects materially diminished by the state of comparative darkness into which the main portions of the building were thrown by the failure of the usual supply. The cause having been investigated by the gas engineer attached to the Theatre was found to be attributable to the defect in a valve connected with the meter, which could only be remedied by the officers of the company, who, upon being applied to for that purpose, replied that no assistance could be afforded until Monday; so that, Sir, but for the indulgence of the public, I, as a Manager, should have been in danger of having the success of my latest and grandest production imperilled, if not destroyed. As experience proves it is futile to appeal to the gas companies, and as I have no doubt this is but a solitary instance of what is constantly occurring to others, who, like myself, are to a great extent dependent on the capricious supply of gas with which we are furnished, I think it my duty, on public grounds, to bring the matter before the only tribunal, public opinion, from whom redress can be hoped for. I am, Sir, your obedient servant, F.B. CHATTERTON.

Theatre Royal, Drury Lane, November 20th.

Amateurs at St George's Hall.
TO THE EDITOR OF THE ERA.
Sir, – Will you kindly insert the following and oblige your grateful servants, C.C. and L.W: –

In answer to your critique of our performance at St George's Hall, on Tuesday last, we desire to express our thanks for the praise so generously bestowed, and also to inform you that as we play again on Friday, 21st inst., at the same place, shall feel greatly indebted if you will a second time put in force your valuable services; but we are happy to say, that as we succeeded in pleasing our friends who were assembled on that night, we can afford to treat your small wit with the contempt it deserves, and beg to subscribe ourselves,
Your obliged and very grateful servants, CISSY CAMISCASCA and LOUIE WALTERS.

(Cissy and Louie do wrong to be angry with us. *We didn't see them. We didn't criticise them!* The miserable efforts of their predecessors drove us away. Pray, ladies, moderate the rancour of your tongues; but if you must shake your tiny fists and stamp your little feet, let it be at the gentlemen who murdered *The Ticket-of-Leave Man*, and so robbed us of the pleasure of seeing you. Cissy and Louie must not too hastily rush into print. – THE ERA CRITIC.) *23/11/1873*

THE Gaiety Theatre, always justly proud of the numerous comforts and conveniences it places at the disposal of its patrons, now boasts of a telegraphic apparatus, and is prepared to book seats literally with lightning-like rapidity. The lines have been laid experimentally between the Theatre and the library of Mr Hay in Cornhill, but we have little doubt that the plan will prove so thoroughly successful as to lead to its speedy extension. The "City Man" is a great supporter of our West End Theatres, but he decides on his evening's amusement "on the spur of the moment." He meets a friend when business cares are over for the day. "Ah, old boy! How are you? Where shall we go?" "To the Gaiety." "Very well; but perhaps it's full." "Oh, I know, let's pop into Hay's. Hay, any seats vacant at the Gaiety?" "Tell you in ten seconds, Sir!" Click, click, click, click. "Yes, Sir!" "All right. Book two seats, instantly! Hi, hansom," and away they go to find the stall-keeper expecting them, and to mentally place another feather in the cap of the Gaiety management.
14/12/1873

CAUTION, to MR and MRS -------, Irish Duettists. – Our Original Blarney Sketch of the Irishman and the English Lady is legally protected from this date, so beware, and don't come blathering about your Love for the Human Family then. Mr PAT KINSELLA and FLORA YARNOLD, Ireland's Foremost Duettists and Dancers, Five Calls Nightly, Gaiety, West Hartlepool.
21/12/1873

5
1874
A D.....M S.....T, A B.....D T.....F, AND A B.....Y LIAR

WANTED, Strong, Competent WOMEN, to Drive Roman Chariots in New York Hippodrome; also Fast Ponies, High-leaping Horses, Hounds, and Whipper-in. Address, P.T. BARNUM, Mr Lindley, 6, Catherine Street, Strand, London.
4/1/1874

ALL lovers of Pantomime are by this time aware that Mr Rice in his magnificent and amusing Pantomime *Little Red Riding Hood* at Covent Garden has introduced a number of real sheep, which nightly excite the admiration and enthusiasm of all the little people whose good fortune it is to be present. On the occasion of the recent visit of their Royal Highnesses the Prince and Princess of Wales and family the said sheep were introduced to the Royal box, much to the delight of the Royal children, whose expressed sympathy on account of the fate which they imagined would await the "muttons" when the Pantomime had run its course led to an offer of purchase by his Royal Highness, an offer, however, which was respectfully declined, Mr Rice being in no hurry to sacrifice his pets.

AMONG the "tricks" likely to live long in the memory of those who witness it, and introduced into the capital Pantomime which nightly delights crowded audiences at the Surrey Theatre, is the sudden transformation at the touch of Harlequin's wand of a huge tree into the head of Mr W. Holland, "the people's caterer," on whose world-renowned moustache a couple of acrobats perform a series of feats which astonish all beholders. The "trick" is as amusing as it is novel, and never fails to elicit loud laughter and applause.

MARION. – For God's sake, come back. – A.C.
18/1/1874

WANTED, to Purchase, Four or Six Very Large POODLES, not less than Fifty Pound Weight. Must be all Dogs, White or Coloured. Two or Three Black preferred. Not broke. Apply to JAMES ATHERTON, Dog Gymnast, Prince's Theatre, Manchester.

CAUTION. Observing that a Couple of Men, one calling himself "Barnum," are exhibiting Marionettes in Wales, purporting to be mine, or were bought from me, I will state that I have owned no Marionettes for Thirty Years, and that at present I have no interest in any exhibition in Great Britain. P.T. BARNUM.
25/1/1874

JEREMIAH BOLT. – Have done what I Said. For God's sake come, before too late, at Mrs B. IPPO.
1/2/1874

DURING the performance of the Pantomime at the Crystal Palace on Monday last, an accident happened, through which the favourite actress, Miss Caroline Parkes, received severe injuries. After Mr Conquest had gone through a "vampire"* in the boards, the man in charge of the trap failed to replace the slider, and his neglect was not perceived from the stage, the opening being concealed by the "vampire." In the next scene Miss Parkes stepped on this, one of her feet went through, and before she could recover herself her other foot also slipped, and she fell through up to her arms. One of her legs was badly lacerated by the iron edge of the trap, and she was of course much bruised and shaken. Although suffering intense pain, she attempted to go on with her part, but was compelled to desist. She is now confined to her bed, and we fear that it must necessarily be a long time before she entirely recovers.

(This accident again calls our attention to the risk of those whose limbs, and even lives, are at the mercy of men who appear to incur no penalty whatever for the most culpable neglect. If a signalman or pointsman on a railway is convicted of causing an accident he is justly punished, and surely the same law should apply to the stage workman who from sheer inattention leaves a trap unfastened, neglects to secure an iron frame, or is absent from his post at the critical moment when human life depends on him. We believe that many such accidents are hushed up because the thought of them might be painful to the audience; hence it is little known how frequent they are, and public feeling is not roused. To Theatrical Managers, therefore, we earnestly appeal, not only in the name of the Profession, but for the sake of common humanity, to prosecute every one whose carelessness is the cause of danger to those engaged in their service. Let it be known in every Theatre that severe punishment will surely follow guilt, and when one or two have been made an example, the rest will quickly be roused to a better sense of their responsibility.

A "vampire" trap-door opened and closed so rapidly it gave the illusion that a performer had appeared out of thin air.
15/2/1874

ON Saturday last, serious consequences resulted at the Theatre Royal, Paisley, from the presence of a couple of amateurs in the performance of *Jack Robinson and His Monkey*, one, a student of Glasgow University, firing his gun right in the face of another, a private of the 21st Regiment of Foot, and completely destroying one of his eyes. The student has been lodged in prison pending an inquiry.

ON Monday last at the Leeds County Court Miss Clare Bateman, burlesque actress, sought to recover from Mr John Coleman, Lessee of the Theatre Royal, Leeds, the sum of £30 for seven and a half weeks' salary. The plaintiff deposed that she advertised in *The Era* in November last, and in the same month entered into negotiations for an engagement with defendant, who offered her £3 a week. She wrote to say that she could not undertake to dance in consequence of a sprained knee. On January 14th defendant telegraphed for her; offered her £4 per week, and told her that the engagement was for the run of the Pantomime. She went to Leeds, and appeared on the following Monday as Diana in *Twinkle, Twinkle*, receiving applause and an encore in her song. The same night she received from defendant a note to the effect that in his opinion she was not qualified for the part, and that he could not allow her to continue it, a cheque for £4 being enclosed. She presented herself nightly at the Theatre, but had not been permitted to appear.

Mr P Gordon and Mr G Thorne, comedians, were called for plaintiff, and stated that she had performed the part very fairly. For the defence it was urged that Miss Bateman was utterly incompetent, that she could not sing in time or tune, and that her English was terribly defective. His Honour said he thought he should be dealing fairly between both parties if he gave judgement for the plaintiff for £6, in addition to the £4 she had received, with costs.

AN extraordinary public entertainment, according to Lima papers, has been produced in Lima, Peru, by an Italian named Contarini, who proposes to carry his exhibition to Europe. He has trained an opera company of thirty parrots and parroquets, who perform two of Bellini's operas, *Norma* and *Sonnambula*, on a miniature stage, with full chorus and recitative. The director and manager accompanies the artists on a piano-harmonium, and the perfection with which each bird sings his part and the excellence of the chorus are prodigious. The debut of this *lyrico-ornithological* company in *Norma* was attended by the wealth and fashion of Lima. When the parroquet that sang the contralto finished the allegro in "The Salutation to the Moon," such was the enthusiasm, the shouting, and the applause at hearing a bird sing the "Casta Diva," that the bird company, affrighted, took flight and sought refuge among the side scenes. This interrupted the performance for fully a quarter of an hour, and Signor Continari had to tranquillise the "artists" by giving them bread soaked with wine. Thenceforth the expressions of approbation were moderated, in order not to spoil the play. The bird-artists have now become accustomed to the applause. The correctness and propriety with which they give certain portions of the opera are said to be wonderful.
1/3/1874

WANTED, a GYMNAST, Lady Preferred, Age from Twelve to Twenty-four; or a Boy or Youth (effeminate-looking preferred), used to Gymnastics, for an Original Performance. Letters only, W.S., 18, Richmond Grove, Barnsbury, London.
15/3/1874

SOME days back a summons was granted to Miss Kate Santley, of the Alhambra Theatre, under rather peculiar circumstances. The lady, or rather her legal advisor, complained that an organisation had been entered into by the friends of a rival actress, Miss Rose Bell, to prevent Miss Santley's efforts to please from meeting with their due recognition from the public. It was stated that Miss Bell's friends supplied free admissions to numbers of persons on condition that they should applaud her and hiss Miss Santley. Much disturbance arose in the Theatre in consequence, and Miss Santley was driven, in defence of her rights, to bring the matter before the Magistrates. The summons came on for hearing before Mr Knox, at Marlborough Street, yesterday (Friday) afternoon.

Mr George Lewis, Jun, appeared on behalf of Miss Kate Santley, and Mr Montagu Williams represented Mr Carlo, one of the defendants. Mr John Baum, the Manager of the Alhambra, was also present in court.

The defendants were called, but only one answered, namely, Mr Carlo. It was stated that the other defendants were Mr Crisplin, who appeared by proxy, Mr Wright, Mr Jeradoch, and Mr Lefevre.

The Magistrate ordered warrants to be issued against the non-appearing defendants.

Mr Lewis said he appeared to support the charge of conspiracy at common law against the defendants, of whom only the defendant Carlos was present. He lived in the same house as Miss Rose Bell, and accompanied her backwards and forwards to and from the Theatre. It would thus appear that he had an interest in the success of Miss Rose Bell. Whether what he had done was with the knowledge of Miss Rose Bell he could not say. Miss Santley, who had acted with success at many Theatres, was engaged about eighteen months ago at the Alhambra, and latterly she had been much surprised at finding that on her appearance she was greeted with hisses from all parts of the house. It appeared that Carlo had been in the habit of buying up free tickets at the lowest possible rate, and giving them away to persons who were charged to hiss Miss Santley whenever she came on the stage. Miss Santley had by this conduct been rendered very unhappy and brought into a very nervous state. A short time ago she engaged a Mr Belt to make a bust of her, and he, seeing that she was ill, asked her the reason, when she told him. Knowing Mr Carlo, he made inquiries, and the result was that the conspiracy was detected. On Saturday week last affairs culminated, and Miss Santley was, before she had uttered a single word, hissed off the stage, and was led away crying, unable to go on with her part. He would prove that Mr Bolt, whom he would put into the box, had received tickets from Mr Carlo, who wrote to him asking him to try and sell a certain picture, as it would help to carry on the war against "the little savage, Kate." It appeared that some four months ago some gentlemen, without Miss Santley's knowledge, gave away tickets to persons engaged to applaud Miss Santley, Miss Bell, and others, but that was a very different thing. There was a distinction between the two matters, and though Miss Santley stopped this as soon as she knew of it, there was nothing to prevent a person from applauding an actress if he saw fit; but to conspire to hiss a lady and drive her off the stage was entirely different. He should produce some evidence, and then ask for warrants to be issued against the defendants that they might be called on to answer the charge against them.

Mr Richard Belt, residing at 60, Sydney Street, Chelsea, said – I am an artist. I was introduced to Miss Santley in November, 1873, for the purpose of making a bust of her. I noticed the state of her health, which induced me to speak to her; and in consequence of what she said I went to the Alhambra Theatre. That was on the 28th of February. I went to the shilling balcony. I saw the defendant Carlo there. I had known him previously. He drew my attention to the stage, and asked me which I liked best, Miss Bell or Miss Santley. I said he was a better judge than I was. He then said he was living in Miss Bell's house. He said he hated Miss Santley, and it was his intention, with the people he had there, to ruin her, and went on to say he hoped he would have my assistance and that of any friends I could bring. He pointed to fifteen persons to whom he was giving instructions what to do and where to stand, and the time for applauding Miss Bell and hissing Miss Santley. He said they were to applaud Miss Bell in the "drinking song," and hiss Miss Santley at any time she came on the stage. He introduced me to a person named Geradin. He said he was his (Carlo's) secretary. I saw Miss Santley come upon the stage. She was met with hissing from his (Carlo's) people. They applauded Miss Bell. Carlo applauded Miss Bell, and hissed Miss Santley, and asked me to do the same. He then said if my friends would like to come to assist him he would give him a number of tickets. He gave me some then, and brought some on Monday morning. He knew me under the name of Howard.

On Monday, the 2nd March, he came to my studio and brought twenty tickets and a picture. He gave me ten tickets, and said he would give me some of other colours at night. I sent the tickets direct to Miss Santley. They were similar to the tickets produced for the balcony. I went to the Theatre on the same evening, and saw Carlo there. He was at the right hand of the balcony. I saw Girardin, Crisplin, Lefevre, Wright, and a man named Alphonse. […] They were speaking of Miss Santley and Miss Bell in French. When Miss Santley came on Carlo's people hissed. I heard much hissing in the gallery. […] On the 3rd March I went to the Theatre again. I had two friends with me. I introduced them to Carlo outside the Theatre. We were passed in by Carlo, who did not pay, nor had he any tickets. We went with Carlo to the right hand side bar of the balcony. Carlo said he had twenty or thirty persons there. That was the night on which some addresses were taken. I asked Carlo to collect his friends that I might introduce them to mine. He said "Very well," and he did so. He introduced some as picture-frame gilders, and one as a card printer. I gave him an order for some cards. I asked him for their names and addresses, as I might want to call on them.

Mr Lewis – You have never been in the detective force, I suppose? (Laughter.) Witness – No. my friends were told off under the care of Jeradoch and another. Carlo said "You'll see how savage we'll make her (Miss Santley)", and they did so. (Laughter.)

Mr Williams – They did so? Witness – I beg pardon. I mean they used to do so.

Mr Williams – You said "And they did so."

Miss Santley – And so they did. […]

Miss Kate Santley then entered the witness box, and said she had been employed at the Alhambra about eighteen months, and previously at the Queen's Theatre and the Strand. In January last her attention was called to Carlo, who generally stood on the left-hand side of the stage. The piece she performed in was *Don Juan*, and the character she represented was Haidee. During the performance there was hissing in the gallery and the balcony after the singing. She had seen Carlo hissing. In the month of January Mr Belt was introduced to her by Mr Worboys, a dear friend who had been very kind to her, and he asked her whether she would give a sculptor the right to take her face. Mr Belt came to her home and saw her in the presence of her servant, a good-natured Irishwoman, who was like a companion to her. Mr Belt had from time to time forwarded her tickets. She was aware Mr Belt attended the Theatre in her interest. The hissing her so much had affected her health and nearly broke her heart, and when she had left the stage on different occasions she had nearly cried her eyes out.

After a lengthened investigation, Mr Knox remanded the prisoner till Friday next, accepting bail of £100 for his appearance.

Mr Carlo later apologised to Miss Santley, who withdrew the summons.
22/3/1874

PERFUMED PROGRAMMES. – S. FIRTH, Theatrical and General Machine Printer, 3, RUSSELL COURT, CATHERINE STREET, STRAND (in conjunction with the CROWN PERFUMERY COMPANY) is prepared to supply Programmes, Printed and Perfumed in a superior manner to any now produced. Ball Cards, Programmes for Amateur Performances, Private Concerts, &c.
12/4/1874

TERRIFIC JUMP FROM A TRAPEZE AT HANLEY. – On Monday evening last Professor Johnson, a gymnast and man of colour, was going through one of his clever trapeze performances at the People's Concert Hall, when he felt one of the ropes on which the iron bar of the trapeze was suspended give way. With praiseworthy fortitude and admirable presence of mind he instantly decided to avert from the people in the pit below the catastrophe which seemed imminent, and, perceiving that he must fall, he made a terrific spring for the stage, on which he fell with a dull heavy thud, a distance of some twenty yards. The cause of the accident was the slipping of a plank to which one of the ropes of the trapeze was fastened. Surgical assistance being called in, it was found that the Professor's right thigh was broken, and that he was considerably shaken. He was conveyed to the North Staffordshire Infirmary, and it is feared that many months will elapse before he can resume his professional duties.

JOSEPH JONES, described on the charge-sheet as a gentleman, residing at the Williamson Hotel in Cheapside, was charged at Bow Street on Friday with assaulting Mary Kaines, one of the barmaids at Drury Lane Theatre. The complainant stated that on Thursday night about half-past eleven she had gone from her bar to the saloon, and was returning, when she met the defendant, who wiped his hands upon her dress. She asked him how he dared do such a thing, and he then seized her apron. After a short struggle he struck her on the head with a stick. The blow cut her face, and blood flowed profusely. After further corroborative evidence, Mr Flowers fined the defendant £3, or two months' imprisonment.
26/4/1874

THE LONDON MUSIC HALLS.
TO THE EDITOR OF THE ERA.
Sir, – Permit me to draw your attention to an article in one of your contemporaries* of the 22nd ult., in which the writer condemns our Music Halls in the most unwarrantable, ignorant, and scurrilous language I ever read. Not content with abusing Proprietors, Managers, and performers in the most untrue and libellous terms, he proceeds to a wholesale attack on the audience in language almost unfit for print, and freely spiced with phrases such as "the parent of vice," "flaunting in dirt and wretchedness its shamelessness and filth from the gallery to the stalls," "high-priced and very bad liquors," &c. The chairman's table he says "is surrounded by billiard sharpers, horse copers, and welchers," while in the bars are "more welchers, &c; and then "the Proprietor has a tap of his own, and never gets drunk like his customers; but, when the Hall closes, he laughs in his sleeve at his dupes' expense." In justice to the Profession to which I belong, and in fairness to the British public who support us, I trust that you will

find space for this my indignant repudiation of what I am sure you will agree with me is a most malicious and untrue libel upon an honest and hardworking section of the community. Yours truly, FREDERICK LAROCHE.
*The *London Figaro*.

TO THE EDITOR OF THE ERA.
Sir, – One of your contemporaries has thought it fit to vilify and abuse the Music Halls, their Proprietors, and *artistes*. Such glaring mis-statements only serve to show the ignorance of the author of them.

But I would point out that the journal in question does not hesitate to solicit the advertisements of those they most condemn. The enclosed will prove this. I remain, yours obediently, FRED. ALBERT.

(The article to which the above letters refer will not create much perturbation in the minds of Music Hall Managers, *artistes*, or patrons. The writer has drawn largely upon his imagination for his falsehoods. We cannot say for his memory upon his wit, because from first to last wit is almost undiscoverable. The ignorance displayed in almost every line amuses, while the spite which evidently inspired the pen provokes us. A more vulgar and untruthful effusion we have seldom if ever seen. Slang is the writer's *forte*. From long acquaintance, we presume, he knows all about horse copers, welchers, and billiard sharpers. It is certain that this would-be sharp critic has been on very close and intimate terms with the said chairman, for he had discovered that his face is well rouged; that his hair is "duly parted behind;" that in his button-hole he wears flowers purchased at the linen-drapers; and with a perfume uncommonly like that of hair-oil. As a type of the Music Hall patron he describes a butcher – a "nasty butcher" – who, yielding to the blandishments of the waiter, parts very readily with a *guinea* for "the guv'nor's benefit," a lame excuse to cover a swindle. […]

The artistes are one and all grossly libelled, and for the first time we learn that our comic singers are all remarkable for the foulness of their ditties; and that the more openly nasty and dirty their patter the more success attends them. At midnight the audience is turned into the street "all more or less drunk," and the writer, wise in his own conceit, and thanking heaven that he is not as other men, walks away convinced that the funds for "the nightly debauch" are raised by theft.

All this is, of course, so manifestly untrue that is deserves nothing but contempt, and among those who know anything of the establishments condemned it can only raise a smile of derision. If half the charges here brought against Music Halls were true such places would be promptly suppressed by the strong arm of the law. But they are not true. They are simply the creation of ignorance and malice combined. Does the writer know that the Music Halls, apart from the caddish elements with which he appears to be so intimate, nightly attract hundreds, aye, thousands of tradesmen and artisans who do not hesitate to take with them their wives and families? Does he know that some of the brightest ornaments of our Stage have been selected from the Music Hall ranks? Is he aware that the "nasty and dirty" comic singer has had the honour of Royal patronage and favour? The services of hundreds of Music Hall artists are secured with every recurring Christmas for the Theatrical boards, a fact which is by no means eloquent of the "foulness of their ditties."

This purist appears to be a nice man with nasty ideas. "Turned into the street more or less drunk," he has erected a Music Hall of his own design; has peopled it from the depth of his befuddled fancy, and has seriously set to work to demolish the whole. His effusion is beneath notice, and we feel that we are doing something analogous to breaking a butterfly upon a wheel in mentioning him at all. The establishment so unjustly attacked is to be easily recognised by the description of the locality, and its interior and exterior arrangements; and we learn that the proprietors intend to take steps to vindicate their conduct, and to repel this unjust assault upon their well-won reputation. But what are we to think of the consistency of a journal which, while admitting to one of its pages this foul abuse, in another fulsomely praises one of the most popular Music Hall artistes of the day, and at the same time sends out urgent appeals for the advertisements of the "nasty and dirty" comic singers it so cruelly condemns? […]

MORE AMATEURS AT KING'S CROSS THEATRE.
A DRAMATIC entertainment took place at the above Theatre on Wednesday evening for the benefit of Mr H. Maynard, which proved an "entertainment" in the fullest sense. Amateurs generally afford us some little amusement to compensate for their various shortcomings; but rarely indeed do they cause so much merriment as on Wednesday.

The little theatrical bandbox known as the King's Cross Theatre was completely filled by an audience evidently ripe for fun. The performers certainly gave them ample opportunities for jocularity, and never did we see dramatic aspirants so perseveringly chaffed. Frequently, too, the audience appeared better acquainted with the text of the pieces than the performers, and prompted them with their exits and entrances, and with portions of the dialogue in advance in the most ludicrous fashion, while personal comments, generally of the most unflattering character, were freely launched upon the unfortunate amateurs. Such suggestions as "enter Brown, or exit Jones," were something novel in the way of dramatic entertainment when coming from the audience instead of the prompter. Who could resist a shout of laughter when the villain of the play, supposed to be lying dead upon the stage, shifts his position in order to lie more comfortably? Who would not grin when a gentleman in the gallery thus refers to the Goddess of Night, "after you with the moon," or cries ironically, "werry pretty?" A baby cried, and somebody makes the comment "what a woice," whereat there is another shout. When the performers stand in need of the prompter the audience cry "encore," or "hear," as if the King's Cross Theatre had been the House of Commons. When the villain says, "I'm dying," a lady advises him "not to be long about it;" and when he falls dead it is remarked "that he goes down easy." But when he is carried off the stage the pent-up hilarity absolutely explodes in a roar that shakes the house. When a lady comes rather near her lover some wag says "Don't tickle him;" when a hero or heroine forgets every alternate sentence, somebody cries "Take your time." But the merriment reaches its height when in the second piece two of the performers appeal to the audience, inquiring pertinently "whether they shall go on or not?" "Try again!" "Never say die!" "Let 'em have it!" the jocular audience respond, and some suspicious-looking floral offerings fall upon the stage, which are indignantly kicked aside by a would-be aspirant for dramatic honours. […]

The comedy *All That Glitters Is Not Gold* was set down as the concluding piece, but the merriment of the audience precluded all hope of hearing or commenting upon the performance, and we quitted the King's Cross Theatre with echoes of uproarious laughter ringing in our ears as we departed.
3/5/1874

ASSAULT ON A THEATRICAL REPORTER.
On Friday, May 1st, at the Leicester Town Hall, before G. Foxton, J.T. Pilgrim, and W. Bowmar. Esqs., Frederick McFayden, who was brought in the custody of Detective Bailey from Portsmouth, the previous day, was charged with violently assaulting Edward Higginson Jolly.

Mr J.B. Fowler appeared for complainant. Defendant pleaded "Guilty," but alleged that there were extenuating circumstances.

Mr Fowler said Mr Jolly, his client, was a reporter for *The Era*, which, as the Bench were aware, was the great theatrical newspaper in London. Defendant was the Manager of a travelling company which had visited the Leicester Theatre for a fortnight or three weeks, and it appeared that on Saturday evening, as Mr Jolly was sitting in one of the boxes close to the stage, whilst the burlesque of *Chilperic* was being performed, the defendant came and struck him three violent blows across the nose. The effect of the blows was such that Mr Jolly was covered with blood, and as he walked out of the Theatre the blood streamed all along the way. It would be for the defendant to give what explanation he could of this most brutal and this most unprovoked assault. […]

Complainant was then sworn, and said – I am correspondent of *The Era*. On Saturday night, the 25th of April, I was in the Leicester Theatre, in the dress-circle close to the stage, at the corner of the boxes, where I had no chance of getting out. The defendant is the Manager of a company called Carry Nelson's company, and is, I believe, husband of Carry Nelson. The company was performing at Leicester Theatre that evening. Towards the close of the evening, while the burlesque was going on, defendant came into the box where I was, having to pass a friend of mine, who sat beside me. He came and sat down by my side, and directly he seated himself, he said, "You are the reporter of *The Era*, I think." I said, "Yes, I believe I am," in a very quiet manner, because he (defendant) seemed very excited. He said, "Then you are a d-----m s-----t, a b-----d thief, and a b-----y liar," and immediately struck out back-handed across my face, two or three times, saying, "Then take that, you b-----r." I was in the corner, and could not get away, and that was how he took advantage. I said, after he had struck me once, "What is that for?" and he muttered something, but I did not hear what it was, for I was confused. He repeated the blow, and then seized his hat, and left the house hurriedly, the people in the pit hissing and hooting. These blows caused me considerable pain. I never slept on Saturday night; in fact, my head was like a fire all night. My handkerchief was covered with blood. (Handkerchief produced.) The blood also flowed very freely all the way along the boxes from the stage to the top of the stairs. When I got outside the house part defendant was standing at the top of the box stairs, and he said, "You b-----r, this was because I wouldn't stand treat," to which I replied, "I should be very sorry to drink with a fellow like you." I presume he meant by that remark that that was the reason I had not eulogised his company, but I am convinced there were other grounds for the assault.

Defendant – Did I ask you what caused you to write and be so insulting to my wife, Miss Carry Nelson? Complainant – You did not; you asked no question about Carry Nelson.

Defendant – No question about you having grossly insulted her several times by getting up and leaving the house when singing was commencing? Defendant – No.

Defendant then addressed the Bench, and said it could not be on his own account that he could have any animosity against the complainant, because he had spoken highly of him; but whenever his wife appeared complainant got up and turned his back, and caused a disturbance. This had been so repeatedly done that he went upon the last night of performance and asked him how it was he had been so grossly insulting to Miss Carry Nelson, who was supposed to be the first burlesque actress on the English stage. He asked complainant if he meant to say that she could neither act nor sing. Complainant said "Yes," and he got up at that and struck him once back-handed across the face; it was not premeditated; he never thought of such a thing when he went to sit quietly and calmly beside him. […]

The Bench expressed their surprise that a man calling himself a Theatrical Manager should so far forget himself as to be guilty of a breach of the peace in a public place of amusement, since it was his duty to set an example to maintain order. Such things would not be allowed, and he was fined 40s. and costs, or be imprisoned for fourteen days.

10/5/1874

A MOST amusing *contretemps* occurred at the Theatre Royal, Darlington, on the occasion of the worthy Lessee's benefit a few days ago. At the close of *Still Waters Run Deep* Captain Hawksley (Mr F. Lever) was handcuffed in the usual manner, and under the care of Gimlet removed from the scene of his downfall. This was an end to Hawksley, but it was only the beginning of the comedian's trouble, for to his dismay he discovered that not a key could be found to release him from his iron bondage. To add to the dilemma, he was to appear in the next piece *Delicate Ground*. Nothing for it, therefore, but to trudge through the streets to the police-station, but even there no key dangled on the constabulary bunch competent to do the requisite business. The suffering comedian was now led to a disciple of Vulcan, who soon took off the tormenting irons, and Mr Lever was set at liberty to take part in mime transactions, having had enough and to spare of stern reality.

31/5/1874

GREAT excitement was occasioned on Monday night at the Adelphi Theatre, Liverpool, by the suicidal act of Richard Wilson, twenty-three years of age. Just before the close of the performance the young man, who had been seated in the gallery, said to two boys that in two hours from that time they could see him in his coffin, if they liked. Two minutes afterwards Wilson threw a bottle from the gallery into the pit, but it did not strike any one. Immediately afterwards the man rose from his seat, and, catching hold of the railing in front of the gallery, turned over. After hanging by his hands for a few seconds, he suddenly sprang backwards, and dropped into the stalls. The performance was just finishing, the man was picked up insensible, and conveyed to the Royal Infirmary. It was believed that he had sustained very severe injury to the back, and one of his thighs was broken.

GREAT disappointment was experienced in Leamington on Wednesday evening, in consequence of the seizure of the "properties" of the company playing with Mr and Mrs Rousby in *Mary Queen of Scots*. The performance was advertised to take place in the Royal Music Hall, Leamington, and at that place a very large and fashionable company assembled. On entering the building it was early intimated to the audience that it was not probable there would be any performance. Meanwhile, negotiations were pending with a view to prevent this mishap. Those present hoped against hope, until shortly after the hour fixed for the commencement of the play, when Mr Duck, Manager of the Theatre Royal, Bath (who has engaged Mr and Mrs Rousby and the company), posted the following: – "Notice. – The Manager regrets to announce that in consequence of an illegal seizure of his property, comprising wardrobes, &c., there will be no performance this evening." On receiving this information, the audience dispersed, after expressing considerable dissatisfaction. It appeared that during the day thirty-five packages arrived at the Great Western Railway Station at Leamington from Cheltenham (where the Rousby company last performed). As these packages were all addressed in the name of "Rousby," they were seized by the sheriff's officer, who was armed with an authority from the trustee of the estate of a jeweller, who some time ago made an arrangement with his creditors, and to whom Mr Rousby is alleged to be indebted. On arriving in Leamington, Mr Duck claimed nearly the whole of the packages as his property, but the officer refused to release them unless the amount of the debt was paid. Mr Duck offered to pay under protest, but the payment was declined under such circumstances. It is stated that the luggage was addressed to "Rousby," according to professional custom, and not because it belonged to that gentleman. The affair caused much local gossip, and much sympathy was expressed for Mrs Rousby, who feels the disappointment very acutely. Legal proceedings have been instituted by Mr Duck for the losses which he has sustained. On Thursday the costumes and properties had not been recovered, and again the performance announced had to be postponed.
7/6/1874

"LADY GODIVA" AT THE ALHAMBRA MUSIC HALL, GLOUCESTER. – *Lady Godiva* having been represented at the above place (since burnt down), attention was recently drawn to the picture posters on the walls of the city. At the Police Court the Mayor, addressing Mr Griffin, the Chief of Police, instructed him to get the prints removed from the walls. The Bench were very much surprised to see them, and he had thought of mentioning the matter before, but had overlooked it. He hoped they would be torn down at once, as they were a disgrace to the city. Mr Reynolds thought it was a great pity the prints were put about, and said he should not have been on the bench, but that he had had a strong letter addressed to him on the matter. He hoped the representation was nothing like the pictures. Mr Griffin said they should be taken down at once.
14/6/1874

TO THE EDITOR OF THE ERA.
Sir, – I beg leave to state that I did play *Lady Godiva* at Gloucester, my *own* copyright version, the horse being my *own* copyright animal, made of *wood*, with tail and mane made of my *own* copyright hair. My

posters are by a well-known and respectable firm, which ought to be proof of the good workmanship of the same. Any further correspondence upon this matter, so far as I am concerned, will be considered like the horse's tail and mane – superfluous. Yours truly, MRS MARK JOHNSON.

AMATEURS AT THE KING'S CROSS THEATRE.
[…] The important role of Jasper Carew was entrusted to Mr Lewis Stoner, whose jack-in-the-box entrance was the signal for much laughter. And why? Well, Mr Stoner's moustache is likely to haunt us for at least a week. We have heard of "an airy nothing seeking a local habitation and a name." This was an airy *something*. It curled upwards and went round and round until it claimed acquaintance with his eyebrows, so that, when wishing to face the bloodthirsty Colonel, he valiantly exclaimed that he had a nerve which never blenched, a conscience void of reproach, and other useful articles, we quite expected to hear him add that there was also in his possession a moustache, the sight of which would make his enemies tremble in their boots. […]
28/6/1874

SCRUMPTIOUS. – "I should have run down ere this, but am not satisfied that I should not be an annoyance." First Advertisement. CAPTAIN SCUTTLE.
12/7/1874

IT will, doubtless, be remembered by many of our readers that at Christmas last Miss Carry Reynham, engaged as Columbine at the Prince of Wales' Theatre, Rochdale, fell through an opening in the stage, injuring her back and side. Since that time the poor girl has been under the hands of several medical men, but to no purpose. A fortnight last she entered the Royal Free Hospital, and on Saturday last, about four o'clock, she died. A post mortem examination, held on Monday last, proved that her death was the result of injuries she has sustained in the fall.

SUSAN is earnestly requested to Communicate with her Parents at 46, Wycliffe Road, Shipley, near Bradford, and Telegraph to W., Post-office, Southampton, who only wishes to send basket. A terrible communication to make. For goodness sake attend to this.

LIVING WONDER. – On SALE, until August 12th, a Handsome DOUBLE-HEADED CALF, Thirteen Weeks Old. In Good Health. Eats and Drinks with both mouths. Apply to Mr A. KELSALL, Burton Joyce, Notts.
2/8/1874

TO THE EDITOR OF THE ERA.
Sir, – Knowing the deep interest you take in maintaining the respectability of the Theatrical Profession, I wish to call your attention to something that took place in this town this week, when Mrs Liston's *Angot* company were at the Theatre Royal. One of the ladies of the company received, through the post, a most insulting letter, of which she took no notice. On the following day another of the same stamp was handed to her by one of the boys of the Theatre, who had received a shilling for its delivery. The lady was in great trouble, and the cause becoming known to some of the gentlemen of the company they determined to make an example of the offender. They accordingly kept the engagement suggested in the letter, and thoroughly humbled the fellow by making him apologise on his bended knees in the public street. A slight notice in your paper of this disgraceful conduct and its chastisement might act as a warning to other men, whose own instincts will not prevent them from insulting Professional ladies. I am, Sir, yours respectfully, F.B.
Leeds, August 6th, 1874.

ON Thursday afternoon, in the Brompton County Court, before Mr Sergeant Wheeler, a case was heard which caused considerable amusement to a crowded court. Mr John Mason, a veterinary surgeon, carrying on business at No. 1A, Elizabeth Street, Pimlico, brought an action against Miss Wilmot (actress), who resides at 10, Michael's Grove, Brompton, to recover the sum of £3 10s. for "medical attendance to your dog, suffering from distemper, inflamed lungs, and bronchitis, from the 31st March until April 17th, thirty-six doses of fever medicine, twenty-four doses of tonic medicine, liniment, and application to the chest and throat." Mr Edmund Newman appeared for the defendant; and the plaintiff conducted his own case.

The plaintiff deposed to attending the defendant's dog at her request, and he stated that his charges were fair and reasonable. The animal was seventeen days in his infirmary. He sent the dog home; but the defendant gave it so much rice pudding that it became worse. (Laughter.)

Mr Newman – Did you after the death of the dog call upon Miss Wilmot and want to make a post-mortem examination? (Roars of laughter.) Witness, emphatically – No, sir.

Mr Newman said the fact was the plaintiff only had the dog twelve days. The charge was exorbitant, and the defendant declined to pay it.

The plaintiff was then somewhat severely cross-examined by Mr Newman. He said the dog was cured when he sent it back, but he admitted that it was sick on the door-step. The charge for keeping a dog was 2s. per day, with extras. He provided beef-tea for the dog, which he purchased from Fortnum and Mason's; and he gave it the best port wine and quinine. (Laughter.) The beef-tea cost 6s. per pound.

A professional witness was called, and he considered the plaintiff's charges fair and reasonable. Mr Cherry, the well-known veterinary surgeon, stated that 2s. per day should include everything.

Miss Wilmot was called, and she stated that the plaintiff only had the charge of the dog for twelve days. When the dog was returned it appeared starved. She gave it some rice pudding, which it ate ravenously, and died on the following day. The defendant wanted to make a post-mortem examination, but she refused to allow him to do so. After hearing other evidence, his Honour gave judgement for the plaintiff for 30s. and costs.
9/8/1874

A DISTURBANCE AT A "DARK SEANCE."
Two tradesmen, named Blake and Pickeys, were charged at Newcastle-on-Tyne on Thursday with assaulting a Gateshead tradesman named Auckland at a "dark *seance*" after the latter had thrown a light on the proceedings by unexpectedly exhibiting a dark lantern. It was maintained by the prosecutor and his witness that when the light was exhibited one of the mediums was off her seat and loose, and that a man was beating the floor with a fiddle when he was supposed to be sitting quietly in the circle. Neither the cross-examination nor the evidence for the defence disproved those statements, confirmation, in fact, being furnished by one of the witnesses for the defence, but the Magistrates, who considered that they had nothing to do with the deciding of the character of the phenomena, were of the opinion that the prosecutor was at fault in breaking the conditions, but on the other hand the defendants had no right to prevent him leaving the room, and therefore they thought that justice would be done by each party paying their own costs.
23/8/1874

AT the Theatre Royal, Cambridge, on the 11th inst., the performances wound up with the tragedy of *Maria Marten; or, the Murder at the Red Barn*. The curtain fell after William Corder, the murderer, had been brought to the scaffold, and with the rope dangling over his head "improved the occasion." The audience refused to leave, and when the orchestra played the National Anthem, it was received with hisses and clamour, and the crowded audience remained in their places. At length Mr Frederick Hughes, the Manager, presented himself, and apologised for being unable to gratify his patrons by actually hanging the actor – Mr Concannen – who represented the murderer, William Corder, unless with his

own consent, which he was hardly likely to give. The "gods" shouted furiously, "Bring him out with the rope round his neck." Of course the demand was not complied with, and after more demonstrations of their desire to see the representative of the Suffolk murderer actually hanged the crowded audience slowly, and with manifest reluctance, left the house.
20/9/1874

MR WILLIAM HODGES, dramatic agent, and at present connected with the company performing at the Amphitheatre, Liverpool, on Wednesday summoned James Dolan for assaulting him on the 22nd inst., and detaining goods belonging to the complainant. Mr Hodges said he was engaged to superintend the production of a piece at the Amphitheatre, and on Monday morning, before leaving Manchester, he received a post-card stating that comfortable apartments might be had at No. 9, Gill Street, Liverpool. He came to Liverpool late on Sunday night, and went to the house. When he went to bed he had no rest whatever, as the bed was infested with bugs. The defendant said that things would be made comfortable by the next night, and the next night he found that the place had been washed and clean linen put on the bed. However, on looking at the bed he saw numbers of the troublesome customers that had annoyed him the previous night. He called the defendant that he might see them for himself. As it was so late, he (Mr Hodges) said he would stay for that night, and he then went to bed, leaving the candle lighted, so that the bugs might be scared away. (Laughter.) However, when the candle was burnt out they returned to the attack, and he was again unable to get any rest. The next morning he sent for a cab, and gave the defendant 4s. for the two nights he had stayed at the house. The defendant then refused to allow him to take away his portmanteau unless he paid 12s. for a week's rent.

The Magistrate – The fact of your being driven out in this way by bugs is a sufficient answer to such a claim. I don't believe you were even bound to pay for a night's lodging. Mr Hodges said that as he was leaving the house the defendant's wife and other people prevented him from taking his portmanteau. The defendant also assaulted him. The Magistrate asked what the defendant had to say. The defendant said he thought he had a right to detain the things. The Magistrate – You had not the shadow of a right to detain them. A man goes to your rooms, and cannot occupy them in consequence of bugs, which is a sufficient ground for a tenant or lodger leaving instanter. The Magistrate ordered the defendant to give up the goods in question, and pay the expenses.
27/9/1874

ON Monday afternoon Mr Carter held an inquest at the Victoria Tavern, Waterloo Road, on the body of Frederick Clacy, aged thirty, better known in the theatrical world as the "dwarf policeman." The evidence given showed that the deceased had for many years been on the boards of some of the minor Metropolitan Theatres, and at each recurring Christmastide was engaged at the Victoria as "Policeman X," where his appearance in a coat of blue created much merriment, owing to his very limited stature, which was only 39½ inches. He had also been engaged by the Christy Minstrels, and for the past week had been exhibiting himself as a dwarf, in the company of Miss Swan, the "Fat Lady," in South London. Whilst being exhibited on the 7th inst. he suddenly fell back insensible, and was carried home and placed in bed, but appeared to rally a little during the evening. All night he walked about the house, and at eight o'clock the following morning was found on the floor of his bedroom lying downwards, dead and cold. Dr Hadwin stated that he had no doubt death was the result of an apoplectic fit, and the Coroner having summed up the case to the Jury, a verdict was returned accordingly. Some of the Jury expressed their surprise that deceased had not died long ago, having regard to the way in which he was always being knocked about.

LAST Thursday night, about nine o'clock, some commotion was caused at Covent Garden Theatre by the loud report of fire-arms and a scuffle amongst the audience in that area of the Theatre. The cause of the commotion turned out to be the going off of a revolver in the pocket of a young gentleman, who was

at once taken in custody. A gentleman named Stewart, who was standing beside the prisoner, had a narrow escape, the ball passing by his legs and burying itself in the floor. On being charged at Bow Street the prisoner gave the name of Hiram Thompson, and stated that he had only just come to this country. The revolver was loaded in five of its six chambers with ball, and the prisoner declared that its going off in his pocket was the result of an accident while he was "playing" with the trigger.
18/10/1874

DURING the run of *Clancarty* at the Royal Amphitheatre, Liverpool, the action of the play at its most critical point was more than once rudely interrupted and interfered with by a general rush by the audience from the Theatre just before public-house closing time for the purpose of being refreshed. This stampede was more general than usual one night last week, and this led Mr Richard Younge to exclaim "Ladies and gentlemen, we are waiting on you. Are we to go on with the play or not?" There was immediately a calm, and the play was proceeded with.
25/10/1874

AT the Liverpool Police Court on Monday last Mr Henry F. Ferrand and Mr Harry Jackson, the well-known actors, now engaged at the Theatre Royal of the above town, were charged with being drunk and riotous on the evening of the 30th ult. From the evidence it appeared that both defendants, having interfered to protect a woman from the brutal conduct of the police, were themselves "run in," the usual charge of drunk and riotous (a ready and convenient excuse for the blunders of the force) being preferred. Mr M. de Frece, Mr B. Henry, Mr J.K. Walton, Mr F. Walton, Mr E. Price, Mr E. Campbell, Mr Wray, and others connected with the Theatre Royal were called, and stated that both defendants were perfectly sober during the evening's performance, and also shortly before the "disturbance" took place; and Mr Aspinall (one of the presiding Magistrates), in at once dismissing the complaint, stated that he only refrained from commenting on the conduct of the police because it had been intimated that summonses for their alleged violence would be carried out.
8/11/1874

TO THE EDITOR OF THE ERA.
Sir, – Allow me to thank the Manager of the South London Musick Hall, through the columns of your Paper, for the Great Pleasure and enjoyment his Ballet has afforded me. No words can sufficiently praise it. It is a revival of the True Ballet of the most Classic Times of the Ballet of the Italian Opera House; no vulgar display of mere legs like the modern Can-Can dancing. The *Choir de Ballet* at the South London, on the contrary, is such that no man who has a true feeling for the Beautiful, the very Poetry of Dancing, can be otherwise than delighted; and I pity the man in whom such pure and Classic dancing can call forth a coarse remark. Such a man must be without a soul. The young girls are all pretty – one prettier than another; and there is more than one whose sweet face I should like to have my last look rest on if I were on my death-bed; and if an Old Veteran can ever hope to go to heaven he feels sure that such faces will be there. Hoping that you will kindly insert this, or any Part of it you think best of, believe me yours obediently, MAJOR C.W. HIND.
Kensington House, Snelbrook, near Southampton.
P.S. – If you charge for insertion let me know by return the amount and I will send check.
22/11/1874

IN the Christmas Pantomime at Sanger's National Amphitheatre the Proprietors will introduce a novelty in the shape of an instrument named the "Orchestrion," which comprises the collective power of a full brass band of twenty performers. The instrument, which is built somewhat after the principle of a barrel organ, is contained in a handsome mahogany case 9ft. high, 7ft. 6in. in width, and 3ft. 6in. in depth, the whole being supported on lofty pedestals. It contains ninety-seven keys, representing seven organ octaves, to which are juxtaposed two octaves of trumpets, trombones, and clarionets, with the usual

auxiliaries, such as cymbals, the major and minor drums, &c. The instrument, which plays the following ten operatic and other selections, viz.: – The Gipsies' Chorus of the *Trovatore*, the opening chorus of *Ernani*, the Bishops' Chorus of the *Africaine*, the final Septuor of *Lucia*, the Rose Song of *The Talisman*, *Flick and Flock* Galop, the Quadrille and Conspirators' Chorus from *La Fille de Madame Angot*, the *Blue Danube* Waltz, and the *Leonie March* by M. Chiaro Frati, has been constructed by M. Chiaro Frati, organ-builder, Farringdon-road, and will be driven by a small donkey engine specially constructed for the purpose.
6/12/1874

WHILST Day's Menagerie was exhibiting at Cawood last week, a young man amused himself by teasing one of the elephants. It happened that a heavy sliding bar turning on a pivot at one end was accessible to the insulted animal. It watched for its opportunity, and at a favourable moment detached the loose end of the heavy bar and let it fall on the young man's head, causing a deep wound. The animal then calmly walked away, satisfied with the punishment inflicted. The young man was afterwards much affected in his head, but is now out of danger.
13/12/1874

6
1875
FIVE MURDERS, SEVEN SUICIDES AND EIGHT GHOSTS

ONE of the magicians whose lot in life it is to work spells by which the magnificence of our various Pantomimes is considerably enhanced is Mr J.B. Winder, of Lawley Street, Birmingham. The Coloured Fires manufactured by this gentleman have an advantage over most others by their freedom from those noxious ingredients which give forth during the process of combustion vapours of a highly irritating and and injurious character. Good colour, great brilliancy, and perfect safety are their chief recommendations.

THE successful Pantomime of *Little Red Riding Hood*, produced by Mr Horace Butler at the Theatre Royal, Bishop Auckland, was, on Monday night, attended by an melancholy occurrence. During the performance Mr Fred. Watson, who took the part of the Cat, was taken with a pain in his head, and complained to his fellow actors. He sat down behind the wing, and when the cue was given he rose to go on the stage, but before reaching it he fell on the ground and never spoke afterwards. He was at once attended by his companions, and medical assistance sent for, but none arrived until it was too late, the poor young fellow dying a few hours after. Effusion of blood on the brain was the cause of death. Deceased, who was twenty-one years of age, was a native of London.

AT the Crystal Palace a skating fête took place on Friday evening on the great fountain basins, illuminated for the occasion by means of bonfires, coloured lights, and other appliances. Messrs Brock and Co's pyrotechnic arrangements were on a sufficiently large scale to render the scene extremely picturesque. The bonfires and limelights on the lakes brought out into lurid relief the skaters as they threaded their way in the crowd, while the bursting rockets from above shed their momentary brilliancy upon the ice and the frost-bedecked banks around. A very pretty effect was added to the evolutions of the skaters by the circulation, in large numbers, of Chinese lanterns, which, held in the hand or suspended from walking-sticks, presented a glowworm-like appearance in the expanse of snow. The band of the St George's Volunteer Rifles quickened the pace of skating by a constant succession of lively airs.

GOLDEN HAIR, GOLDEN HAIR, GOLDEN HAIR. – FAIRY FLUID, Perfectly Harmless, and Never Failing, from the Recipe of an Eminent Physician. Will convert the Darkest Brunette into "A Fair One with the Golden Locks" in a few hours, and make a Fair One Fairer. Price Half-a-Guinea per Bottle. To be obtained only of Mr FRED HUGHES, 9, Wellington Street, Strand, Five Doors from the Strand towards Waterloo Bridge.
3/1/1875

AT the Cheltenham Police Court, on Tuesday, William McNatty, a Pantaloon, was charged with stealing a watch and chain from his lodgings in Henrietta Street. The case having been proved, prisoner pleaded that he had been drinking, and did not know what he was doing; he had no felonious intention, as he had left his money and clothes with his landlady to take care of. Two witnesses said the prisoner was dancing and capering about, and appeared more mad than anything else. When asked to plead, he said he supposed he must plead guilty, but threw himself on the mercy of the Bench. He was committed to gaol for one month.
10/1/1875

ON Sunday last a dog-cart accident occurred on the road between the Felling and Usworth. Mr Alexander, the Clown at the Theatre Royal, Newcastle-upon-Tyne; Mr Cooper, Manager for Messrs Cockburn, Haymarket Horse Bazaar; Mr Grant, of the Monument Hotel, Newcastle; and Mr Thomas Wallace, were seated in the dog-cart, to which was yoked a valuable mare. They were on the turnpike road a short distance from the Felling, when a black retriever dog belonging to Mr Wright, Felling, jumped at the mare's head and and seized the horse with its teeth. The horse, in consequence of the bite, commenced to plunge and kick violently. The next moment the mare dashed over the hedge at the roadside, and with the dog-cart and its occupants fell heavily into a ploughed field on the other side. The drop from the hedge to the field was fully five feet. The occupants of the dog-cart were sent sprawling on the ploughed land in a variety of shapes and directions, and had scarcely recovered from the spill when they saw the mare, which had broken from her trappings, galloping across the field, and it was not until she had ran across four fields that she came to a standstill. Beyond receiving an uncomfortable shock from the fall, and being bespattered with the dirt, the four gentlemen were unhurt; and they have good reason to congratulate themselves on their wonderful escape from injury.
31/1/1875

ONE of the thespians in the Pantomime at the Theatre Royal, Manchester, recently gave birth to a lamb, which necessitated a temporary relinquishment of its histrionic appearances. Mother and child are now doing well, and the little stranger made its appearance before the footlights, in company with its mamma, to the great delight of the audience.

WE should very much like to know on what grounds poor orphan children of City schools ought to be debarred from seeing a Pantomime. At a meeting of the Common Council, on Monday, Mr Medwin gravely inquired whether it was true that the children attending the orphan schools had received permission to see the Pantomime at the Surrey Theatre. Of course, the question was greeted with derisive laughter by the more rational members of the Council; but Mr Medwin had not done with them yet, and requested the Committee "to consider carefully the evil consequences of taking children to such places." At this point our philosopher was again interrupted by renewed laughter, and and was finally "shut up" by Mr Ashby, the Chairman, who told this bigoted noodle that it was by the express desire of the Lord Mayor that the children were to be taken to a morning performance, and they acquiesced with the wishes of his Lordship. Mr Medwin must be a jovial and genial spirit truly, to grudge these poor children a few hours' harmless enjoyment of stage fairyland and the humours of Clown and Pantaloon. What have they to cheer them, poor creatures? They are orphans. Their very food and clothing depend upon the bounty of others, and they must, in most cases, look forward to a career of toil. There are unhappily too many of the Medwin school of philosophy who would shut out from the young, and especially if the young are poor also, every glimpse of a more cheerful and genial existence, so that they may become mere plodding machines, to do the rough work of the world, and to make life a little easier for the Medwins.
14/2/1875

ON the 15th inst., at the Guildhall, Norwich, before the Mayor, A.F.C. Bolingbroke and F. Brown, Esqs., a youth named William Robert Pottle was charged with willfully breaking a gas globe at the Theatre. From the evidence, it appeared that during the performance on the 13th a number of the occupants of the "celestial regions" were regaling themselves with the delicacy known as "trotters," and to dispose of the bones amused themselves by throwing them at the globes, which they did with marvellous dexterity and, of course, damage. The prisoner was detected in the act, and Mr Chaplin (the Lessee), having had nearly the whole of his gas glasses broken, gave him into custody. The Magistrates sentenced the prisoner to fourteen days imprisonment with hard labour, and a week additional, unless the costs, 8s. 6d., were paid.
21/2/1875

FROM AN OCCASIONAL CORRESPONDENT.
THE readers of *The Era* will perhaps peruse with interest a few remarks on a theatrical performance of a character which, if not novel in this country, is certainly most infrequent. On Monday, the 15th inst., was presented in the Town Hall, Shoreditch, by special licence from the Lord Chamberlain*, and permission of the Chief Rabbi, a dramatic rendering of the History of Joseph, in the Polish tongue, for the first time in London, and, as I believe, in England. […]

There are about thirty-six characters in the piece, of whom Jacob, Joseph, Potiphar and his wife, and Pharoah, are the principals. Reuben, Benjamin, and the other brothers are little more than a chorus, and the remaining parts, though necessary to the story, are of minor importance. Of the acting and singing – the drama is a musical one – much in praise may be said. The thoughtful, melancholy, dreaming Joseph, was rendered with much quiet earnestness by the performer, who was young, and had a pleasant and musical voice, and was of agreeable presence. In a scene devoted to some spectral illusion – the dream of Joseph, I understand – an Angel was supposed to appear to him, and the performer created interest out of a most inartistically-arranged incident. He was also very successful in another scene, where, at the grave of his mother Rachel, he invokes and is answered by his mother's spirit, who promises to watch over his future destiny, and urges him to good and virtuous conduct. The scene with Potiphar's wife was very discreetly managed, the youth who played the lady singing a very pleasant melody with considerable taste. The role of Jacob was also well played. The part of Potiphar was fairly interpreted, but might have been made in dignity much more important. Reuben showed some ability in depicting grief at the loss of a favourite brother. Pharoah was not to our mind a tithe as kingly as he should have been. Perhaps the costumes and entire absence of scenery depressed him.

The costumes were peculiarly Polish. I was assured they were quite correct. Jacob wore a tall fur cap, loose paletot without pockets, drab smalls, white stockings, and patent leather shoes. All his sons, except Joseph and Benjamin, wore Polish hats, square topped, blue or orange, with braided cords. The elder ones wore double-breasted coats; the others striped tunics – all wearing cross-gartered stockings, like Polish peasants. Potiphar was attired in black frock-coat, white waistcoat, black trousers, and hat, carried a walking-cane, smoked good cigars, and used wax tapers. The Butler, Baker, Jacob's Servant, and an Interpreter wore the present European costumes. The novelty of the performance and its peculiarities are sufficient, I trust, for troubling you with so long an account. The vocal music and accompaniments were, I understood, adaptations of old Hebrew and Polish melodies. A small but efficient band conduced to the success of the representation, which was announced for two successive evenings.
*The Lord Chamberlain had in fact stated that his permission to stage the play was not required, as although the work contained Biblical characters – forbidden to be represented on the British stage – "it was performed by Jews, for Jews, and in a Jewish language."

WANTED, Four Handsome GIRLS, from Sixteen to Twenty, for a Twelve Months' Season on the Continent, in a high-toned Entertainment. They must have had some training as Club Swingers,

Acrobats, or Ballet Dancers. Wardrobe furnished, all expenses paid, and a good salary. Enclose Photos. Address, CONTINENT, care Walter's, News Agent, 409, Strand.
21/3/1875

AMATEUR ACROBATS AT THE ALBION THEATRE.
A VERY large audience assembled at the Albion Theatre on Wednesday evening, attracted chiefly by a very novel and exciting contest in rope climbing. Mdlles Nathalie, Leontine, and Blanche have been engaged at the above Theatre, and their very graceful performances could not be otherwise than attractive. It was a happy thought, however, to turn the remarkable talents of Mdlle Blanche to account in a challenge given by her to any ten men who chose to compete with her in climbing the high rope from the stage to the roof of the Theatre […]: "After her usual performance Blanche will challenge ten men, professional or amateur gymnasts, sailors, or others, to climb a rope by hands and feet more times than all put together. Two ropes will be suspended from the ceiling of the Theatre, the challenged persons to have the choice of rope. Blanche will commence to ascend her rope with the first man, who will climb as many times as he can; the second will then take his place, and so on. Blanche will not leave her rope until the ten men have been tired out, and each man will receive one shilling for each time he reaches the top of the rope. Should Blanche be beaten she will, besides, give fifty pounds to be divided among the victors. If Blanche is victorious, she claims only the title of 'Veni, Vidi, Vici.' The first ten men who give their names to the manager shall be accepted for the challenge."

It must be noted that previous to the contest taking place Mdlle Blanche had gone through the whole of her performance without the slightest curtailment, while her opponents came fresh to their work. […] The ten men having been called from the audience assembled upon the stage. They were of all sorts and sizes, one quite a lad, while others were strapping fellows one would hardly have thought likely to be so easily beaten by a young lady. But we live under "Petticoat Government," and in an age when the "Rights of Woman" are loudly trumpeted forth. The real secret, however, remains to be told. The feat is one requiring not strength so much as skill. The competitors were told to appear "in clean and suitable attire," but two or three of them would have been none the worse for soap and water and a polish with a Turkish towel. The excitement amongst the audience became great when when two ropes were let down from the ceiling, one for Mdlle Blanche and one for her rivals, and they watched impatiently for the climbing.

No. One began briskly, and quickly reached the roof, coming down steadily, and again performing the same operation; but twice was enough for him. No. Two was a "heavyweight," and his appearance on the rope was droll in the extreme, owing to the extraordinary movements of his legs. We question whether the octopus in the Brighton Aquarium ever made fuller use of his "feelers" than did this eccentric competitor. He, however, only reached the ceiling once, and "came down with a run," amidst vociferous laughter. No. Three went steadily to work, and got twice to the ceiling, and then gave it up as a bad job. No. Four essayed, but only climbed the rope once. No. Five went up once, jerking and jumping at the rope like a frog trying to get over long grass, but having ascended once he only got up half way a second time, and stuck fast. No. Six acted in a precisely similar manner, while No. Seven failed ignominiously, roars of laughter greeting his rapid descent, after having only reached half way up the rope. No. Eight made a gallant struggle. He evidently would not tamely yield the prize, but he was dead beat after only climbing twice. No. Nine faintly and feebly climbed but once, but the last man looked as if he meant business, and Mdlle Blanche put on a little extra steam. But No. Ten could only ascend twice, which number, as we have seen, was not passed by any competitor.

Meanwhile Mdlle Blanche had, with the greatest ease, climbed fifteen times without leaving her rope, and, in order to prove that there was no difference between her rope and that of her rivals, she climbed once more upon the latter, making sixteen times, thus accomplishing what the whole ten men had failed to do, and more. Hearty cheers greeted the conclusion, and Mr Abrahams (the Manager) then called the

men forward, and paid them as per agreement, the competitor who failed to reach the ceiling receiving his shilling as well as the rest, and everybody being satisfied that the trial was a fair one.
28/3/1875

MUCH interest has been excited at Aldershot, and, indeed, throughout the country, in consequence of the supposed suicide of Mrs H. Percy, a professional singer, at Aldershot, who is believed to have drowned herself rather than submit to the conditions of the Contagious Diseases Act, as required by the police, who suspected her of immoral intercourse with the soldiers of the garrison.

It appears that since the death of her husband, some ten months ago, Mrs Percy has been engaged at the Red, White, and Blue Music Hall, which forms part of the Alliance Inn, situate in the main thoroughfare of the town. In the course of her performances here she received an intimation from the authorities of the Metropolitan Police, who are charged with the administration of the Act, that she had brought herself within the scope of the law, and would be required to attend at the police-station and be duly registered*, or to appear before a Magistrate and disprove the evidence that would be brought against her. She chose rather to leave the town, and accordingly went off with her daughter to reside with friends at Windsor. About a fortnight ago the agent for the Music Hall at the Queen's Tap, on the outskirts of the camp, engaged Mrs Percy to appear there. In the course of this engagement Inspector Godfrey, whose duty it is to carry out the provisions of the law, warned the Proprietor of the Music Hall that Mrs Percy had been required to submit to the Act and had failed to comply. Fearing probably that his licence might be withdrawn, the Proprietor dismissed the unfortunate woman at once.

She had relatives at Aldershot, with whom she stayed for a day or two, and on Saturday night last she was accidentally met in the street by Mr Solly Lewis, who played in the last Crystal Palace Pantomime, and who has known Mrs Percy for some years, and has acted with her. She informed Mr Lewis and his wife, who was with him, that she had come back to clear her good name. There can be little doubt that at this time she was somewhat inebriated. About eleven o'clock at night she parted from a young soldier with whom she had been walking on the hills. Next forenoon her lifeless body was found in the canal.

The inquest was held on Tuesday evening, when it transpired that the deceased had been living with a professional singer named Ritson as his wife. Mr Superintendent Stephenson denied most emphatically that he had ever threatened to oppose the licence of the Hall where deceased was engaged. The Jury returned a verdict "That deceased was found dead in Basingstoke Canal, but there was no evidence to show by what means she had got into the water."
**As a prostitute.*
4/4/1875

WANTED, a BLACK FEMALE, Age Sixteen to Eighteen Years, to learn the Equestrian Art. Terms, Board, Lodging, Clothing, &c., and £10 per annum. For further particulars apply to T.C. BARLOW, Colour Printer, 311, St Vincent Street, Glasgow.
11/4/1875

RATHER a farcical incident recently occurred at Greenwich, in which a low comedian was concerned. Mr Harry Simms, of the Victoria and Greenwich Theatres, was speaking to a friend in London Street when suddenly a policeman asked him to step into the hotel opposite for a few moments, as a little matter of importance required an additional witness. He, with his usual courtesy, at once complied, and with twelve others was sworn in, but for what reason was *never* even hinted to him. They all then apparently took their departure, and Mr Simms at once, satisfied that he had done some one good service, went home to his domestic circle, little dreaming that it was his duty to view a dead body. Imagine, then, his astonishment, when the next day he was arrested by order of the Coroner for a fine of 40s., for not fulfilling his oath as a sworn Juryman. After a full explanation, the Coroner saw the blunder that had been made, and at once ordered his release.

From a review of a performance at the Cambridge Music Hall, London:
Messrs Elton and Hilston proved a very comical couple. They personated the Rival Showmen, who tell lies most extraordinary to the gaping crowd, and by the aid of these induce their patrons to "walk up and be in time." Inside the show of one of them we are promised a terribly realistic drama entitled *The Ruthless Dog-Headed Ruffian of the Deep; or, the Fatal Cough Drop*. Outside their *piece de resistance* is called *The Blood-Stained Barn Door; or, the Monkey and the Nuts*, in seventeen acts, embracing five murders, seven suicides, and eight ghosts. This, in spite of its terrible title, proved a very diverting affair, the pronunciation and style of the actors of the "blood and thunder" school being hit off with excellent skill, and with a rare appreciation of the humorous.

TO THE PROFESSION. – Notice to those Persons who have at different times Borrowed Money from me and have broken their promise time after time, and particularly those who have obtained certain sums from me under what I have since proved to be False Pretences. – This is to give them fair warning, that if the said Sums of Money are not Repaid to me One Month from this date, I will publish each and every one of their names, with full particulars, in *The Era*, for I find it useless to institute proceedings against persons who are devoid of honour and betray the confidence imposed in the Profession. SAM HAGUE, St James's Hall, Liverpool. April 24th, 1875.
25/4/1875

MR S. HAYES, of the West End Box Office, 199, Regent Street, has recently brought out a novelty which should prove an incentive to lady playgoers to book their seats at his establishment. The novelty is called the West End Box Fan. It is elegant in design, is beautifully scented, and, besides being useful, answering all the purposes of an ordinary fan, it is also instructive. Each section of it contains the box plan of a West End Theatre, the following being included in the number: – Covent Garden, Gaiety, Olympic, Strand, Criterion, Drury Lane, Vaudeville, Princess's, Court, Lyceum, Globe, and Prince of Wales's. By its aid the exact position of every numbered seat may be seen at a glance, and to playgoers generally it will doubtless prove invaluable. One of its greatest recommendations is its price, for it costs – nothing. It is presented gratis to every person booking a seat at Mr Hayes's office.

Notice to Showmen and Others. TO BE SOLD or LET, the Largest PIG in the Kingdom, near One Ton in Weight. Selling Price £50. For further particulars apply to MR CHARLES STAMPS, Sheepwash Lane, Old Crown Inn, Great Bridge, near Tipton, Staffordshire.
9/5/1875

TO THE EDITOR OF THE ERA.
Sir, – Will you, for the guidance of my brother and sister professionals, insert the following facts? Some time back, while travelling from Euston Square to Northampton, a fish basket was placed on top of my wife's luggage, and the ice and refuse running therefrom went through the wicker of the basket and spoilt a "prince's" stage costume contained therein. I immediately put in a claim on the Company for £1, my wife being careful not to over-estimate the damage, and a representative of the Company expressed himself perfectly satisfied as to the claim being reasonable. The matter was, I thought, settled, when the Company's representative again called and requested to know the value of all the contents of the basket, which I told him was £40. I then received a letter from the Company saying that, as the luggage exceeded £10 value, they cannot be held liable for the loss sustained. I hope this may act as a caution to professionals, and, with apologies for troubling you, I am, yours respectfully, E. BROWN (Brown and Kelly), Comic Duettists.
16/5/1875

TO THE EDITOR OF THE ERA.

Sir, – In the second volume of *The Life of Edmund Kean*, by F.W. Hawkins (Tinsley Brothers, 1869), at page 99, I find the following (to me) singular passage: "He (Edmund Kean) did not, *like an actor of the present day*, seek to deprive his actresses of the opportunity of making any particular 'point' or effect *by twisting their wrists*, and adopting *other painful means*, to momentarily distract their attention from the performance." If any actor of the day is given to such a rascally trick I know full well that certain considerations of the law of libel would not allow of the publication of his name; but I should be glad if you would publish this, so that, if such contemptible practices exist, a ventilation of them, without names of the offenders, may have the effect of putting an end to them, and benefiting those unfortunates whose wrists are in danger of dislocation from such brutish ferocity. But I fain would trust that "an actor of the present day" (whose name it would do me good to see in print) stands alone in his wrist-wrenching propensities. I am, your obedient servant, OBSERVER.

6/6/1875

TO THE EDITOR OF THE ERA.

Sir, – Now that morning performances are becoming so fashionable I crave, through the medium of *The Era*, to make a respectful protest to the ladies. I frequently occupy a seat in the pit at popular Theatres, and constantly attend morning concerts, but, however delighted I may be with what I *hear*, owing to the head-dresses adopted by the ladies *seeing* is out of the question.

This is particularly annoying when, for instance, I go to witness the performances of an actor like Salvini. It is quite impossible to catch more than an occasional glimpse of his fine features owing to the manner in which the ladies arrange their bonnets and feathers and build up their back hair. Sometimes it literally stands on end "like quills upon the fretful porcupine," or it is drawn over huge combs into a kind of crown, on the top of which is perched a tall hat, which may, after the fashion of the Court of Charles the Second, have broad flaps, or, what is quite as bad, a "nodding plume" of vast proportions. If possible, the bonnets are even worse obstructions than the hats; for however gossamer-like the materials may be, the shape is certain to be expansive enough. It cannot be called a head *covering*, since it generally projects several inches above or beyond the head, being commonly fastened – by means I do not pretend to fathom – to an enormous plait of hair, which never grew on the owner's head, or else it rests on the topmost folds of a mighty chignon.

But I have not yet concluded all my complaints against the bonnet which is worn by many of the fair sex solely as a flower-pot. It does not shelter the head from the cold, but it serves to hold a fearful and wonderful display of artificial flowers. There they dance before my eyes – primroses, tulips, camelias, forget-me-nots, wreaths of ivy, oakleaves, bunches of cherries, ferns; in fact, I might exhaust all the varieties of the garden and conservatory in attempting to describe them.

Possibly the ladies are amused, as with their lorgnettes they criticise each other, but *I want to see the play*. The most passionate scene in a great Shakespearean tragedy is but a thing of "fire and fury signifying nothing" if I cannot see the faces of the actors. I might as well be peeping through a tropical forest with cockatoos and other birds of wonderful plumage on every branch to try to see the stage through all this feminine array. It is nearly as bad at morning concerts. We may hear Patti, Nilsson, or Titiens, but unless we are close to the orchestra we cannot see them. In a large Theatre or Concert Room some must inevitably occupy back seats. I, therefore, appeal to you, Mr Editor, and remain your obedient servant, Q IN THE CORNER.

20/6/1875

THE colonnade of Drury Lane Theatre was displaced by the violent storm of Sunday morning, and fell into Russell-street with a tremendous crash. It was fortunate, indeed, that the accident happened when it did, or a most serious catastrophe might have been the result. No one was hurt, and early on Monday the necessary repairs were at once proceeded with, so that not the slightest interference took place with the performances of the day, a morning one, in which Signor Salvini appeared, and an evening representation of *Lohengrin*. The portion of the colonnade swept away weighed many tons.

NOTICE. – The Friends of JEAN SURLANDO, Gymnast, will regret to hear of the Sad Loss of his Performing Dog "CHARLIE," through being accidentally killed at Fenton, Staffordshire, by being run over by a passing Train.
18/7/1875

LOVELINESS ON THE INCREASE. – A marked increase in female loveliness is the eye-catching result of the immense popularity which HAGEN'S MAGNOLIA BALM has obtained among ladies everywhere. Complexions radiant with snowy purity, and tinged with the roseate hue of health, are commonly met with, whenever it is used. Sold by all Chemists and Perfumers, in bottles and elegant Toilet Case, at 3s. 6d. Depot, 114 and 116, Southampton Row, London. – (ADVT)

IF this should Meet the Eye of MRS BLAND, Exhibitor of Fat Child, by writing to her Son, JOHN BLAND, she would hear of something to her advantage. Address, JOHN BLAND, Tommy Dodd Exhibition, Weighbridge, Jersey, Channel Islands.
25/7/1875

MR LIONEL BROUGH, the celebrated Blue Beard of Miss Lydia Thompson's company, now appearing at the Theatre Royal, Brighton, and Mr Charles Collette were recently dining together at a country inn a few miles from the famous sea-side resort, when their meal was interrupted by a sudden and unlooked-for intruder. A large bird dashed through the window, smashed the glass, overturned wine and sauce bottles, and with a sudden pounce secured a roast fowl which was upon the table, as if to say "That's *not* the sort of bird I am." Mr Brough nearly blinded Mr Collette in endeavouring to strike the intruder with the pepper castor, and after much difficulty secured the bird, which proved to be a fine specimen of the rock eagle. How it came to be at large is a mystery. Mr James Scanlon, Miss Thompson's Acting-Manager, is having the bird stuffed, and will take it throughout the tour as "a bird of good omen."

A Disgraceful Scene at the Greenwich Theatre.
ON Tuesday night the Manager, Mr Charles Crofton, took his benefit, and we were sorry to see such a poor house; at the same time, if caterers for public amusement want to draw large audiences at this season of the year, they ought not to place such dismal dramas as *The Poisoner* as an attraction, nor allow bad amateurs to gratify their vanity for the promised support of their friends, and so mar the abilities of the real actors. […] The farce of *Bathing* concluded the programme. For this Mr James Francis and Mr William Hurlstone, two very old Greenwich favourites, had promised their valuable services. On making their appearance, some blackguards at the back of the circle assailed them with missiles, ranging from a *cabbage* to a *trotter*. At first all was taken in good part, but as they attempted to proceed, a fresh supply of projectiles came, and, after several appeals made in vain, the comedians very wisely left the stage. The curtain was lowered, and the entertainment (?) was brought to a very abrupt termination.
1/8/1875

Fireworks at the Crystal Palace.
"Fireworks at the Palace." There is magic in the sentence, for fireworks at Sydenham have always been a great feature. But fireworks of the old school are no longer sufficient to satisfy the craving for novelty, and Messrs Brock hit upon the "happy thought" of representing toys in fireworks. After the entire gardens, terraces, fountains, &c., had been brilliantly illuminated, the water temples being especially beautiful under the effects of the various coloured fires, a series of the novel fireworks we have referred

to were displayed. They consisted of movable devices and set pieces, founded upon nursery rhymes principally. Thus the juveniles were delighted with a marvellous fiery specimen of "Jack in the Box," and an illustration of "a frog he would a-wooing go," quite as remarkable in its way, and welcomed with shrieks of delight from the little folks. "See-Saw, Margery Daw," was quite as much to their taste, and "There was a little man, and he had a little gun," was another amusingly-depicted firework. The novelty and excellence of these curious fireworks attracted much attention.

M. Blondin, who also performed some of his most extraordinary feats, was illuminated by fireworks as he wheeled his barrow down the rope. The effect was as singular as it was brilliant. Blondin was as adventurous as ever, and turned a somersault upon the rope with the greatest dexterity.
15/8/1875

CHECK TAKER, with view of being in the Pantomime. A YOUNG MAN wishes to get attached to a Theatre in or near London. Has impersonated Females in Farces and Burlesques with success. Cannot give any time, but willing to be useful. Address, P.C., Mr. A.L. Clark, 4, Clover Street, Chatham.
22/8/1875

AT the Hinckley County Court (before Mr Sergeant Miller, Judge), a singular action has just been tried between Mr Edward L. Driver, farmer, Elmesthorpe, and Mr R. Orton, of Blackwall, aeronaut, being a claim of £5 for trespass by breaking down and injuring plaintiff's crops and causing a balloon to descend therein.

It was shown that some of the damage was done by the corn being injured by the escape of gas from the balloon, and some by the corn being broken down and torn up by the grappling irons, and some by the corn and fences being trampled down by the people who ran after the balloon. His Honour expressed some doubt whether the defendant could have the same control over the balloon that a huntsman would have over his horse and dogs, so as to make him liable for a wilful trespass, but eventually gave judgement for the amount claimed.

WANTED, for a Small Public-House, a Novelty of any kind, a FAT WOMAN, or Child to Play the Violin. Address, A.B.C., Post-office, Lancaster, till called for.
29/8/1875

ON Thursday, at Messrs Bonham and Son's Rooms, Leicester Square, there was a rather novel sale of theatrical properties, which caused a little competition amongst the costumiers. The properties were the surplus from recent pieces which have been produced at the Alhambra Theatre, such as *The Black Crook, King Carotte*, &c. The lots did not realise very alarming prices, and the gentlemen present must, we think, be congratulated upon some good bargains.

The first lot, for example, "Thirty trick fans," being put up, somebody had the conscience to bid sixpence for them. They were knocked down at seven shillings. A lot of children's barrows, saws, planes, hammers, axes, trowels, &c., used in *The Black Crook*, fetched only four shillings. Lot six included a large elephant, turtle, crocodile, birds, beasts, and fishes, &c., from *The Black Crook* and *Roi Carotte*. This lot fetched only eleven shillings, and just as it was being knocked down the elephant, as if disgusted at the price offered for him, fell down from the heap on which he had been placed, causing much laughter, and disturbing greatly other wild beasts who were in his company. What to do with the elephant puzzled the porters for some time, and there was a warning voice heard, "Don't put him on the pianner," there being an antique Broadwood in the vicinity.

The elephant being disposed of, the sale proceeded. Nondescript heads, helmets, a property goose, who must always have been a tough customer to have stood so much knocking about, tambourines, and a host of miscellaneous articles forming lot seven brought twelve shillings. Lot nine, six dozen gauze foil paper peacocks, large hand wire fans, used in *Nana Sahib*, and fifteen pairs of fairies' wings. Think of "fairies' wings" selling for a few pence each. It is positively saddening, but the lot only realised fifteen shillings. There was a brisker fire of bidders for lot twenty-four, twelve bees, twelve lady birds, twelve grasshoppers, and twelve dragonfly costumes from the ballet of *Le Roi Carotte*, which fetched twenty-six shillings; but forty trick umbrellas with handles, a quantity of *papier mache* busts, twelve trick hand cards, a lot of demon masks, dummy rolls of cloth and ballot box, were knocked down for half-a-crown. "Worth the money to burn," said a keen bystander, who, however, had his own reasons for not making a higher bid. Some of the pretty Grecian dresses from *Le Roi Carotte* went off better: twenty-seven of them, in good condition, brought two guineas, a wonderfully high price compared with other lots that had been knocked down. Here and there some rusty-looking property would realise a pretty good figure. We inquired why. "It's for the metal, don't ye see." In this, as in other matters, metal, whether gold or lead, has its legitimate value.

FOR SALE, Six Highly-trained SHEEP: used last season in Mr Wilson Barrett's highly successful Pantomime "Little Bo-Peep," at the Leeds Amphitheatre. For terms apply to the trainer, Mr J. TEMPLETON, Princess's Palace, Leeds.
19/9/1875

FOR SALE, a Great Novelty for a Clown, for Pantomimes, Ring, or Stage, a Four-Wheeled CARRIAGE, in which Four Cats are driven at full speed, late the property of John Milton Hengler. Address, JOHN WALKER, Circus, Danzig, Prussia. Always a great draw for Benefits.

A DWARF. – The Mother of an Interesting Little GIRL in her Eighth Year desires to receive offers for her Exhibition. She has not Grown since she was two years old; her hands, arms, and feet are wonderfully small. Excellent references required. Address to Mrs EDWARDS, Soho Street, Handsworth, Birmingham.
26/9/1875

LAD WANTED, about Fourteen Years of Age, to Sell Biscuits, Programmes, and Cigars, and to make himself generally useful. Board and Lodging in the House. No business on Sundays. Apply at the Royal Music Hall, Holborn.
3/10/1875

THE ASSAULT BY A CLOWN (SURREY SESSIONS).
Edwin Crouste, aged thirty-four, a Clown, surrendered last Wednesday to take his trial for assaulting Thomas W. Gardiner, and inflicting on him grievous bodily harm. Mr Montagu Williams and Mr Baggallay prosecuted, and Mr Edward Clarke and Mr Lyon defended the prisoner.

Between the prosecutor and defendant there existed a difficulty of some standing with reference to money matters. The defendant, seeing Mr Gardiner in the bar of the York Hotel, Waterloo Road, on September 30th, went up to him and proceeded to use very violent and abusive language towards him. He followed him into an adjoining room, where he went to eat a chop, and there continued his abuse. Having said to Gardiner that he would spit in his face and knock his teeth down his throat, Gardiner, showing the dinner knife with which he was cutting his chop, replied "If you spit in my face I'll knife you." Thereupon Crouste struck him behind the left ear with the handle of his umbrella, knocked him down, knelt upon him, and struck him repeatedly about the head with his fists. Gardiner struggled to his feet and tried to get possession of the umbrella, whereupon Crouste again knocked him down, and again beat him while on the floor. There was no evidence to show that Gardiner ever struck, or even attempted to strike, Crouste. The result of this assault was that Gardiner's skull was slightly fractured, and he suffered a serious concussion of the brain, being in great danger and remaining in a comatose state for three or four days. Although now comparatively restored to health he was still under medical treatment. The defendant alleged that the blows were struck in self-defence.

The Chairman summed up the whole of the evidence with great minuteness, pointing out to the Jury that there was no evidence of any assault by the prosecutor, unless they considered that the showing of the dinner knife, with the remark that accompanied the act, was an assault. If they thought so, then he explained to them that although a man might strike a reasonable blow in self-defence, he was not justified in continuing the attack and taking his revenge on the assailant. There was evidence of malice for the Jury to consider, because it had been proved by one of the witnesses that Crouëste, two days before the assault, had said to him that he would do for Gardiner, and that thereupon he had felt it his duty to warn Gardiner's father.

The Jury found the prisoner Guilty on the second count of the indictment for occasioning actual bodily harm, but recommended him to mercy. Mr. Baggalay said the prosecutor also wished to recommend the defendant to mercy.

Mr Hardman, addressing the prisoner, said it was fortunate for him that the prosecutor, after the serious injuries he had received, had been kind enough to ask for the merciful consideration of the Court. That request should be attended to, as well as the recommendation of the Jury, although he failed to see where the "extenuating circumstances" were, for he had never tried a case of more deliberate and unprovoked assault. He then sentenced him to three months' hard labour.

SILVER ARMOUR FOR SALE. – 50 Complete Suits. 100 Suits of Roman for Children. 50 Jewelled Suits for Ladies. KENNEDY and Co., 140, Steelhouse Lane, Birmingham.
31/10/1875

To Managers and Others. TO BE SOLD, a Bargain, a Magnificent FEMALE DRESS for the Character of HAMLET complete, consisting of Black Velvet heavily trimmed with Black Bugles, and Royal Blue Satin, with Shoes, Sword, and Skulls, and a few Stage Ornaments. Apply, HENRY WALTERS, 11, Cleveland Street, Birkenhead.
7/11/1875

A VERY ingenious and enterprising gentleman has conceived the idea of starting a theatrical steamboat in the interests of playgoers and those members of the profession who live "up the river," and at a considerable distance from the scenes of their labours. The splendidly-fitted saloon boat *Victoria* will on and after the night of Monday, the 22nd, leave Waterloo Pier at 12.30 for Charing Cross, Pimlico, Chelsea, and Putney. Refreshments will be supplied on board at moderate prices, and every care will be taken to ensure the comfort of the passengers. Members of the profession will be carried at exceptionally low rates. The venture is worthy of encouragement and support.

REINDEER. – FOR SALE, a Herd of Twenty Reindeer, Female Indian Elephant 6½ft. high, Five Polar Bears, several Brown Bears, and other Stock. Apply C. RICE, Menagerie, London and Hamburg.
14/11/1875

AT the Middlesex Sessions on Wednesday, William Watts and William Whittlebury were indicted for stealing 28lbs. of lard and other articles, value thirty shillings, from Mr Frederick Trotman, their master, the refreshment contractor of the Zoological Gardens, Regent's Park. The prisoners, employed as porter and baker, had it appeared secreted the goods in a sack full of stale buns, &c., which was being sent away from the refreshment department. It was a singular fact that the detection was in consequence of the visitors complaining of some cakes which had been made with dripping instead of lard. Mr Trotman thought these robberies had gone on for some time. Mr. Sergeant Cox sentenced Watts (the baker) to twelve months' imprisonment, but the Jury found Whittlebury not guilty.

"Spitz, Spitze, Spider, Crab."
This is the title of the forthcoming Pantomime at the Grecian Theatre, famous for the startling effects produced by means of the perseverance, ingenuity, and skill of Mr George Conquest. In recent years he has attracted the town by his marvellous doings, now as a giant, now as a dwarf, now as a bird, now as a tree. This year we expect to find all previous efforts surpassed, for we are to encounter Mr George Conquest as a Crab. To bring his ideas into working order the famous actor and pantomimist has left no stone unturned, and for something like eight months have his studies been turned in the crab direction. He has made more than a dozen models, and has discovered for each successive one fresh improvements; he has passed a week in the Brighton Aquarium, in the company of shell fish in general and crabs in particular; he has listened to the sage counsel of Mr Frank Buckland*; and, in a word, he has left nothing undone which could be done to carry out his conception in a style which shall do credit to himself and credit to the establishment where he rules so well, and where his patrons and admirers are numbered by thousands.
*Francis T. Buckland, author of Curiosities of Natural History *and famous for eating exotic animals.*
21/11/1875

AT Hammersmith Police Court on Thursday, Paolo Frati, an Italian, was charged with playing a noisy instrument in a public thoroughfare, to the annoyance of Mr W.S. Gilbert, of Essex Villas, Kensington. The evidence was interpreted to the prisoner, who did not understand English. Mr Gilbert said he was a dramatic author. On Wednesday afternoon, while engaged in writing, he was disturbed by the defendant playing an organ outside his house. He went out and said *Basta* (enough), but the defendant continued playing. He went out a second time and motioned him to go away. He replied "Go for one penny," or words to that effect. Witness retired to the house, but as the prisoner continued playing he gave him in charge. The prisoner removed from the house after witness went for a constable, but not before.

The prisoner, after the evidence was interpreted to him, said it was quite true. He was very sorry, and if he had understood he was annoying Mr Gilbert he would have gone away. In reply to the Magistrate, the interpreter said the prisoner had been six months in this country. Mr Ingram thought the prisoner had had time to know he was bound to go away when requested. Mr Gilbert wished to know whether it was competent for him to plead on the prisoner's behalf. Mr Ingram replied in the negative, and said that from the attending circumstances it was evident that the prisoner intended to have a penny before he went away. He fined the prisoner 10s., which included 5s. for the interpreter. The money was paid.

NOISE IN THEATRES.
TO THE EDITOR OF THE ERA.
Sir, – I trust you will grant me the favour of giving insertion to a few words of complaint in reference to the above. In most of the West End London Theatre pits little or no effort is made to secure a suppression of noise consequent upon parties entering or leaving while a play is proceeding. For instance, at the Gaiety on Saturday last, during Mr Phelps's fine delivery of the "Farewell" in *Henry the Eighth*, there was an almost incessant banging of doors, and clamour of footsteps on the bare pavement of the corridor. Last Wednesday week, at an interesting part of *Romeo and Juliet*, the attendant appeared to be taking a "constitutional" up and down the aforesaid pit corridor, with no light footstep either, and whose boots were evidently well nailed, making no little clatter. Again, on one occasion at the Princess's there was constant interruption arising from the tramping of people entering after the curtain was up during Mr Jefferson's life-like impersonation of Rip, of whose performance every word is worth hearing; and the annoyance arose merely because there was nothing in the pit passages to deaden the sound.

We, of the pit, generally the largest portion of the house, have to put up with (in most cases) bad and comfortless seats, some without backs, some narrow in the extreme, and with little or no room for the knees; adding to which one is half baked by the bad ventilation of the house. Why "pile up the agony" further – why are we to be debarred from hearing? I know of no Theatre, except the Prince of Wales's or the Court, where a really comfortable pit-seat is obtainable. Surely some sort of matting could be provided to deaden the sound, both in the pit itself and approaches, as at the Lyceum and Drury Lane. The bang, bang, of doors might be prevented, I should say, by means of list or the like. I am sure the discomfort arising from the causes I have named only require to be known by the Management to be easily remedied, and directions given to the attendants to caution parties to "tread lightly." Even at the Standard this latter is observed, for there the attendant so soon as the curtain rises commands "silence" with usher-like voice. I enclose memorandum of my attendance – always by payment – at the several Theatres of late, which shows that I have some claim to the title of Playgoer, and as such, and being a constant reader of your excellent Journal, I address these few words to you (hoping they will meet Managerial eyes) and knowing that you will be conferring a benefit on many if you will kindly give insertion to A SIGH FROM THE PIT.

AT the Knutsford Sessions, on Wednesday, Charles Thatcher, thirty-nine, described as lower agent-in-advance for Wombwell's Menagerie, was found guilty of stealing fifty-two postage stamps at Nantwich, Cheshire, in April last. He made the following novel defence, denying that he was the man. He said the evidence was purely circumstantial, and instanced what an effect such evidence had as follows: –

A lady, a widow, kept a "general pie shop" in London, and she was courted by two men – a baker and an ex-policeman. The baker was discarded, and the policeman preferred. The baker, in revenge, set up an opposition pie shop, and drew away the widow's custom. The widow called her accepted suitor to her aid, and he one morning, when the baker's shop was full of customers, went and threw twenty dead cats on the counter, with the remark that "he would bring the other five tomorrow." (Laughter.) The consequence was a general stampede. The shut mouths would not open, and the open mouths wouldn't shut, and the inference drawn was that the cats were there to be encrusted, and that they were constantly in the habit of being supplied with "cat mutton," and the business fell off accordingly.

From the first the prisoner said it had been a case of might against right, the strong against the weak, the oppressor against the oppressed, and eloquently appealed to the Jury for a dismissal. The Chairman having summed up, the Jury returned a verdict of guilty. He was sentenced to three months' imprisonment, the prisoner retiring with the dramatic assertion "that the day would come when he would make the country believe that he was innocent of this identical charge." It may be mentioned that prisoner was convicted at Shrewsbury subsequent to the time when the above offence was committed, but this, of course, could not be put in evidence against him.
28/11/1875

A LADY having Two Clever CHILDREN, the Youngest being Three Years, able to Play on an Organ-Accordion, and is really a Novelty suitable for Pantomime, the other (aged Ten) is a Singer and Dancer, she would like to have them brought out. Apply, by letter only, S.J., 173, Southwark Bridge Road, London.
5/12/1875

TO BE SOLD, a Great Bargain, a Splendid Blue and Silver ARMOUR DRESS, used by a "Star" Actress for Joan of Arc. Equal to new. Tunic, Belt, with splendid New Sword complete, richly Spangled Blue and Silver Tights, Boots, Gauntlets, and Steel Helmet. Address, R.R., 65, Hanover Square, Bradford.
12/12/1875

Samuel Bernard Payne Fowell was charged on Thursday, at Bow Street Police Court, before Sir T. Henry, with forging and uttering a cheque for £10.

Mr Humphries, Proprietor of the Red Lion, Strand, said that some weeks back the prisoner came into his billiard-room, had some refreshment, and played several games of billiards. He then said his name was Anson, that he was the actor at the Olympic, and that he had a benefit on that night. He produced a cheque for £10, purporting to be drawn by Mr Coleman. This he endorsed "G.W. Anson," and witness cashed it for him. It was passed through his bankers and returned marked "Referred to drawer." On Wednesday, at the Belmore Testimonial Benefit, Drury Lane, witness saw him going into the dress circle of the Theatre, and gave him into custody.

Detective-sergeant Kerley, E division, said that when he arrested the prisoner he told him that he would be charged with forging and uttering the cheque, and also other cheques, purporting to be signed by Mr Neville, Olympic Theatre; Messrs Lewis and Lewis, Solicitors, Ely Place; and others. He at once said it was all true. He had forged them all. He also said that he had obtained the cheque-book he used by means of a forged order. That book was found on him. It was one of the Imperial Bank.

Mark Goodman, hosier, 37, Chandos Street, said he knew the prisoner. He was in the habit of coming to his shop and buying small things. He always passed himself off as Mr G.W. Anson, the actor. He used to buy articles that he said he wanted for the stage. The shirt he had on in the dock he bought there, and told him he wanted it to play Oliver Cromwell. Last Saturday fortnight he came into witness's shop and said he was very tired, as he had played twice that day. He then selected a scarf and one or two other things, which he said he wanted to buy. He said he only had a cheque with him for £10, that Mr Neville had given him. Witness expressed his surprise, and he said "Oh, I get a similar cheque every night I act!" He left the shop with the intention of getting it changed. In a quarter of an hour he came back, and said he could not change it as it was so late. Witness had only £4 odd in his shop, but the prisoner said he would take that, and call on the following Monday for the remainder, and a coat he had ordered. The cheque was never honoured, and witness had not seen prisoner again till that day.

Mr Anson was called, who said the signatures on the cheques were not his, but forgeries.

Mr Superintendent Thomson, who watched the case, here asked for a remand, as there were at least forty more cases that could be brought against the prisoner. A remand was accordingly granted.

19/12/1875

7
1876
A GLASS OF STOUT IN HER BONNET

The Panic in a Theatre at Sheffield.
It was a matter for congratulation at the time the fire occurred, resulting in a panic at the Alexandra Opera House, Sheffield, on the 28th December, that beyond the fright and a few trifling injuries sustained, no one was badly hurt. It appears, however, that this was a premature conclusion to arrive at. Two ballet girls, it may be remembered, were burnt, but were considered to be progressing so favourably that no doubts were entertained of their ultimate recovery. Sad to tell, however, one of them, Marion Oldale, died on Monday last. The unfortunate girl was a native of Sheffield, and in her eighteenth year. The inquest was held on Thursday, when the evidence showed that the deceased was one of the nymphs suspended from the flies during the Transformation Scene, being strapped to an iron rod placed against her back. A gauze festoon near the wings was blown against some lights, and catching fire the flames extended to the girl's dress, and being strapped to the rod she was unable to move. It was stated that she never uttered a scream. A verdict of "Accidental death" was returned.
16/1/1876

ON the 22nd inst., at the Thames Police Court, a poor-looking man named Jameson was charged with driving five sheep along a public thoroughfare at illegal hours. David Markham, a constable, 139 K, said he was on duty in the Commercial Road when he saw the defendant driving five sheep at prohibited hours. The defendant said he was engaged to take the sheep out for exercise. They performed at the Pavilion Theatre in the Pantomime *Little Bo-Peep has Lost her Sheep.* Little Bo-Peep was marked on one side of their backs and the Pavilion on the other. He had no idea he was doing wrong in giving them a little recreation after their performance, or else he should not have brought them out. Mr Paget said the defendant must find some other place to exercise Bo-Peep's sheep, and must not drive them up and down the road. He was inclined to think it was an advertisement for the Pantomime. He should not impose any penalty in the present case, but the defendant would have to pay the cost of the summons.
30/1/1876

STOLEN, from the Wardrobe of the Theatre Royal, Bath, a DARK RED ROBE Figured with Gold, a Long Blue Cloth Shirt, Trimmed with Black Fur, worn by Mr Wybert Rousby as King Lear and Photographed by the London Stereoscopic Company; also a RICHELIEU DRESS, made of Scarlet Cloth. Whoever will give such information (as shall lead to their recovery) to FRANK MUSGRAVE, Esq., Theatre Royal, Nottingham, will receive TWO POUNDS REWARD.
6/2/1876

A SAD event occurred at Southport on the 23rd ult. A retired actor named Mr William Willmore, the father of the well-known actresses Misses Lizzie and Jenny Willmore, was returning home, and had to go over the railway on the Manchester line at the level crossing in the town between Virginia Street and Little London. A goods train was shunting and he waited for that to pass. He was proceeding across, when a goods train from Wigan came down the line, and, before he could get out of the way, knocked him down, injuring his face and breaking some of his ribs. He would have been horribly mutilated but that a cabman, named Gould, dragged him away. Mr Willmore exclaimed "I have lost my hat and parcel. Will no one take me away." He was then placed on a shutter and taken to the infirmary, and attended to by the house surgeon, Dr Murray, but about half-past ten (an hour after his admission) he died.

NOTHING is to be heard just now but of skating and the opening of new Rinks for the enjoyment of that extremely popular pastime. Rinks are growing like mushrooms. Bazaars where people will no longer purchase toys and fancy articles, chapels whence congregations have departed, furniture warehouses long disused, livery stables and picture galleries, yield to the fashions of the day, and are transformed into Skating Rinks. On Saturday evening, close to Oxford Circus, there was opened a new Rink, once occupied by a range of stabling, the freehold ground for which was secured at a cost of £25,000. The beauty of the building is much enhanced by the splendid decorations and illuminations of Messrs J. Defries and Sons. On the front is an illuminated shield with the words "Oxford Circus Rink." Festoons of variegated lamps have been placed in the corridor, and the walls hidden by silvered mirrors. The recesses are filled with statuary, choice flowers, &c.

Proceeding further, we find the interior of the Rink resembling an exquisite ballroom or winter garden. In the centre, a chandelier of novel design, in the shape of crystal feathers, is a prominent decoration. Groups of statuary, illustrating skating scenes, are brilliantly illuminated, and a splendid trophy of flags, with shields representing Russian and Polish skating costumes. [...] At the opening on Saturday evening the Coldstream Guards' band, conducted by Mr Fred. Godfrey, played; and visitors in Rink hats, Rink gloves, or entire Rink suits, with Rink fans, earrings, scarf pins, and other ornaments modelled in miniature upon the Plimpton* skate, went round and round one way till the sound of a bell sent them travelling round and round in the opposite direction. This novel plan was adopted owing to the somewhat confined area of the Rink, and those who wished to avoid giddiness were glad to change their course according to the bell.

*The four-wheeled roller skate was invented by James Plimpton.

Who Licences the Skating Rinks?
TO THE EDITOR OF THE ERA.
Sir, – Where is the Lord Chamberlain? What are the eminently moral Licencing Magistrates of the Clerkenwell Sessions doing just now? What are the Police about? And why, in the name of common sense, are the Managers of the Metropolitan Theatres and Music Halls fast asleep, just when they should be on the alert and careful of their very lives? Skating Rinks are opening in all directions. They offer an evening's amusement and splendid facilities for flirtation at a small expenditure. Each of them has its band; and at all of them quadrilles and waltzes are skated to the music of Coote, Godfrey, or Marriot. Who gives them the licence either for music or dancing? Does anyone, or are four-fifths of them illegally open; and likely in a very short time to become worse in their baleful character than any dancing saloon the guardians of public morality have seen fit to close up and to sweep away? Yet these same Skating Rinks are thinning the audiences of our Theatres, and taking away the better class of visitors from our Music Halls. What trouble and expense are involved in adapting a building to the requirements of the Lord Chamberlain in the matter of Theatres, and to the caprice of the Licencing Magistrates in that of Music Halls, the Managers of both know to their cost. In the race for popularity both have to be heavily handicapped. Can the Skating Rink Manager dash on the course and ride his

horse unweighted, and with any jockey that he chooses? That's what I want to know. If he can, let our Managers combine at once, and get the rules of the ring altered. I would make one in such a combination were I still a Manager and not a mere invalid spectator. Yours very truly, E.P. HINGSTON.
5/3/1876

Skating Rinks.
TO THE EDITOR OF THE ERA.
Sir, – The Lord Chamberlain having nothing whatever to do with granting licences for the above-named places, his name must be ignored. In all other respects I cordially agree with the contents of the letter which appeared in your valuable journal last week bearing the signature of Mr E.P. Hingston. I fear that gentleman is not acquainted with the trials and troubles in even endeavouring to put down these unlicenced places. I will give you an outline, so far as regards my own experience, of the insurmountable difficulties one has to contend with. I can assure, you, Sir, to suppress a place illegally carrying on music and dancing with impunity, and with the thorough cognizance of the police authorities, is no easy matter.

Last year a gentleman very well known throughout both the Dramatic and Musical Professions, in conjunction with myself, laid information against some well-known Gardens not one hundred miles from the Elephant and Castle, and, after supplying the Magistrate of the district with incontestable proofs of the illegality of music and dancing being carried on night and day, we were informed that the only course left open to us was to indict the then Proprietor of keeping a disorderly house. That was the satisfaction we received after parading the environs of a police-court for two days trying to suppress an illegal act; and I should much wish to know in what other way the Proprietors of these establishments can be proceeded against for infringing the Act of Parliament. I, for one, shall use strenuous efforts to put down two of these places situated very near me, and have written to the Secretaries of both Rinks, informing them that they have no power to permit music or dancing in their respective buildings, and that it is my intention to lay information against them if not immediately stopped. I am, dear Sir, yours faithfully, JOHN AUBREY.
Elephant and Castle Theatre, March 9th, 1876.

ON Monday evening last, at the Haymarket Theatre, a novel and effective bit of business was introduced by Mr H.B. Conway, and so well was it done, so ably seconded by Mr Howe, and so pleasing to the public, that we immediately marked it in our "Shakespeare." Mr Conway, as Romeo, rushing precipitately into the cell of the Friar (Mr Howe), caught his foot in the doorway and fell forward. He alighted on his hands and knees, his hat and he parting company, his whole demeanour being indicative of anything but that repose and respect which should characterise such a visit. A gentle titter rippled round the house, and Romeo certainly won the smiles of all the ladies present. When, however, a few moments afterwards, Mr Howe, with a half smile on his reverend lips, remarked, with an emphasis not to be resisted, "Wisely and slow! They stumble that run fast!" a peal of laughter rang through the house so loud and so hearty that the succeeding lines of Mercutio and Benvolio (Messrs Harcourt and Matthison) were not heard for some moments, and Romeo, for the first time in his immortal career, made a success as a light comedian.
12/3/1876

MDLLE DE KOLMAR*, the beautiful Alsatian orphan, whose musical abilities are so remarkable, will shortly give two matinees in London. At the first she will present her classical entertainment, when she will sing in French, German, Italian, and English, accompanying herself on the pianoforte, harp, flageolet, and violin. At the second Mdlle de Kolmar will give an orchestral performance, when several of her own compositions will be played, the young artiste herself conducting. Both matinees will take place at St George's Hall.

Mdlle de Kolmar, who was also an actress, was only twelve years old.

THE number of persons who appear to think that Theatrical Managers have nothing better to do than to write free admissions would astonish those who are inexperienced in dramatic affairs. Mr John Hollingshead, the able and accomplished Manager of the Gaiety Theatre, is incessantly pestered with such applications. The more attractive the entertainment the greater is the demand, and this week Mr Hollingshead received from a certain Mr Cyril Wintle a letter, the unblushing coolness of which has perhaps never been equalled. Mr Cyril Wintle commences with a glowing eulogium upon the acting of Mr J.L. Toole in *Tottle's*, and then proceeds to say:

"If you were to supply me with some orders I could guarantee their being used by gentlemen who would wear evening dress, and so add to the general appearance of your pretty Theatre. Awaiting your reply, I remain, Sir, yours truly, Cyril Wintle, 3, South Street, Thurloe Square, S.W., 15th March, 1876."

Some Managers, upon receiving such a letter, would – after throwing it upon the fire – have relieved their feelings by the utterance of strong language. Not so Mr Hollingshead. That ready-witted gentleman resolved to pay Mr Wintle back in his own coin, and since he made such a point of improving "the general appearance of the Gaiety Theatre," Mr Hollingshead gratified his wish by writing him an order *for two to the gallery*, with the express injunction that "evening dress was indispensable." Mr Wintle and his friend will therefore be conspicuous personages, should they accept the Manager's generous offer.

1,000 Miles in 1,000 Hours. WANTED, by Madame Angelo, the Mulatto, a Native of Calcutta, and Champion Female Walker of the World, for the above Feat, to commence as soon as possible, good Walled-in PLEASURE GARDENS or Grounds. Address, Madame ANGELO, 52, Cawney Hill, Dudley.
19/3/1876

MR GEORGE CONQUEST, of Grecian Theatre, is prepared to treat with Provincial Managers for the Sale of the Trick as used by him of THE DWARF IN THE BOX. Can be performed by any Actor. Only one will be sold in each town. Any one infringing Mr Conquest's rights will be legally proceeded against. The Manchester and Liverpool rights already disposed of.
2/4/1876

AMONG the attractions at Norwich during the holidays was a portable Theatre, in which our Correspondent witnessed an entertainment by "the only dramatic company in Norfolk." It consisted of the drama of *Michael Earle*, a comic song, a dance by the leading lady and the farce of *The Secret*. The time occupied did not exceed *ten minutes!*

IS there an ACTRESS of TRAGEDY coming to Manchester for a few weeks' stay who will give a Young Lady one or two lessons a week. Address, JULIA, Post-office, Manchester, up to April 28th.
23/4/1876

A SAD catastrophe occurred on Thursday last in connection with the establishment of Mr Samuel May, the well-known Theatrical costumier of Bow Street. Three of the men employed were seized with illness, and gave symptoms of poisoning after partaking of some beer fetched from a neighbouring public-house. It was subsequently discovered that the jug used for the beer had previously contained some poisonous matter employed by the men for polishing armour. Two of the victims were taken to King's College Hospital. In the case of Alfred Bright, aged forty-three, residing at 2, Sheffield Street, Clare Market, stageman, the efforts of the house surgeon proved unavailing, for the unfortunate man died. Samuel Harrison, aged forty-two, residing at 14, Napier Road, Mason's Hill, Bromley, lies in the hospital in a precarious condition. The third man, having only drunk a small quantity, is out of danger.

WANTED, Engagements after Whit Week for Mons. D. ARLANDE'S Great Sensation. His terrific Flight upon the back of a large Fiery Dragon, completely surrounded by Fireworks, the greatest Novelty for 1876. Sole Agent, J. Wilder, Gala and Fete Agent, 185, Great Francis Street, Birmingham.
30/4/1876

ON Sunday last Alexander Kerr, scene painter and actor, aged fifty, was found lying wrapped in a carpet, quite dead, upon the stage of the Victoria Theatre, Bury. The deceased's right cheek and eye were eaten out by rats. He came on the preceding Thursday searching for work, but was unsuccessful, and after the play on Saturday night was over he hid himself and went on the stage to sleep after the building was locked up.
7/5/1876

BORES AT THE PLAY.
Far be it from us to hinder anybody from going to the play, but if we might mildly suggest to some who may be frequently met with in modern Theatres that they indulge in habits which greatly annoy their neighbours, we shall, we think, do the Dramatic state some service. [...]

We must say the "gods" at times try our patience considerably. Not long ago at a fashionable Theatre we saw a distinguished-looking visitor evidently suffering from annoyance of some kind not easily understood by other visitors. By-and-by he made a rush from his stall, and we heard him in irate conversation with the attendant outside, and then for the first time learned the cause of his protest. An impertinent denizen of the gallery, seeing that the occupant of the stall had "no wool on the top of his head where the wool ought to grow," as the popular Ethiopian ditty hath it, had amused himself with making a target of the gentleman's cranium, and aimed walnut shells at it with the unerring precision of a first-rate rifle volunteer. We can bear witness to the good humour with which the gentleman bore the infliction until it got past endurance. On special nights the gods are apt to make themselves particularly troublesome. They will drop bits of orange peel into a lady's turban, or make pellets of their playbills and fire these light missiles at any obnoxious personage. They will shoot cherry stones into the orchestra stalls and other light artillery, and it's all very well to say "why doesn't the policeman look after them?" It would puzzle that functionary "to catch them at it" as they hang over the front of the gallery, communicating with great glee any special success of their arms to their companions in the back seats.

But let us not be unjust to the "gods" of the ordinary stamp. There are Careless Bores in the upper regions of the Opera, as well as at the minor suburban Temples of the Drama. We saw last season an incident at the Royal Italian Opera which might have been attended with serious – nay, even fatal results. Somebody – we did not ascertain whether the culprit was of the stern or the softer sex – carelessly let fall an opera glass. This, all will admit, is not one of those "unconsidered trifles" which can alight upon the head of a visitor beneath without making him unpleasantly acquainted with the fact. The opera glass in this instance fell upon the head of a gentleman, who, unlike the one mentioned above, had a very thick, bushy, head of hair. That head of hair saved him, perhaps, from concussion of the brain. He was stunned by the blow, and his evening's enjoyment utterly spoiled, but happily he, as we afterwards learned, sustained no further injury. We record this fact partly with the view of making a suggestion. Everybody now has an opera glass, a fan, or something of the kind, which in falling might do serious injury, and we are glad to see in some of the modern Theatres the edge at the front of the balcony raised a little. This is especially advisable at those Theatres where the playgoer "likes a drop of summat between the acts." We once saw a young lady in the pit receive a glass of stout in her bonnet. Luckily the glass did not fall. [...]

Now we must complain of another "Bore at the Play." That is the slovenly playgoer – the person who slouches into the Theatre with his hands in his pockets, and with possibly a bottle sticking out of the breast-pocket of his coat – the person who has so little consideration for others, and so little respect for himself, that he will come from his desk, his shop, his factory, without taking the least trouble whatever as to his personal appearance. He slouches down in his seat, arms akimbo, smelling of tobacco and beer, with sometimes the added flavour of spring onions. He never appears to have satisfied his appetite, and immediately he had taken his seat will bring out a packet of stale shrimps or winkles, and scatter the unrefreshing *debris* over his neighbours on each side, perhaps pretty, decent, and neatly-dressed girls, who have all the refinement and cultivation of ladies, but whose circumstances may compel them, when they go to the play, to sit beside a personage of this stamp. If the "Dirty Bore" should by chance see these lines, we honestly and earnestly counsel him to brush his hair, wash his hands, put on clean linen, eat his winkles, shrimps, and onions at home, and not polish his face with a snuffy pocket-handkerchief. He will, the next time he goes to the play, have the pleasure of finding himself – for the first time – a welcome guest, and decent people will not shrug their shoulders when they see him enter.

Our next bore at the play is the "Laughing Bore." Ha! Ha! He! He! Ho! Ho! Don't we all know him, my dear playgoing friends, and don't we find him a nuisance? […] We met him last night at the French Plays. He laughed his loudest. It was to show everybody that he perfectly understood all he heard. Unhappily for him, he laughed in the wrong places, and somebody had the courage to whisper that it was not at all funny, and the laughing Bore was shut up. But it was hopeless to suppose him cured. He laughed the next night at Salvini in *Othello*, and most people are agreed, we believe, that Salvini's Moor is anything but a laughing matter.

As for the Talking Bores, time out of mind they have been a nuisance. They are hopeless, we fear. Some people evidently go to the play for no other purpose than to chatter. We remember in the old days at Her Majesty's Theatre what a time the talkers had of it. They could, and did, keep up an incessant conversation. They flirted, chaffed, told stories, and made appointments, and retailed the last bits of scandal, and all the while they did not turn their eyes from Cerito or Taglioni, or Lucile Grahn or Duvernay.* […]

Famous ballerinas of the day.
11/6/1876

BORES AT THE PLAY.
On a former occasion we discussed some of the peculiarities of the bores who hinder the enjoyment of those who go to the Theatre for recreation. It is really singular why some people go to the play at all. We see stylish-looking visitors come in when a piece is half over, or just drop in and stay for one act of a five-act comedy or tragedy, the chief result of their attendance being to distract the attention of others. Especially when, as frequently happens, they begin asking the person sitting next them to give them particulars of the plot. "Is this the first or third act?" they will inquire, and when you have given the requisite information other queries will come as a matter of course. […] You begin to get somewhat curt in the tone of your replies, and possibly say that it is not easy to give the particulars of a difficult plot in half a dozen sentences. [..]

A bore to be avoided more than any is the bore who pretends to be on intimate terms with the performers; who will give you, if you choose to listen, a swarm of personal details connected with them which have not the slightest foundation in fact. This bore knows the exact age of every pretty actress – at least he will tell you so – and the amount of scandal he is master of is really surprising. To hear him one would fancy the Stage to be a perfect Saturnalia, and all the men and women vicious to the last degree. […] Bores of his sort should be scouted by all right-minded playgoers. Their tales of actors and actresses, and their hints of scandal behind the scenes, have scarcely a grain of truth to a bushel of lies. If people only considered the amount of really arduous and tiresome work the actor has to go through, they would come to the conclusion that he has but little time to spare for such vagaries.

Perhaps there is no greater nuisance to the playgoer than the Restless Bore. This is an individual who is never contented with his seat. There is always a column in the way, or a door somewhere near, or he objects to the neck of the double bass sticking up in front of him. When he has induced the attendant to procure him another seat he generally finds that the second place is less satisfactory than the first, and he commonly goes back. The moment he is seated he jumps up again, and to the great disgust of his next neighbour, rushes out. He has forgotten something, or he wants to see a friend, or he has not the patience to wait for a programme, but must go and get one himself. Back he comes, but not to sit quietly. The Restless Bore always has a great deal of trouble with his legs. They appear scarcely to belong to him, he throws them about so. At one moment they are upon the heels of the visitor in front of him; the next instant he has crossed them, possibly scraping a lady's dress with his feet as he does so. After affectionately nursing one leg for a few moments he drops it noisily, and at the first glimpse of the act drop descending out he goes. […]

The bore who remembers the Kembles is a neighbour to be avoided at the play if possible. He generally begins his boredom with a muttered exclamation intended to express dissatisfaction with all modern acting. "Psha!" "Dolt!" "Bungler!" and so forth, he will murmer until he thinks he sees a sympathetic soul who will listen to him. Then he pours into that playgoer's ear a perfect flood of memories of the past, anecdotes that would greatly astonish the persons of whom they are told, narratives of first nights and terrible crushes at "the Garden" or "the Lane," constantly interlarded with such phrases as "Ah, sir, those were, indeed, the palmy days of the Drama." […] Our recommendation to any playgoer who falls in the way of this bore is to change his seat as quickly as possible.

The bore who wants everything done twice over is another great nuisance. His happy hunting ground is the Opera. At the play he cannot very well encore a long soliloquy, but he revenges himself by calling the actor to the footlights incessantly. Sometimes it happens after a death scene; and so persistently does he call for the performer that oftentimes, for the sake of quieting the uproar, the actor who has just expired will come on when the bulk of the audience can perceive that the effect of the situation has been ruined. At the Opera, and especially at English opera (when there happens to be such an entertainment), he has it all his own way. The more familiar the melody the more certainly will he demand its repetition. Such as air as "I dreamt that I dwelt in marble halls," or the equally well-known "Then you'll remember me," taxes the utmost capacity of his throat and the full vigour of his hands and feet. He gives quiet people the impression that he leads a sedentary life during the day, and comes to the Theatre for exercise; because it does not seem at all likely that a person who worked hard all the day would stamp, clap, and rave so incessantly. Some of the most famous artistes have made a vigorous stand against this kind of bore, but we fear it will be a long time ere he is put down thoroughly.

The bore who invariably goes to sleep is a nuisance, but – supposing he does not snore – he is less obnoxious than others we have referred to. His sole object in coming to the play appears to be the enjoyment of forty winks on the quiet. One can fancy that he had a scolding wife or crying children, or some domestic hindrance to a quiet nap at home, so he goes to the Theatre to get it, little caring what other visitors may think of him, and still less what the actor feels. […] The modern habit of dining late has of course much to do with the drowsiness that may be observed stealing over playgoers in the fashionable portions of the house. It is a great pity, because it tends to encourage a flimsy class of entertainment. The more robust ideas of the dramatist do not stand a fair chance while the process of digestion is going forward. Late dinners certainly help to increase the number of Bores at the Play.
18/6/1876

OFFENBACH, who is at present in the United States, gave a grand midnight entertainment recently to his friends in the New World. Among those present who are known in this country were Gordon Bennett, Gilmore (the great Boston jubilee conductor), Howard Paul, the Marquis Talleyrand-Perigord, and Augustin Daly. Each bill of fare was illuminated with characters from Offenbach's operas, and a statuette of the *maestro* in ice cream was served up, and bore a striking resemblance to the author of *The Grand Duchess*.

A PARIS correspondent states that Mdlle Stein, a pretty and graceful young woman, and one of the best comediennes on the German stage, has committed suicide under romantic circumstances. She had gone to Ems to give a series of performances. On the morning of her death she had attended rehearsal. As she did not appear at the Theatre the Manager sent to her residence. Her emissary was informed that Mdlle Stein had gone for a walk in the wood. As she did not return home in the evening it was feared she had lost her way. A search was organised, and eventually her corpse was found. To carry our her fatal project she had chosen one of the most romantic and picturesque sites of the environs of Ems; she had laid her plaid shawl on the grass, and then threw herself upon it, her face turned toward the Mahlsberg Hills. Her parasol was by her side, and in her right hand she held a six-chamber revolver, with one bullet of which she had shot herself in the heart. In the other hand she grasped Goethe's famous work "Wilhelm Meister's Lehrjarhre," open at the passages which describe how the arrival of Theresa, Wilhelm's betrothed, causes the death of Mignon.

It would appear that Mdlle Stein was betrothed to a young nobleman, the Graf von B., who was possessed of very slender means. On the morning of her death Mdlle Stein had received a letter stating that Graf von B., who was stopping at Hanover, had just been betrothed to a cousin, whose father possessed a large fortune. After reading it she at once left the house, and having formed the project of committing suicide, at once put it into execution. The most terrible circumstance in connection with the whole affair is that the letter in question was simply a hoax.

EXTRAORDINARY NOVELTY. – Mr WALTER P. DANDO, Inventor of an Apparatus for enabling a Performer to Jump or Dive to or from a considerable height, or to aid in the personification of a Monkey, Bird, or other Novelty, wishes to negotiate with Managers or Artists for the production of his Invention Abroad. The Apparatus is on an entire New principle, and one machine will work Eight distinct Jumps and Dives from different parts of the Stage, without cutting the Stage or complicated fixings or Nets, which is a great feature in travelling. MR GEORGE CONQUEST has purchased the entire Right of my Patent for England, and has executed with my Apparatus the wonderful feat of Jumping Thirty-two Feet, without the aid of Nets or any visible means, and, most wonderful of all, perfectly noiseless. Substantial Artists would find this a rare opportunity, as the Inventor has many Novelties besides the Jumping Apparatus. Address, till end of July, 128, Shepherdess Walk, City Road, London, N. Inventor's ideas carried out in strict confidence. India-rubber Springs of every strength made with Improved Eyes.

FOR SALE, Splendid Black Scotch BULL'S HEAD, magnificently Stuffed, Mounted on Solid Spanish Mahogany Shield. A noble Ornament for Public-house or Entrance Hall; also Two genuine Novelties, a Chicken with Four Legs, Four Wings, and One Head; and a Kitten with Eight Legs, Two Tails, Two Bodies, and One Head. Apply, FREDERICK COBURN, Naturalist, 35, Exeter Row, Birmingham.
16/7/1876

IT may be satisfactory to some playgoers to distinctly remember that during this oppressive weather the chief scenes of some of the most popular plays deal with ice or snow, and accordingly have a grateful and cooling effect. For instance, there is the "Snow Ballet" at the Alhambra, a lovely scene at all times, but especially pleasing now to think of snow-flakes and chill breezes with the thermometer at 100 in the shade. Then there is the Crimean Hut scene in *Ours*, which is all rushing wind, storm of snow and shiver – a picture which at this time of the year is far more pleasing to the audience than a house on fire or a burning summer garden. Then again, in *A Scrap of Paper*, Mr Kendal shivers over the fire in his study, and the last act of *Our Boys* is supposed to take place in a miserable garret in the depth of winter.

There is no doubt a reverse to the picture, which will not be so much appreciated by the actors, who are doomed to suffer terribly. The fanciful swallows must trip about in muffs and furs; the officers in *Ours* are compelled to swathe themselves in huge fur coats, fur gloves, fur caps, and to perspire under several flannel shirts; the hero of *A Scrap of Paper* has to wrap himself up as he croons over the fire; and *Our Boys* must wear clothing suitable to the time of year which is so distinctly stated. The most refreshing title of any entertainment next to the "Snow Ballet" is *Cool as a Cucumber*.
23/7/1876

ON Monday night, the 21st, about a quarter past eight, just before the commencement of the performance at the York Theatre Royal, an explosion of oxyhydrogen gas took place in the paint room, at the rear of the Theatre. It appears that William Pinder, the stage carpenter, was getting the gas ready in a bag to be used in the performance, when by some means it exploded. The occupants of the Theatre were startled by the report, but when it became known that the Theatre was in no danger, the fears of the audience were allayed. Pinder was blown against the wall by the force of the explosion, and his right leg and side were severely injured. Dr Draper was called in, and by his directions Pinder was removed to the City and County Hospital. No damage was done to the building. On Tuesday it was found necessary to amputate the right leg of the injured carpenter. The poor fellow succumbed to the operation, and died on Wednesday. An inquest was held on Thursday.
27/8/1876

MASTER CARPENTER. WANTED. Sobriety Indispensable. Very Stout Men need not write, as room is limited. Address, with experience, reference, and terms, to Mr H. NOBLE, Acting-Manager, Theatre Royal, Bradford.
3/9/1876

IN the performance of *La Sonnambula* by Madame Telma and Mr H. Walsham's opera company at Douglas, Isle of Man, a few nights ago, the *prima donna* was placed in a rather novel situation. The part of Amina was played by Madame Telma, who, in the second act, brought the performance to a very sudden termination. She had entered the Count's bed-chamber, as supposed, in a state of somnambulism, but her sleep was disturbed as if by a terrible "nightmare." Singing the beautiful sleep song introduced at this point, she stretched herself on the Count's bed, but no sooner had she done so than a deep crack was heard, followed by the *prima donna* rising abruptly and walking angrily off the stage, indignantly remarking, "I will never come on this stage again." The chorus of neighbours here entered to witness Amina's disgrace, but were, perhaps, agreeably surprised to find that that lady had disappeared. The curtain descended, covering their confusion, and an apology was then made to the audience, with a promise that the act would be concluded after the bed had been repaired. In about ten minutes the curtain again rose, and the play was then completed successfully, Madame Telma having evidently thought better of her hasty resolution.
10/9/1876

TO THE EDITOR OF THE ERA.
Sir, – *"Non cuivis homini contingit adire Corinthum."* It is not the good luck of every man to get as far as Corinth; neither does a truant disposition, a tram car, or the North London Railway tempt many travellers to the Clapton Park Theatre. There is a certain charm about the unknown, a mystery that hangs over the unexplored, whether it be Central Africa or Eastern London; and when sundry bills, fluttering about the nuts and apples in the windows of the Eastern greengrocers, insisted in red letters that *Hamlet* was to be played on Wednesday week at the Clapton Park Theatre (Licensed to Mr Thomas Turner, and prices as usual!) the charm was irresistible.

After many inquiries this local Temple of the Drama was discovered, hiding itself as it were in the quiet of a respectably melancholy street, and by its dismal appearance seeming to be ashamed of being a

Theatre at all. On our arrival some one was engaged in a vain struggle with the exterior gas jets, which refused their "uneffectual fires" altogether, and only asserted their possible utility by allowing an escape of gas. The interior of the Theatre was only a little less dark. The sunlight was a black object in the centre of the roof, which roof was principally decorated with weather stains and damp. The footlights were flaring their best considering the stoppages in several of the burners, and served to show that the orchestra was devoid of musicians, and apparently only utilised as the last resting place of a decayed piano. That the curtain showed a disposition to part company with its batten, and to droop, probably out of compliment to the melancholy Dane, and in no way attributable to defective stage management; that the solemn silence of the dress circle was the result of the presence of a select audience (invisible in the gloom), and not of empty benches; that the stamping and whistling in the gallery was due to a pardonable impatience, and not to an ironical reception of the Proprietor, who tried in vain to quell the tumult – all this we would readily believe, for have we not Mr Pennington (in large letters, please), and Mr Alfred Rayner (same size letters, please) to give us Shakespeare? A muffled altercation behind the scenes, and the curtain rises spasmodically, with an increased tendency to droop at one of the upper corners.

But we do not propose to criticise the performance, for have not the principal performers won their laurels and their right to large type elsewhere? We will only pity them in their futile efforts to make dramatic bricks without straw. The Proprietor, like Mrs John Gilpin, "although on pleasure bent, has a frugal mind." Hence the stage was covered with a scrap of baize, chameleon-like in colour, and jagged at the edges, of scant and insufficient proportions where he had failed to *make the two ends meet*. That Polonius, Horatio, First Player, Rosencrantz and Osric were identically the same person, who was everything by turns and nothing long, is somewhat surprising in England, however it may have been in Denmark. That the Horatio of the grave scene should be as unlike as possible to the Horatio of the earlier acts, and be apparently the twin brother of Guildenstern, was, no doubt, of the "*double, double, toil, and trouble,*" incidental to an economical cast. As was also the burial of Ophelia, the rites of which ceremony were so maimed that nothing was left, and *nobody* was buried behind a tree, in the absence of a crowd of courtiers who were only visible to the mind's eye of Hamlet. That lights half-down resulted in the total extinction of the footlights, and three several false attempts to relight them with a weak-minded candle between the acts, was, I presume, simply to show the gaping holes in the back-drop, and so shame the Proprietor into necessary repairs. That one of the cloths dropped abruptly, and having at first refused to be rolled up at all, compromised the matter on compulsion by resting in crumpled obstinacy at an inconvenient angle among the sky borders, was possibly a practical joke on the part of the scene-shifter to enliven the seriousness of an immortal tragedy.

But something too much of this. I would merely call the attention of a public which delights in novelty to the existence of the Clapton Park Theatre. There are more Theatres than are dreamed of in your West End philosophy; and remember, notwithstanding the attraction, the prices are usual! I am, yours, &c., C.M.

EARLY on Wednesday an elephant named Rose, belonging to Messrs John Sanger and Sons' Circus, evidently took the idea into her head that a walk would prove beneficial to her health, for she broke from the chains that secured her in her tent, and, taking a stroll for nearly half a mile, decided to add variety to the excursion by a little amateur burglary. Accordingly, putting her head to the door of a house, she soon forced an entrance, and made her way into the front parlour. The owner of the house, Mr John Pattison, hearing a strange noise, came down *en deshabille*, when to his surprise he beheld the huge animal. Fear instantly took possession of the man, who immediately ran upstairs again, leaped out of the first floor window, and rushed in his airy costume to the Circus, where he found one of the keepers searching for his lost charge. They returned, and Rose accompanied the keeper to her tent, after having regaled herself at the house with three loaves of bread, two jars of preserves, and all the sugar she could find. Before

quitting the town (Carlisle) Mr H. Bertrand, Messrs Sanger's Manager, called upon Mr Pattison to see what recompense was required.
17/9/1876

A SINGULAR case has been before the Gosport Magistrates. A person named Hall was charged with maliciously injuring a ringdove. Mr Frikell, a professor of legerdemain, was giving an entertainment at Gosport, and a ringdove was passed to a lady (Mr Frikell's wife) for the purpose of apparently decapitating it with a pair of scissors. Before, however, the trick could be performed, the defendant, who was among the audience, seized both the scissors and the bird and actually cut off the head. The bird, it seemed, was a valuable one, it having been specially trained for this trick, slipping its head under its wing when it was supposed to have been decapitated, and keeping it concealed until the head had to be restored. At the suggestion of the Magistrates the parties came to an arrangement.

THOMAS AGUZZI, your Wife is ill, and in great distress. Will you write or not, Father? Please write MARY AGUZZI, 74, Everett Street, Nine Elms Lane, Battersea, London.
1/10/1876

WHILST Mr Knight, a gentleman connected with Herr Bandmann's company, was out riding at Scarborough last week, on the sands beyond the Spa, he found on his return journey that the tide was fast flowing and was already dashing against the Spa walls. He, however, pushed forward, and while so doing lost a stirrup. The huge waves terrified the animal, and its rider was quickly thrown into the sea. The scene was one of great excitement to crowds upon the Spa who could not render assistance. To add to the bewilderment of Mr Knight, the horse stumbled over the piles and stones at the foot of the Spa wall, horse and rider fell, and the tide completely drenched both. After considerable difficulty the unlucky horseman managed to get to *terra firma* in anything but a pleasant plight. Mr Knight had received a slight cut on the forehead and the knees of the horse were bruised. He had cause, however, to be thankful for his escape from drowning.
15/10/1876

ADVERTISER is characterised as an original Poet, Punster, Writer, Novelist, Correspondent, Speaker, Song-writer, Conversationalist, Tragic Actor, and Comedian; young, steady, studious, persevering; passionately attached to drama and literature; seeks employment. Anything suitable. Modest remuneration. Letters, "HAMLET," 1, Duke Street, Little Britain, E.C.
22/10/1876

ON Saturday, the 21st inst., Tom Taylor's popular play of *The Ticket-of-Leave Man* was performed at the York Theatre before a crowded pit and gallery, and, strange to say, in the audience was a Detective Sergeant from London with a warrant to apprehend the very man who was playing the part of Hawkshaw, the Detective. The play was allowed to proceed, and at its termination "Hawkshaw" was handcuffed and handed over to the custody of the City police. On Sunday morning the real detective conveyed the ideal detective by train to London to answer the charge against him.

To Provincial Managers and Ladies of the Choreographic Art. MADAME ESPINOSA begs to say that she has just received a large consignment of French Operatic Dancing Shoes from Francois Craik, Sole Contractor to the National Academy of Paris, among which are shoes especially constructed for toe dancing. She will be happy to supply them to Ladies on moderate terms. She has also received a large stock of the new Parisian greace-whites and rouges of different tints, suitable for different Complexions. Orders will be immediately attended to. Address, 132, Kennington Road, London.
29/10/1876

WANTED, a Man to Train and Mind Two Small Elephants, Four Feet Six Inches High. Apply, F. GINNETT, Circus, Brighton.
26/11/1876

ON Tuesday evening the audience at Her Majesty's Opera House, Aberdeen, had the rare opportunity of judging at one sitting the merits, or rather demerits, of a couple of Ingomars. This somewhat extraordinary occurrence happened as follows:

On the night mentioned *Ingomar* was the chosen selection, in which the accomplished young actress Miss Adeline Stanhope personated the difficult character of Parthenia. Mr T. Percy, whom the lady specially deputed to support her, was the rude but brave barbarian, and from the opening of the piece it was plain enough that memory played him false, and that he had had insufficient study of his lines. Miss Stanhope and the prompter were continually coming to the rescue, but all to no purpose, for towards the end of the third act the proceeding culminated in utter failure. Miss Stanhope turned to the audience, and said it was not her fault, but she could not go on. The curtain rapidly descended and hid both the confusion and the mountain home of the "rude savage." After a short wait, Mr Gomersal came to the front, and, in an emphatic manner, said that he felt the position far more acutely than the audience could. During his ten years of management such a scene or anything approaching to it had not occurred. Mr Percy had not made himself master of the text; hence his failure. He was sure they would exonerate him (Mr G.) from any blame in the matter, as it was not a member of his company that had come to grief, and of course he could not be held responsible for his engagement. With their permission Mr Steele, who was in the cast as Myron, would assume the character. It is but justice to say that the audience at once granted Mr Gomersal's request for exoneration, and loudly applauded his short speech.

The play was then commenced where it had abruptly terminated, and the transformed Ingomar, with book in hand, poured forth the beautiful language of the part. Occasionally, however, some really ludicrous scenes resulted from this schoolmaster-like method of delivery of strong passion and excitement; notably in that part of the third act where Ingomar falls, overcome by his changing nature, occasioned by his dawning love for Parthenia. Whilst lying on the ground, face downwards, Ingomar gave us real pantomime, the "barbarian" raising his head and snatching a hasty glance at the lines of the text. In another scene, while embracing Parthenia, he took advantage of the only position possible, and, holding the book, music stand like, behind her head, answered from its indispensable leaves her tender sentiments. Joking apart, however, Mr Steele deserves to be complimented on his hasty assumption, for he required little of the book towards the end of the play.

Miss Stanhope enacted the part of Parthenia throughout as if nothing untoward had taken place, and both *artistes* were called to the front at the end of each act. Mr Innes also merits a word of praise for his portrayal of Myron, in which he was word perfect, although previously cast for another role. After a laughable farce the audience dispersed in good humour. Mr S. Garland is now supporting Miss Stanhope with fair success.
3/12/1876

A STUDENTS' ROW AT A THEATRE.
On the 1st inst. the Theatre Royal, Glasgow, was made the scene of one of those disgraceful exhibitions of rowdyism which are becoming of somewhat frequent occurrence during the University session. A body of students, who, as it is rumoured, had assembled at St George's Cross with the ostensible purpose of public disturbance, and led by a piper, marched into the side galleries of the Theatre Royal. Lest they should be mistaken for gentlemen, they at once began to manifest their caddish propensities. For some evenings in the theatre there have been musical effusions more vociferous than melodious, but on this occasion it was plain that nothing less than a riot had been planned.

For some time prior to the raising of the curtain, the exuberant youths amused themselves by shooting peas and throwing flour on the occupants of the orchestral and pit stalls, with the tuneful accompaniment of howlings, caterwaulings, and other animal sounds, without which, it would seem, it is impossible for students to enter into any recreation; and lest any of Flotow's exquisite music should be heard, the piper hired for the occasion had evidently received explicit instructions where and how to accompany the artistes. The overture to Martha became, consequently, quite inaudible, and the first part of the performance passed off in dumbshow. Vain were the repeated cries to "order;" expostulations were useless. [...] Not content with flinging flour, peasemeal, and peas on the garments and heads of the defenceless, haddocks were added to the missiles. Annoyance now gave way to a feeling amounting to alarm amongst the people, and a young lady became so frightened that she fainted and was carried out. The police were called in, and with some little difficulty succeeded in capturing a few of the ringleaders, and conveying them to the station. Even after this had been effected the disturbance was not wholly quelled, for the discomfited students held an indignation meeting in the gallery between the acts, and gave vent to their opinions as to the course adopted towards them by the police and management, the piper relieving the tedium by discoursing on the bagpipes.

Between one of the acts of the opera a number of gentlemen and students left the Theatre for the purpose of obtaining refreshments. One of the latter thought it proper to blow a sixpenny horn in the ear of one of the former. The result was the exchange of some hot words, and the giving of the student into the charge of the police, who took him to the Northern Police-station. The youth had by this time become alarmed at the turn which affairs had taken, and expressed regret at what he had done, and apologised. The gentleman very willingly accepted the apology, and as he did not wish to press the charge the prisoner was set at liberty, his name, however, being taken, lest it might be deemed right to go further into the matter.

It would have been thought that this check to such acts of rowdyism would have proved effective. But it did not; for after the performances in the Theatre the students collected and proceeded in a tumultuous manner along Sauchiehall Street. As they had marched up that thoroughfare between seven and eight o'clock on their way to the Theatre, forming a compact body, singing, shouting, and brandishing their sticks, the night officers in the district were warned to be on the alert lest the exuberant youth should return. When the few men did come up with them they found the students amusing themselves by putting out the lamps, smashing at shutters and signboards, and making themselves generally mischievous. They tried to effect the capture of one whom they observed to be in the act of extinguishing a lamp, but they were surrounded and knocked down while the lad was rescued. In fact, they were perfectly helpless in such a crowd, and when they managed to get out of the *melee* it was found that one of them, John Buchanan, had received a severe cut on the head, caused by a blow from a stick. His comrades accompanied him to the residence of the Western District police surgeon, Dr Johnstone, which happened fortunately to be in the neighbourhood. The doctor dressed the wound, and certified that the officer was unfit for duty. It is needless to say that the disturbances caused much alarm to the residents.

10/12/1876

8
1877
ENLARGED PHOTOGRAPHS OF LOVELY YOUNG MEN

ON Tuesday evening, as the Pantomine of *Sinbad the Sailor* was progressing at Her Majesty's Opera House, Aberdeen, great cause for alarm was created by the rear quarters of the "elephant," which accompanies the pseudo Prince of Wales on his Indian tour, taking fire, possibly from some of the side-wing jets in passing on to the stage. The house was crowded to repletion, and many instinctively jumped up in the middle of the pit and stalls ready to make for the door, while not a few rushed down stairs on the first appearance of the flames, without waiting to see whether there was sufficient cause for their retreat. The "legs" of the "elephant" – represented by two supers – threw down the body, and and the burning parts were soon extinguished. Had a panic ensued, disastrous consequences could not have been prevented, notwithstanding the excellent arrangements which exist at this house for the suppression of fire. With the Brooklyn calamity* still fresh in their minds, the fear of the audience was, doubtless, intensified, and it was very bad taste on behalf of one of the company on the stage at the time to cry "Fire." The mishap, slight though it was, is only another instance of the great necessity which exists for every reasonable and continued precaution being taken against the dreaded enemy.
On 5th December, 1876, at least 276 people were killed in a fire at the Brooklyn Theatre in New York.
7/1/1877

AT the Lambeth Police Court on Tuesday, Charles Graham, alias Charles Lever, aged twenty-one, describing himself as an actor and theatrical agent, residing at 146, Beresford Street, Walworth Road, was charged, before Mr Chance, with stealing by means of a trick, from Stephen Maskell, the sum of £10.

The case is one of a very peculiar character, and Detectives Berry and Reid, of the P Division, who took the prisoner into custody, stated that there were several persons present who had been duped by the prisoner. […]

Detective Berry said that, in company with Detective Reid, he proceeded on Monday to the lodgings of the prisoner, in Beresford Street. Upon seeing the prisoner and telling him the charge, he at first made no reply. He was asked if he was a "theatrical gentleman," and he said that he was not, but knew many Proprietors of Theatres. He added further that he had performed at the Elephant and Castle Theatre about two months ago. He denied that he was the man wanted, but said it was a person on the other side of the river. On the table in the parlour witness found upwards of a thousand letters and documents relating to the advertisements mentioned.*

The officers produced a large number of letters and documents, chiefly comprising letters from males and females from all parts of the country, received during the past seven or eight weeks. Some of these were of a most extraordinary character. One was evidently from a young lady, judging from the handwriting, and stated, "I have never performed on any stage, but am desirous of doing so. I am between fifteen and sixteen, fair, and considered good-looking." Another wrote, "I do not object to an engagement in the provinces, provided it is not too far and a pretty good salary. I am not in a position to pay the commission mentioned until engaged." [...] A male applicant wrote, "Comedy or burlesque would be my line, as I can sing and dance." Another young lady, described as having been highly educated, was "anxious to go on the stage, but could not pay the fees at present asked, as she was reduced in circumstances." "One Anxious to Join" wrote, "I am very dark, age seventeen, 5ft. 1in. high, but I do not like to dance." Three sisters, aged respectively sixteen, eighteen, and nineteen, stated that they were quite inexperienced in stage matters, but believed they could do all that was wanted. A gentleman from the neighbourhood of Bow in his letter said, "I tender my valuable services. If my part is to be tragic, I may safely say I am A1. Although never on the regular stage, I have never been beaten." Another applicant from Bolton wrote: – "i see you har in want of young peoples for the stage – i is very ansics to be a hactor – i has never hacted before. – Oblege with earlyest anser at convenance." Most of the other letters were written in similar terms to those quoted. Some offered to go on the stage without any salary as long as they got there, and one young woman in writing remarked, "I want to do the regular business, but it must have nothing to do with 'balley.'" One writer, the son of a clergyman and highly educated, stated that he was driven to such extremes that he thought the stage was the best thing to turn to.

Detective Berry, in answer to the Magistrate, said there were two young women present who had each paid 5s. to defendant to give them lessons for playing in *The Hunchback*. He told them he could get them on the stage in a fortnight. They were to pay him £2, but all they could afford was 10s., and they promised to pay the remainder when they got into engagements.

The prisoner declared there was no fraud intended.

Mr Chance said it appeared that prisoner was trading upon parties without any qualification whatever. It was a monstrous mode of getting money. He should remand him for a week for further inquiries.

The prisoner applied for bail.

Mr Chance required two substantial bail in £40, with twenty-four hours' notice to the police.

The prisoner was removed to the cells.

For employment as a clerk and messenger, the applicant to pay £10 as security since he would be handling large amounts of money. Graham was later sentenced to eighteen months' hard labour.

A MUSICAL NUISANCE.
On Tuesday, at the Westminster County Court, before Mr F. Bayley, Judge, a case came on for hearing, in which an application was made by Mr James Redding Ware, a literary gentleman, for an injunction to restrain Mr S. Corpe, the defendant, from playing an organ in chambers adjoining those occupied by the plaintiff. Mr De Courcy Atkins appeared for the plaintiff, and Mr Kemp for the defendant.

The plaintiff said that he occupied chambers at 50, Lincoln's Inn Fields, on the third floor; defendant occupied others on the second floor directly under his. He had seen the organ complained of. He thought its dimensions approximately were twelve feet high, ten feet wide, and four or five feet in depth. It occupied about half of the room. When the organ was first taken into the house on the 22nd August last he wrote to the defendant stating he should resist, at law if necessary, the playing of an organ in the room, and received a letter in reply stating that the defendant would take care, as he was bound to do, that the organ was not so used as to be a nuisance; indeed, in ordinary practice it would make less noise than a piano. When the organ was tuned after having been fitted up, he asked how long the operation would last; on being told two or three hours, he went out for that time.

The organ had been played at different periods since, about two or three times a week; he stayed in once for about three hours during which it was being played, and found that it so interfered with his comfort and the performance of his work that whenever it commenced he had to leave the house. It was usually played from seven o'clock until ten o'clock in the evening. The vibration was very great, causing an effect very like that produced by a slight application of galvanism. On the first day it was played a Dresden plate in his room was thrown down, the vibration communicated itself to all the articles in his rooms composed of china, glass, or metal. He had occupied the chambers for four or five years, and had expended a considerable amount of money on them. The music was very bad, and very common airs were played. If he did not obtain the injunction he then applied for he should be obliged to leave his rooms.

Mr John Fullilove, an artist, who occupied the chambers with the plaintiff, corroborated his statement. [...]

The defendant, Mr Saunderson Corpe, said he was one of the solicitors to the Great Eastern Railway Company. He had private chambers at 50, Lincoln's Inn Fields. The organ in question was made expressly for his rooms. It was not so powerful as a church organ. He had not experienced any vibration, although he had gone into other rooms while it was being played; certainly not the effect of a galvanic battery being applied.

Mr M.J. Gayland said he was a solicitor having chambers on the floor under that occupied by defendant. He had stayed at his office one evening to test the effect of the organ, and it did not interfere with the performance of his work nor was it any obstacle to conversation; he had given his clerk instruction while it was being played.

Mr Moor, another solicitor to the Great Eastern Railway, and defendant's attorney, gave corroborative testimony.

At the conclusion of the case his Honour said in his opinion this was not an actionable nuisance, although he considered it an intolerable one. A verdict was given for the defendant, with costs.

DURING the performance of *The Queen of Connaught* at the Olympic, on the evening of Tuesday last, Miss Ada Cavendish narrowly escaped injury by fire, her hair being set in a blaze by the escape of some blazing liquid from the flambeau she carries in the cave scene of the third act. Mr Henry Neville's attention was called to the accident, he immediately smothered the flame with his hands, and the actress proceeded with her part with as much confidence as though nothing had happened. From the same source Mr Culver's wig took fire, and we advise that the torch be forthwith banished from the scene.
21/1/1877

ROBERT NYLAND, aged nineteen, known in the Profession as Benhamo, an equestrian *artiste*, of the Cirque d'Hiver, Paris, has come to a most untimely end. While playing a game at billiards a wager was laid that he could not jump over the cue, and while endeavouring to accomplish the feat the cue caught his trousers and entered his body. He was picked up almost in a state of insensibility, and was taken home. After suffering for a week the most acute pain he died of mortification on the 17th January, and was buried on the 19th, his remains being followed to their last resting place by Mr Franconi, Mr Fernando, Mr Myers, and all deceased's brother and sister artistes of the above establishment. His loss is deeply regretted.
11/2/1877

TO THE EDITOR OF THE ERA.
Sir, – In these go-ahead times old fogies like myself must expect to see many curious changes in the manners and customs of Englishmen, but one thing I certainly did not expect to see, that is the shopkeeper making use of the Stage as a temptation to purchasers of Bohea or Twankay. I inclose you a handbill of the Imperial Tea Company, given to me in Birmingham, and judge of my surprise, Mr Editor, when upon reading it I found that by purchasing "one pound of this celebrated tea" I should also receive in addition to "the cup that cheers but not inebriates" a free ticket to the pit of the Prince of Wales's Theatre. As this is, so far as I am aware, the first instance on record of the Teapot and the Stage

being so intimately associated I have thought you might consider the occurrence worthy of a place in your columns.

For my own part, though I cannot for a moment impute any blame to the management of the Prince of Wales's Theatre, seeing that grocers have a right if they please to patronise the Drama, I cannot help feeling that the Stage is likely to suffer in being mixed up with tradesmen's puffs. Fancy the outraged feeling of old playgoers like myself, who have seen Kemble, Kean, Siddons, and other dramatic stars, when they read such announcements as those in the shop windows: – "Now's your time! A pound of sausages and a ticket for the Pantomime, only one shilling;" or, "Look alive! A bottle of gin, and a tragedy to follow, for half-a-crown. Be in time – be in time;" or the bootmaker may offer a pair of slippers and the farce of *Boots at the Swan*; while the butterman may tempt the customers with a pound of fine Dorset and a ticket for the ballet; and the proprietress of a genteel ladies' school may attract pupils with *The School For Scandal*. Remembering that tradesmen at the present day have advantages of publicity denied to their forefathers, I do respectfully appeal to them to leave Theatres alone, for I fail to see that the Drama can benefit by this unexpected Teetotal alliance of "The Teapot and the Stage." I remain, Sir, your obedient servant, A PLAYGOER OF THE PAST.

NOTICE. THE IMPERIAL TEA COMPANY will on Saturday next, February the 10th, PRESENT TO EVERY PURCHASER OF ONE POUND OF THEIR CELEBRATED TEA A FREE TICKET TO THE PRINCE OF WALES'S THEATRE, BIRMINGHAM, which will admit One Person to the Pit on any one night during the Pantomime.

WANTED, Information respecting my Black Retriever Trick Dog CHARLIE, who was Stolen from 180, Union Street, Oldham. Friends communicating to this address, or any Police-station, will oblige RICHARD THORNE, Scenic Artist, Theatre Royal, Oldham.
18/2/1877

"HAMLET" AT ST GEORGE'S HALL.
WE have seen some dismal performances of *Hamlet* in our time. At one representation we witnessed the Ghost had a tumble, and was observed rubbing the knobbly portions of his anatomy while he told the story of his woes to young Hamlet. On another occasion the fair Ophelia had a cold which so obscured her utterance, and necessitated such frequent use of her pocket-handkerchief, that laughter rather than sympathy accompanied her delineation.

Although there was not anything so specially ridiculous as this on Monday afternoon at St George's Hall, we think we can back the performance against any we have seen for absolute dullness. Almost every performer seemed on the verge of despair. Nearly everybody looked as if some horrible crime had been committed, and detectives amongst the audience were watching them. Hamlet crept about the stage like a melancholy mouse expecting every moment the ferocious cat to pounce upon him. The representative of the First Actor gave out his text in whispers, as if his communication was of too dreadful a nature to be made audible. […] As for the Hamlet of Mr Horace Crichton, what could he have been thinking about to venture so far out of his depth? The maundering way in which the soliloquies were delivered, the abject, dismal, undignified way in which he mooned about the stage, and his absolutely grotesque actions and attitudes caused incessant laughter, and no wonder. Who could help laughing when Hamlet stooped down to confront the King with the antics of a Clown in the Circus? […] Mr Alfred Calmour we could not bear; and Mr Gardner, as the Second Actor, had such a faint idea of dramatic requirements that he could not even manage his costume effectively, and a shout of laughter greeted the appearance of the trousers of everyday life beneath his cloak in the play scene. As the Queen Mrs Green acted with some discrimination; and the Ophelia of Miss Kate Langford revealed care and good taste, although the impersonation, as a whole, was feeble. Miss Langford was very unfortunate in "making up" for Ophelia's madness. Her appearance excited comic rather than sentimental feelings. But it is useless to continue. Such performances are a sheer waste of time to sit out or describe.

A RATHER large and select audience was attracted to the Temperance Hall, Grimsby, on the 27th ult., by the announcement that Dr Lynn, the world-famed "wonder-worker," would give his entertainment in legerdemain and so-called spirit manifestations; but instead of the talented Doctor appearing, he was personated by a man who had represented himself as the agent-in-advance. Apparently thinking the fraud would not be detected, the personator – who was really in the service of Dr Lynn when he visited Grimsby about a year ago – proceeded to imitate the great conjurer in some of his feats of sleight-of-hand, but performed the tricks so clumsily that the audience at length became disgusted, and the man was challenged as to his identity, when he produced a telegram from London stating that Dr Lynn, on account of illness, was unable to fulfil his appointment. Several at once left the Hall, and many, feeling they had been duped, eventually rushed to the ante-room after the conjurer and demanded the return of their money, which several obtained; but the pressure becoming great a "Samaritan," who had seen the whole of the performance and received back his admission money, packed the hero of the fraud into a box, and represented that he had left the building; and all ended quietly. The personator and his assistants left the town next morning without paying their hotel bill. Having by a ruse put their landlord off his guard, they got clear away with their luggage.

WANTED, MUSICIANS to keep away from Richmond, Surrey. Satisfactory explanations by applying to the Promenade Band, Belvidere Arms, Marsh Gate.
6/5/1877

THE Phoites – *Les Jolies* Kickapoos, as they please to call themselves – are still at the Oxford, nightly astonishing and delighting the visitors by their extraordinary antics illustrative of the fact that whalebone and india-rubber enter largely into the composition of their respective anatomies, and that it is possible to do more wonderful things with the human legs than were even dreamed of when human legs were first made.

A NEW DRAMATIC AUTHOR.
Possibly there never was a more curious specimen of dramatic literature issued from the Press than the work before us, written by an author rejoicing in the name of George St George. Three dramatic poems are given in the volume, which is published by Slade Brothers, Great Portland Street. The title of the first is *The Sires and Sons From Albion Sprung*. Number two is *The Man of Thought and the Man of Action*. The third is a dream play called *Don't Book Your Make Ups*; and then as a makeweight there is *A Vision of Love and Hope*. Now, what can we say to the publishers in response to their declaration that "the volume is entitled to rank among literary productions of the highest class?" Our simplest course will be to let the readers judge for themselves the quality of the work; they can admire or laugh according to their fancy.

Sires and Sons From Albion Sprung is a pretty wide theme for an author, remembering the United States of America, Canada, and a host of Colonial possessions. The *dramatis personae* in this piece are remarkable indeed. We have a Chorus dressed in a Roman toga, and we are referred to Catlin's* work for information regarding the dress of the Indian chiefs. But stranger shapes hover about us. The spirits of Shakespeare, Milton, Dryden, Thomson, Pope, and a host of other well-known bards appear, we are told, "in the costume of their time." Now, this hardly agrees with our notions of Spiritualism, for, according to a popular authority on the subject, "spirits are impalpable, and do not wear mortal costumes." We turn a page, and we get an illustration of the landing of the Pilgrim fathers, and then a specimen of dramatic dialogue is given such as we assuredly have never met with before. A number of Indian chiefs are grouped around. There is "dirge-like music," and a chief addresses the Pilgrims, the chorus undertaking the responsible duty of translating the following remarkable dialogue:

FIRST CHIEF: Nan-be-quon, tehe hee sugg-a. Nau-be-guon-ais?

CHORUS (interprets the speech): Who and what are the strangers coming in the big canoe from the rising sun?
SECOND CHIEF: Nis-a-way-een-gee-sug, nah pa-ke-me-tron dugh-kis-dee.
CHORUS: He asks, shall we give them friendly greeting, or dig up the scalping-knife and tomahawk?
[…]

Sometimes the author drops into verse, and Sam Slick, a razor-strop man, sells his wares with a rhyming comment upon their merits. As for plot or characterisation we confess we are quite at a loss to discover the purpose of the author, who must have had some idea of the stage in his mind, or he would not give directions as to scenery and costumes, and speak of the "green curtain." *The Vision of Hope and Love*, Mr George St George is careful to inform us, was written in 1845. It begins with this sentence, "How vague are our ideas of the human mind," which is just what we felt when reading this remarkable vision of love and hope. […] In one place we get a hint that the title *Don't Book Your Make Ups* was chosen with the idea that it was funny! As for stage business, the author had the drollest notions imaginable. Quite a point is made of a bit of paper in which a herring was wrapped, and the most minute directions are given as to making a cup of tea. *The Man of Thought and the Man of Action* is even more curious still, for Seymour, the "man of thought," entertains us with anecdotes of his early days. How he woke up his old aunt by pricking her with a pin when she snored during the sermon, and how "the echoes of the hymn he then heard still reverberates in the chambers of his brain." Should any reader be desirous of unravelling these wonderful mysteries they have only to send a guinea to the publishers, Messrs Slade Brothers, Great Portland Street, and, as we learn the circulation is limited to a few copies – a fact which few will be inclined to doubt, we imagine – they had better lose no time.
*George Catlin (1796-1872), a painter famous for his portraits of Native Americans.

The Sham Dr Lynn.
TO THE EDITOR OF THE ERA.
Sir, – The lad wearing spectacles and the girls with long flowing hair, who are visiting provincial towns where I am well known, were never engaged by me; but I have every reason to believe that the youth was once employed by my late Manager as programme boy and check taker. I am informed by a victim of the young imposter that my name is very extensively announced, and that when the time for commencing the entertainment arrives the lad referred to comes upon the platform and reads a telegram purporting to be an apology to the audience from me to the effect that I am unable to attend on account of illness.

I have communicated with the police in towns where the sham Dr Lynn is expected, and shall feel obliged by your giving publicity to this, and thus assist me in bringing the swindlers to justice. Yours faithfully, HUGH S. LYNN.
13/5/1877

TO THE EDITOR OF THE ERA.
Sir, – I was at the Globe Theatre on Monday night last, and between the acts of *After Dark* sought refreshments in the saloon of that house. A pint bottle of Moet's champagne was ordered and the modest sum of *six shillings* was charged for the same. A reasonable request to see the wine list was at once declined, and a refusal given to serve me again, because I had remonstrated in the first instance. Surely this is not a state of things calculated to advance the interests of any establishment, and certainly it is not asking too much to be made acquainted with the charges so as to be able to purchase or abstain from an article that you do not consider worth your money. If it is to their interest to charge the public a hundred per cent. over the original cost of what they supply let them do so by all means, but at least let the poor victim know before he falls into the snare.

It may seem a very trivial subject to call down notice, but ask the regular visitors to Theatres what are the samples of solids and liquids they are called upon to take, and the universal reply will be, not worth one-third of the money they have to pay for the same. Individually, it is of no moment to me, but upon public grounds I call attention to these facts. I enclose my card. JUSTITIA.

The Coming Hamlet.
TO THE EDITOR OF THE ERA.
Sir, – Within the last twelvemonth I have lost a very beautiful wife with cancer, and I find I cannot for the present enter into my profession of animal painter. I have devoted now five months' study on *Hamlet*; there are many striking points in the arrangement, and I thought it would be policy before I begin to advertise in your paper, to pay you the customary fee for time devoted by your leading dramatic correspondent, for coming down here and taking cognizance of the various features of the character.

Of course it has been an expensive coaching under Mr George Neville in the character, his hints and my own combined, and I am now completing fencing with Mr Ramon Castellote. I shall have no objection in paying for the space his notice might occupy in your paper, as I do not fear a favourable criticism of the character, and as it would be only necessary to go through the soliloquies and leading scenes, any day or evening that your correspondent can run down by his stating time and day in his reply, I would then be ready *to receive him in costume* and will entertain him with a glass of port, and pay him your charge for such notice. Mr Neville is particularly anxious that I might give my first in London, before I go to favourite and well-known boards, where I have played manifold times whilst a member of the Garrick Club at Bristol. I have devoted great care and feeling throughout the character. I am personally acquainted with -------, but as your paper passes into every Manager's hands, I think yours the only critique that demands attention. I can darken my room at any hour of the day, but, of course, I am tied for space for stage effects. I remain, Sir, yours respectfully.
(The above letter reached us on Wednesday. We have suppressed name and address, and some other particulars which might establish the identity of the ambitious and vainglorious writer, whose invitation we will endeavour to accept if, at his convenience, he will forward us a medical certificate of his sanity.)
10/6/1877

FOR SALE, Three MONKEYS; all will Wear their Dresses, and one is very clever with Tools; and Two Small Paintings, Six Feet Square. Address, Mr GEORGE HUNT, 28, Sidmouth Street, Devizes, Wilts.
1/7/1877

NOTICE. To the PERSON with GYMNASTIC CHILDREN. Your Party are not Engaged at the Crystal Palace, London, or even entertained. Why make such untrue statements, to mislead Proprietors and the Public in General? I trust it will not occur again. From W.H. Wieland, Caterer to the Crystal Palace Company.
8/7/1877

DURING the performance of Little Louie, the *clairvoyante*, and Professor Herriott, the wizard, on Tuesday, in the Pavilion at Raikes Hall Gardens, Blackpool, a man handed to the Professor a book of an obscene character, in order to test Little Louie, and to see if she could tell what it was. On being asked, "What is this?" she replied, "A book, papa." The Professor then asked her, "What would you think of the gentleman who gave it to me?" to which she said, "Well, papa, a gentleman that would offer an article to a little girl that he would be ashamed to offer to his own mother or sister, ought to be thoroughly ashamed of himself." The book was then handed to Mr Rushton, the Manager, amidst loud cries of "Turn him out" from the audience, and the owner of the book was unceremoniously ejected.
26/8/1877

I WANT Your Address, Dear JOE. Mamma knows all, even your leaving for Liverpool by steamer. If you want money, I'll send it. For God's sake write.
9/9/1877

£2 REWARD will be paid by the Guardians of the St Saviour's Union, Surrey, to anyone giving information that will lead to the apprehension and conviction of WILLIAM THOMAS RYDER ROBINS, an Actor – professionally known as "W. Ryder" – for Deserting his Wife and Family. Supposed to be in the Provinces. Was recently engaged at the Theatre of Varieties, Bolton, in the name of "Irvinerini." Height, 5ft. 10½in.; Dark Hair, Blue Eyes, Aged Thirty-Three Years. Information to be given to HUGH A. BRYDGES, Assistant Clerk, John Street West, Blackfriars Road, London.
16/9/1877

TO THE EDITOR OF THE ERA.
Sir, – Referring to your notice of the Bedford Music Hall (The Era, September 9th, 1877), I find your representative indulging in the production of a microscopic essay on my wishes and ambitions. How he came to suppose that I should sing "Would I Were a Man!" is to me a mystery, when I find such an eloquent member of the male sex with such a wandering and unenviable memory. I never sang a song with the title on which he so merrily dwells, but I do sing "Would I *Wear* a Bird!" The difference is a great one, for it cannot be denied that the lady would enjoy the change to a feathered existence, whereas to become a man – Ugh! Yours faithfully, FLORENCE SANGER.
(We are sorry to have wounded the susceptibilities of the sex, and if Miss Sanger will promise to be a little more distinct we will promise never again to mistake her ornithological wishes for masculine tendencies.)
23/9/1877

AT the Assembly Rooms, Clonmel, on Monday night last, there was an extraordinary scene not likely to be readily forgotten by those who witnessed it. Announcements had been scattered throughout the town that the "Great Vance and his Concert Party" would appear, and the popularity and fame of the eminent entertainer sufficed to fill the house to overflow.

The proceedings were to commence at "eight o'clock precisely," but nothing was done until twenty minutes to nine. At that hour that individual who had hitherto made himself known as the "agent in advance" appeared, in swallow tails and white kids, and apologised for the amateurishness of the pianist – his pianist not having arrived. He then commenced to sing the ditty known as "Beautiful Girls," differing in the important question of key with the accompanist at the outset. The audience at once became restive. "Arrah, give me my sixpence and let me go home!" roared somebody in the gallery, and this was the signal for a general uproar. More than one gentleman in the boxes then rose, and denounced the fellow as an imposter. [...] Terror-stricken, the swallow-tailed artist was heard above the din, telling all who wished their money returned to come up on the stage. Numbers did so, and a very few received back what they had paid, but the rush was too great. On they came, yelling and hooting in an alarming manner, and the author of all this din was forced behind the scenes – a young girl clinging to his side in the most frantic manner, at the same time tightly grasping a bag of money supposed to be the entire proceeds of the night. For safety's sake she took the rings from off her fingers, and, placing them in her mouth, one of them slipped down too far, and she was nearly choked.[...]

In the midst of the confusion the "agent" was dragged from behind the scenes to the front, minus his swallow-tails, when a gallant gentleman, who appeared determined to make the fellow disgorge, and to have full justice done, caught him by the throat; nor did he relinquish his hold until the bag of money was handed over to him by the young female to whom we have already referred. Up he held it triumphantly before the house, amidst cries of "Bravo! Well done, Captain!" Then came the question of what he should do with the money, when some cried out, "Charity;" others, "Indian Famine Fund;" whereupon he handed the bag to another gentleman, and in the end it was decided that the Sheriff should take charge of it, which he kindly undertook to do. Upon being counted the contents were found to realise only some six pounds odd. The bulk of the silver must have been adroitly removed before the commencement of this remarkable entertainment.

Meanwhile the "Celebrated Comedian" and his famous concert party – we shrewdly suspect he was the entire "company" himself – escaped, and hid in a lane way, escaping in the dead hour of night over a wall into Mary Street, and off in the direction of the railway station. By the mail train, at three o'clock a.m., he took his departure, it is supposed for Waterford. Anxious as they were to get clear of Clonmel, before leaving the female of the party called at their lodging-house for a favourite black cat, which the landlady refused to give up until the week's bill was paid. Rather than leave without her pet, the money – somewhere about £2 – was paid, and "tabby" was wrapped comfortably in a shawl, and prepared for the journey.
30/9/1877

ON Tuesday an action was brought at the Marylebone County Court, before Mr Sergeant Wheeler, Judge, by Miss Ellis, to recover the sum of £12 from Mr Algar, Ballet Master.

Mr Ladbury, barrister, appeared for the plaintiff.

Janet Ellis stated that she was a ballet dancer, and resided at Peckham. She knew the defendant, and in May last she entered into an engagement with him to go to Amsterdam for eight weeks. She was to receive 30s. per week. She proceeded to Amsterdam with him, and performed at a summer Theatre there for a fortnight, when the defendant was dismissed. She was successful, particularly in her skipping-rope performance, and was encored nightly. At the end of a fortnight she was compelled to leave, and, having no money had to apply to the Consul, who sent her to England. Defendant did not pay her anything.

Witness said, in reply to the Judge, that defendant kept them on bread, butter, and eggs, and she was nearly half starved.

The defendant said on the 3rd June the Queen of the Netherlands died, and the performance was stopped in consequence. He was not dismissed for misconduct. The performance being stopped prevented him from carrying out his engagement with the plaintiff.

Plaintiff – But you were dismissed before the Queen died.

Defendant said he considered he acted as a gentleman in paying for the plaintiff's board and lodging.

His Honour – But you did not even pay for her passage home. Judgement will be for the plaintiff for the amount claimed and costs.

HER MAJESTY'S THEATRE. WANTED, Three Hundred YOUNG LADIES, between the ages of Six and Ten, and not exceeding Four Feet in height. Apply to M. FRANCESCO, Stage Door, Her Majesty's Theatre, Haymarket, daily, at Two o'clock.
7/10/1877

DIED, at her residence, Horsley Fields (late of Bell Street, Wolverhampton), on the 5th inst., Mrs Esther Devey, aged thirty-one years. She was well known and respected by many professionals staying at her house, and is regretted by all who knew this pretty miniature lady, who was only forty-three inches in height.
25/11/1877

HAS anyone yet discovered the distinct value to a comedy or drama in the way of an advertisement in the new managerial plan of placarding the approaches to our Theatres with enlarged photographs of lovely young men? Adonis with curled hair and a beautiful necktie grins at us in the Strand; Antinous shows his white teeth and soft eyes to the crowds in Oxford Street; Lothario in a sort of classical toga exposes his bare neck in Drury Lane, and wishes to impress us with the idea that a Grecian statue has just stepped out of a Roman bath! They are "quite too awfully nice," these young men. Their coats look as if they had been stretched on their backs by some patent process. The art of Douglass and Truefitt, to

say nothing of Marsh, has curled to perfection their ambrosial locks; their complexions have been made "beautiful for ever," and pass satisfactorily through the ordeal of the photographer's camera. But it is not quite clear why these pictures should be thus placarded. Inside the show the comedians thus counterfeited may be acting in character. They may be romantic knights in the middle ages, or they may be cabmen. Seldom do they appear on stage in their habit as they live, with these Sackville Street coats and Burlington Arcade neckties. Is the Drama so indifferent an art to Mary Jane, the housemaid, to Lottie at the bar, to Belinda behind the counter, or to Polly at the Post-office that these susceptible young sillies cannot enter a Theatre unless they are assured beforehand of the presence there of some "thing of beauty" which to them will be "a joy for ever?" It may be so, but apart from the peculiarity of the placards is it not reducing the Theatre to its original element of a show? Mr Richardson's "fit-up" would have been nothing without his pictures and his parade. Now that the entrances to Theatres are turned into picture galleries we only want the gong and the showman with a long stick calling out to passers-by "Walk up! Walk up!"
2/12/1877

TO THE EDITOR OF THE ERA.
Sir, – Will you give me space in your valuable columns to show a few of the trials, troubles, and temptations of those whose lot it is to belong to the ballet. In the first place it is not generally known that we have to practice for four or six weeks, for which in London we get not a single penny piece. I ask why should not we be paid for that time as well as when the night duties commence? We often get promises from the Manager that he will give us half-pay for rehearsals, but when these rehearsals commence he shuffles out of it with some lame excuse. Surely the rehearsal time is the time we want money most to obtain food and other necessaries. As soon as the rehearsals are complete we have a night or two before the production of a ballet to go to the Hall or Theatre at twelve o'clock at night and rehearse until five or six o'clock the next morning. Now, why is this necessary? Could it not be done as well in day-time? It is all very well for the principals, who have their friends to treat them to what they like, but not for the ballet. There are more girls annually that I know who have been brought to shame and trouble through midnight rehearsals than through any other cause. The Press generally is ever ready to crush us poor wretches. No one has a good word for us, because the world does not know one half our trials and troubles, or they would have pity instead of disgust. Hoping that some kind friend will take up the matter and remedy the evils of the ballet in its present state, I inclose my name and address, and I subscribe myself, Yours obediently, A POOR BALLET GIRL.
16/12/1877

MR C. RICE was a sufferer by the accident which occurred to the Scotch express on Tuesday. He received a severe wound on the head and was very seriously shaken. Mr Rice was sitting asleep with his head resting on his hand in the window recess when, awakened by the crash of the engine passing through the mineral train, he sprang up to clasp his wife, who was sleeping opposite him. This movement saved him, for at the same instant the whole side of the compartment was cut clean away, and half of his head and his right arm would undoubtedly have been cut away with it.

TRIALS OF THE BALLET.
TO THE EDITOR OF THE ERA.
Sir, – Seeing *The Era* of last Sunday, I beg to say it is true about rehearsals, and that is not all. I am what they call an extra lady, and at the Theatres on this side of the water – the Surrey side – we only get 8s. per week, and at this time of the year we have to find everything for the Pantomime, as they say they can't afford to pay for them. So we must, or go. We mustn't speak, or out we go at a moment's notice. Tights, shoes, and muslin dresses take over one pound to pay for out of our money. We have to do all this for nothing. We have rehearsals from ten in the morning until five, then sometimes in the evening; and then you have your own dresses to make. What time have you, except when you ought to be asleep?

If you are five minutes late in the morning you are fined, and at the same time you are starving, and have to depend on your landlord to let you run on a bit, or pawn all you have got, or do something else, and that is our lot in life. This is how us poor girls are treated that want to get an honest living, as I and hundreds more do. If the public did but know half our lot they would pity us, I think, and we might get a little more and the Proprietor might buy our things, as it is for their good, not ours. All this is true, I am sure, and a deal more. If you think proper to publish this, or any of it, you would have the thanks of many poor girls, who would ever pray for your welfare. Yours obediently, A BALLET GIRL.
23/12/1877

9
1878
A Target for Flora's Arrows

"What's in a Name?"
TO THE EDITOR OF THE ERA.
Sir, – Ford, Welford, Weyford, Waxford, &c., represented by *The Times*, *Telegraph*, *Observer*, *Daily News*, *Echo*, *The Era*, &c., as having played the part of Mealymouth in the Pantomime at Covent Garden, are unfortunate victims of my obscure name, created in the perturbed minds of distracted reporters. Permit me to protect the reputation of any person having the misfortune to be named after the above, by exposing the real imposter. Suffer me to contradict twenty-odd newspapers by stating that I am still fooling along with the part at Covent Garden, and still rejoice in the unpronounceable name of MARK MELFORD.

THE efforts of a young actress are too frequently marred by the injudicious compliments of foolish admirers. We had an instance of this on Thursday at the Queen's, when Miss Maud Milton, in *Fatherland*, immediately on making her appearance, had thrown to her a handsome bouquet. Very wisely she treated it with indifference; and the impulsive youth who had wasted his money on it had the mortification of seeing it picked up, at the termination of the act, by one of the stage attendants. He will do well to shun bouquets for the rest of his life.
6/1/1878

Notice to all whom it may concern. MINNIE WILLIAMS, pupil of Harry Baldwin, was Stolen away from me while asleep in her bed at 62, Merrion Street, Leeds. Any parties Engaging her, who is known by the name of VALLAIRIO, will be held liable. Address, HARRY BALDWIN, Theatre Royal, Spennymoor. N.B. – What is Professionals' opinion after my labour of sixteen months?
13/1/1878

A NEW JULIET.
The descent from the sublime to the ridiculous is a very easy one. To jump from the ridiculous to the sublime is a different matter altogether, and will be found a task of no small difficulty. The attempt has been made during the week by a Miss Florence Sedley, who has failed most ignominiously, and who, in her endeavour to soar, has flopped down into the region of the ridiculous, a region in which she dwelt unhappily when first we made her acquaintance. "When and where was that?" some curious reader may be disposed to ask. We refer the curious one to our recent detailed description of the Pantomime called *Roley-Poley* now being performed with marked success at the Grecian Theatre. In that description will be found the following passage: – "Everybody who appears in Gloriopolis is musical except the Queen

of that realm, who gave us the idea, by the expression of her face and the discordancy of her voice, that singing is an extremely painful exercise. By this time, doubtless, the voice of that Queen has been hushed." [...] The name of Her Majesty was Miss Florence Sedley, and Miss Florence Sedley it was who undertook on the morning of Wednesday last to impersonate Shakespeare's Juliet at the Globe Theatre.

The temerity of this act would have fairly appalled us had we known before she made her appearance who the Juliet was to be. When she came upon the stage we could not believe our eyes. We thought they had been made the fools of the other senses. But as we looked and listened, and looked again, that Pantomime scene of Christmas Eve came vividly before our mental vision, and we saw Queen Gloria standing in the centre of the Grecian stage, surrounded by a motley throng, shrieking discordantly, and just heard above the din of the "gods" and the chaff of the pit; we saw her swaying to and fro, and looking piteously at her companions, and making curious grimaces, and exciting derision. There was no mistake about it now. Queen Gloria was Juliet and Juliet was Queen Gloria, and both were rolled into one in the person of Miss Florence Sedley.

Now, a lady may be a very bad vocalist, a very incompetent performer in Pantomime, and still a very tolerable actress in Shakespearean tragedy. But no proof of the fact was afforded this time. [...] That Miss Sedley had taken the trouble to learn the words of her part we shall not deny, but at the same time we must affirm that she appeared in few instances to know the meaning of the lines to which she gave utterance. Her elocution was faulty, her action was neither appropriate nor graceful, and her chief desire appeared to be when opportunity occurred to maul Romeo. It was just as much as that gallant young gentleman could do to keep her from pulling his wig from his head. In the famous chamber scene she played such tricks with the "bones of her ancestors" that we could hardly keep our risibility under control. When the catastrophe came all control was lost, and we indulged in laughter which we smothered as best we could in a handkerchief. For when Juliet had fallen dead by Romeo's side she discovered that her dress had not arranged itself to her liking. A dead Juliet showing her ankle would certainly not be in accord with the eternal fitness of things. And so Juliet revived for a moment, brought the erring garment to order, and then *died all over again*. [...]

Funny – very funny – was the comment on Miss Florence Sedley's genius contained in the following colloquy which took place as we left the Theatre: – "Well, what do you think of Miss Sedley's Juliet?" was the question addressed to us. "Comical," we replied. "Comical or not comical, she has been engaged at the Court." "No!" we exclaimed in a tone of incredulous amazement. "Yes she has," was the response, *"but she won't have to speak."*

A VERY daring case of robbery occurred in Dundee about midnight on Saturday, the 12th inst., the victim being Mr W. Lowe, well known as the able author and representative of the Sandy MacGulliver of the Music Hall Pantomime in the city named. Mr Lowe, after the conclusion of the performances, went home to his lodgings for a short time, and thereafter accompanied a friend to his home. On his way back to his lodgings he was suddenly attacked in Meadowside by four men, who forcibly dragged him off the pavement into a close, and began at once to rifle his pockets. One of the men caught him round the neck in garrotting fashion, another held back his arms, and before he could give any alarm, the two others had relieved him of his watch and chain, his purse, and two notebooks. The robbery must have been deliberately planned and carried out, for each of the ruffians seemed to know the special part he was to play, and not a word was spoken by any of them. When they had carefully rifled Mr Lowe's pockets they pulled him into the middle of the street, made him spin round several times, and then bolted.

Owing to the suddenness of the attack, and the confusion caused by being whirled so rapidly about, Mr Lowe was not half aware of the extent of his loss for a minute or two. A constable was then informed of the occurrence, and the case was subsequently reported at the Central Office. Mr Lowe is suffering a good deal from the effect of the ill-treatment he sustained at the hands of his assailants. It was fortunate that he had left the greater part of his money at his lodgings before coming out, all that the ruffians got being only 4s. or 5s. A loss which he feels very much, besides his watch and chain, is that that of his notebook, which contained memoranda of some three or four years' reading. No clue has yet been obtained by the police to lead to the detection of the villains.

SCENIC ARTIST. WANTED, for a permanency. Those gentlemen with a taste for inhaling the fragrance of a "brewer's apron" need not apply. Address, with terms, Mr E. CLINTON HALL, Theatre Royal, Leicester.

TO BE SOLD, a Bargain, the Magnificent DRESSES, Armour, Banners, and Poles, complete, for the Kings and Queens of England and Attendants, from William the Conqueror to Queen Victoria. May be seen nightly in the Successful Grand Pantomime "Jack and the Beanstalk," at the Theatre Royal, Leeds. "The Costumes for the Kings and Queens of England are brilliant and rich, surpassing anything ever seen in Leeds, and will make any Pantomime." – Vide Yorkshire Post.
20/1/1878

REGINALD H. BURKETT, described as a clerk, and giving his address as 1, Field's Court, Gray's Inn Square, was charged on the 19th inst., at Worship Street Police Court, with riotous and indecent behaviour at the Grecian Theatre, City Road.

It appeared from the evidence that the prisoner and other persons were in a private box close to the stage, and during the performance of the Pantomime were noisy and disorderly. The prisoner was observed to be smoking, and Mr Gillett, Stage-Manager, sent to inform him that it was not allowed. For a short time there was quietness and order, but when the ballet scene commenced the prisoner behaved in a disgusting way, making motions to the dancers, and when their business brought them to the front he leaned out of the box and with his stick tried to hook the legs of one of the ballet women, who began to cry and had to leave the stage. Presently a Mr Nicholls, one of the actors, appeared on the stage and commenced to sing. The prisoner called out to him and used some nasty expressions, whereupon Mr Nicholls, going to the side of the box, demanded of the prisoner what he meant. The prisoner retorted with more offensive language, and Mr Nicholls struck him. Thereupon the prisoner jumped out of the box on to the stage and struck Mr Nicholls, and for some moments a fight proceeded on the stage. This created so much excitement that the curtain had to be dropped and the performance stopped. Mr George Conquest then ordered the prisoner to be given into custody, which was done.

Mr Bushby, after hearing the evidence of three witnesses, thought that there was no use proceeding any further with the case, except for ordering the prisoner to keep the peace. He had received the first blow from Mr Nicholls, but his conduct had been very bad. He ordered him to find one surety for his good behaviour for three months.

Mr Warren, solicitor, of Bloomsbury Square, offered himself, and having justified, the prisoner was released.

The Missing Circus Girl.
TO THE EDITOR OF THE ERA.
Sir, – At Brighton, on Sunday evening, January the 6th, after coming from church, the little Circus girl, Jessie Simpson, my apprentice, went out ostensibly to buy some sweetstuff; since which time she has not been seen, and all efforts to find her have been without avail. At every place that could be thought of inquiries have been made, a warrant also has been obtained, and is now in the hands of the police for her apprehension. It was thought at first that some dishonourable person had decoyed her away, that, being a clever girl, they might make money of her services, or marry this little bit better than a child. However, all inquiries and everything yet done, on this or other suspicions, have failed to find her, and her mysterious and sudden disappearance therefore makes me very anxious lest some great evil may have befallen her. She is a native of Plymouth, about fifteen years old, five feet high, rather stout, black hair

and eyes, thin face, rather pretty; when she left had on a black velvet dress, cloth jacket, new hat and flowers, gold bracelets, and silver earrings. A reward also has been offered for any information that would find her. I shall be very glad if any person can throw any light on the whereabouts of the girl; or if she should see this letter to write to me, that no great wrong has come to her, as up to the moment of her disappearance there could not have been a better or more obedient girl. Yours obediently, F. GINNETT, Circus, Torquay.
27/1/1878

MEDICAL men have frequently remarked the effect music has upon the insane, but until recently we have not heard that the influence has been practically applied until a well-known American pianist, Mr Mark Pattison, tried it at the Blankwell's Island Lunatic Asylum, where a musical and dramatic entertainment was given recently to fourteen hundred female lunatics. One of the most incurably insane of the patients, a girl eighteen years of age, was induced to seat herself near the pianist, who played softly and expressively a nocturne of Chopin. It was observed that the savage, half-animal looks of the girl changed as the music proceeded. The dreamy, poetical character of the music evidently had a soothing effect, but when Mr Pattison dashed into a lively polka she became excited, but not savagely. The influence in this case tended to make the patient merry rather than violent, and her pulse rose from 80 to 108. The polka being over the pianist played "Home, Sweet Home," changing it to a waltz movement. During the performance of "Home, Sweet Home," a German woman was deeply affected, and falling on her knees was heard repeating the Lord's Prayer; but the waltz without exception tempted all the women to join in it. What will the authorities at Hanwell and Colney Hatch say to this? If music is so potent in America why not try it here?
3/2/1878

TO D.J. FROM A.H.W. Behave like a man; come back and help to set things straight. At any rate write to your wife, even if you won't say where you are.
17/2/1878

I, HARRY LOVE, Bill-Poster, Hastings, hereby give Mr H. JAMES, who broke his Leg at the Havelock Hotel, Notice, if he does not communicate with me, the Things WILL BE SOLD next week to defray expenses.
24/2/1878

THE PROFESSIONAL BOUQUET THROWER.
TO THE EDITOR OF THE ERA.
Dear Sir, – We must always appeal to you when we are in trouble, and I think I have got something very like a grievance. Not a mere personal matter, although I might say very much on that score; but it is a subject intimately connected with that better respect for actresses as women, and that higher consideration of acting as an art, which you have so devotedly and steadily encouraged. […]

Now, what is an actress to do when she is persecuted by the professional bouquet thrower? When she is marked out for those compliments which savour very much of insult, and when, without encouragement, she is deliberately placed before the public in a bad and false position? But who, you will ask, is the professional bouquet thrower? You must know him in the stalls as well as we do on the stage. He is over-dressed and impudent, and prides himself on the acquaintance of actresses, who despise him as much as his fellow-men must. He comes to the Theatre early in the evening, like the milliner's young man, with an advance guard of band-boxes. He takes the stallkeepers into his confidence, and sits surrounded – like a cheap Cupid – with pretty flowers and valuable exotics.

Having selected an actress with whose name he desires his own to be associated he begins flinging the flowers at her in a wild and reckless fashion. He has not the art of a member of a well-disciplined *claque*, and as often as not throws the bouquet at a ridiculous moment. He does not wait for a moment of applause or a good acting point, but pelts the poor nervous actress at her first entrance, making her look very silly, or hurls the weighty mass of flowers and fern at her in the middle of a song or speech. He has so many bouquets to dispose of and cannot properly fix the time of their delivery. In acting as he does the professional bouquet thrower is encouraged by three distinct motives. He wishes to be taken for a fast fellow and the friend of a popular actress, caring little how he may be compromising her. He desires to raise the jealousy or anger of his friends, many of whom may have greater taste or tact. Lastly, he is not above doing the dirty work of the rich man to whom he is the toady, and for a consideration will fling bouquets for which he has not paid to actresses whom he does not know. […] Letters to the stage door, or presents sent to the same quarter, can be put aside without any harm being done, except to the sense of respect of her who receives them. But I, for one, don't like being made a target for Flora's arrows whilst I am doing my work on the stage, and using my best endeavours to amuse the public as best I can.

A graceful compliment has degenerated into a disgraceful trade. If an actress so works up the feeling of the house that the ladies in the audience who are carrying bouquets fling them at her feet, what more charming and spontaneous compliment can exist? But what compliment is conveyed in the idiotic foresight of a youth who fills his private box with exotics, who comes to the Theatre without a lady, or who had a dozen bouquets under his stall? I, for one, own that I cannot see where actress or art are dignified by the proceeding. Besides being foolish it is personally annoying and uncomfortable. Those who sit near the professional bouquet thrower in the stalls are conscious of a swish of water over their heads and necks, for of course

The rose has been washed, just washed in a shower,
Which Damon to Phyllis conveyed;

and those on the stage are pelted not always gracefully or with effect.

Meanwhile, what is an actress to do? If she accepts the compliment with a smile it is instantly assumed that she is encouraging the attention of a notorious libertine, and desires to be recommended by him to his rich and aristocratic friends. If she allows the flowers to remain where they are on the floor she is considered sulky or ungracious. If she throws them back at the impudent face of the persecutor she, by the act, seriously insults her audience, whilst she does no harm to her enemy. In this predicament will not the audience help us? We cannot help ourselves. An audience can see in an instant if the compliment is a true or a forced one, and an audience can punish when we cannot. Let us be secure from the odious attentions of these bouquet throwers, who make themselves ridiculous and interrupt the scene. Let them be put down by popular clamour and indignation, when our faces tell how much we are annoyed.

A man does not carry bouquets. He had nothing to do with them. Ladies carry bouquets, and we are always pleased to accept a floral compliment from our generous sisters. I repeat, that a man does not carry a bouquet. In these curiously affected days he carries a stick, and, as I do not think the public would allow him to "give us the stick," pray let the public prevent him from surrounding his conceit with the beautiful flowers which, for once in their lives, ought to be strangers to the "rake". Yours obediently, AN ACTRESS.

SOMETHING like excitement was occasioned at the morning performance at the Globe on Wednesday, by the arrival of some four or five Turkish gentlemen of distinction, who, accompanied by their dragomen and interpreter, took up a position in a private box, and were soon the observed of all observers. They paid close attention to the proceedings, and before the termination of the entertainment were taken behind the scenes and introduced to several prominent members of the company, Mr Charles Collette wondering why such a parcel of foreigners, who could not speak a word of English, should visit an English Theatre. Mr Clifton treated the strangers with great courtesy; Mr Johnson, the scene painter, offered them snuff; cigarettes and coffee were provided for them in the saloon; and not until the Turks had departed in a Strand omnibus did it leak out that the dusky gentlemen were none other than certain lively spirits of the Crichton Club, who had come to enjoy the performance and a capital joke at the same time.

BALLOONS. – MR WHELAN is prepared to accept Engagements with his Unequalled Fleet of Balloons. They having ascended from every place where engaged for the last Three Years, weather being favourable or not. Caterers, Secretaries, and Managers of Fetes and Galas, to prevent disappointment are invited to communicate early for terms, references, opinions of the Press, &c., to 6, Lord Street, Huddersfield.
3/3/1878

WANTED, by a GIANTESS, who has not been much before the public, an Engagement to travel with a first class Exhibition. The Lady is rather above the regular size of people exhibiting themselves as stout. Address, GIANTESS, care of J. Maxwell, Fishmonger, Highbridge, Newcastle-on-Tyne.
17/3/1878

WANTED, a COCK'S DRESS, with Head, suitable for a Boy about Forty Inches High; also Two small Dummy Donkeys. Address immediately, J. RALLAMO, Post-office, Bridport, Dorset.
24/3/1878

THE Australian Tom Thumb and Commodore Nutt, who have been on a tour through the Western counties, created some amusement among the passengers at the Exeter station of the Great Western Railway on the 23rd inst., by an argument they started with the authorities. It seems that when the ticket examiner came to the carriage only two half tickets were given up for Tom Thumb and the Commodore. On being told that each ought to pay the full fare as they are respectively twenty-one and twenty-eight years of age, it was pleaded on their behalf that both were not equal to one ordinary-sized passenger, and therefore should not be expected to pay more than one full fare. The report, however, was that as they had the voices, the manners, and the age of men, they must each pay the ordinary fare, and, amid the amusement of those who had gathered round the carriage, the Commodore and his companion had to yield to the ticket collector's demand.
31/3/1878

D-RE., come or write immediately. Little D. is constantly fretting and asking for you. He is very ill, and so am I. Nothing shall be said and all forgiven. Yours, D.
14/4/1878

Shocking Death of an Actress.
On Wednesday afternoon Dr Diplock held an inquiry at 138, Kensington Park Road, as to the death of Miss Harriet Barlow, aged twenty-two, who was found dead in the area of the house on the morning of Good Friday. From the evidence of Laura Jessop, a servant at the house, it appeared that the deceased lady was found by the witness at about half-past nine on Good Friday morning, lying at the bottom of the area, fully dressed, and quite dead; it being apparent that she had fallen head first from the garden. There was a little blood on the stones, a piece of area railing was found firmly clutched in her right hand, and a part of the railing in front of the drawing-room window was found in the area near the body.

Police-constable 173 X stated that he was called to the house by the last witness on Friday morning, about ten o'clock, and found the deceased lying in the area doubled up and quite dead; there was some blood on her face. A doctor was sent for, and he pronounced life to be extinct, and expressed his opinion that she had been dead some hours.

Mrs Florence Gay stated that the deceased lodged with her since Christmas last. She usually came home at night rather late, as her professional duties as an actress kept her engaged late. She had no latch-key, and no one sat up for her. On the Thursday she told witness she would not come home that night.

The witness retired at half-past eleven, being under the impression that the deceased would not return home that night. The witness heard no noise during the night. No knock was heard at the door, and the witness's brother slept in the front drawing-room on the couch, but he did not hear any noise.

The deceased had never before attempted to get into the house by means of the drawing-room window. The last engagement of the deceased was at the Prince's Theatre, Manchester.

The Jury returned a verdict "That the deceased came by her death from the falling into the area, and the same was caused accidentally."

A CASE of painful interest came before the Stipendiary Magistrate (Mr Kynnersley) at the Birmingham Police Court on Wednesday. James West Bridges, the well-known and accomplished equestrian who was up to a recent date one of the company engaged by Mr Newsome at Curzon Hall, Birmingham, was brought up and charged with being disorderly and using abusive and obscene language at the house of a man named Louis Marks, a jeweller's factor residing in Belgrave Road, Birmingham.

It appeared from the evidence of the complainant that on the previous evening the accused came to his house, jumped over the garden wall, and behaved himself in a most extraordinary manner, using at the same time very bad language at the top of his voice. Complainant remonstrated with the accused, and ultimately the latter went away. At midnight, however, the complainant was aroused by a loud knocking at his door, and upon looking out he saw the accused hammering at the door violently. He came down to him, and he at once drew a sword and threatened the complainant that if he came near him he would run it into him. He (complainant) went in search of a policeman and the accused disappeared, but he was subsequently found by the officer crouching in an entry. Upon the policeman asking him to give an account of himself he replied that he wanted Jesus Christ out of complainant's house. The poor fellow, who was suffering from a deranged mind, was then taken by the officer to the lock-up, and on Wednesday morning Mr Newsome was communicated with.

A witness (one of Mr Newsome's company) appeared, and in his evidence stated that the accused was one of the cleverest riders in the Profession, and that he had been in the habit of receiving from £12 to £15 per week, but that recently he had been periodically in a state of mind which rendered him quite unaccountable for his actions. The Magistrate ordered that the case stand over for a few days, and directed that a medical man should see and examine the accused in the meantime. During the brief hearing of the case the unfortunate accused showed evident signs of an impaired mind in an occasional vacant look and a few unintelligible and incoherent utterances.
28/4/1878

WANTED, to hear from a PERFORMING FLEA, BEE, or BIRD SHOW, or real good Novelty, for Shop. N.B. – Magnetic Lady can write in. Address, T. VINE, 228, High Street, Swansea.
5/5/1878

WE do not often hear of goats assisting in an operatic performance, but in the representation of *Tannhäuser*, at the Royal Italian Opera, on Tuesday evening, Mdlle Cottino, in order to make the effect as Arcadian as possible, had a couple of goats in the scene where she sings the song of the Shepherd. Unfortunately for the lady's vocal display, the goats insisted upon bleating all the time in the most laughable manner, but Mdlle Cottino was not disconcerted, and finished her song in artistic style. We trust the goats were satisfied with their operatic *debut*.
12/5/1878

IF MRS BUNNY, now Exhibiting the Child Without Arms or Legs, will communicate to Mr GROVES, at 60 (or 160), Walworth Road, London, on or before the 22nd of this month, she can hear of something to her advantage.
16/6/1878

LAST Tuesday evening a concert was given by 1,000 children at the Philharmonic Hall, Liverpool. The spacious platform thus crowded partly gave way, and about 800 of them came down, some of them a couple of feet, others more. The children, panic-stricken, shrieked, and a scene of intense excitement ensued. Fortunately the drop was not sufficient to cause fatal injuries, the worst cases being attended to at the infirmary. After some little delay the concert proceeded.
23/6/1878

THE intense heat which has prevailed throughout the week has proved a formidable enemy to the majority of Managers, and in too many instances the interiors of our Theatres have presented a beggarly array of empty benches. By way of example we may mention a fact unprecedented in the history of any Theatre of repute. A representative of this journal early in the week attended a popular house where an excellent company was engaged in the performance of a most attractive drama. He had the stalls *all to himself*.
30/6/1878

THE position of a *prima donna* whose nose bleeds in the middle of an important scene is by no means an enviable one. Madame Pappenheim was placed in such a dilemma at Her Majesty's Theatre on Saturday last, when she came upon the stage in the first act of *Fidelio*. An old-fashioned remedy in such cases is to put the key of the back door down the sufferer's back. Another way is to dip one's head in cold water. We have heard of a lump of ice being applied to the nose. But how could Madame Pappenheim, at such a critical moment, apply such remedies? We heartily sympathise with her, and cordially applaud the courage she displayed in proceeding under the circumstances with her part.
7/7/1878

A FREAK OF NATURE. To be Exhibited alive, a Cat, Mother of One Kitten and Two Puppies with Cats' Paws. Private Exhibitions, in Town or Country, attended on application to Mr S. EMANUELS, 168, Drury Lane.

To Comic Skaters, Negro Comedians, &c. FOR SALE, AIR-TIGHT DRESS. Blows out to an enormous size. Easy to work in. Blown up in two minutes. Lowest £2. A Big Novelty. H. STANLEY, 40, Cambridge Street, Bilston, Staffordshire.
14/7/1878

MISS AGNES BECKWITH'S GREAT FEAT.
Lovers of swimming witnessed a remarkable feat accomplished on Wednesday last by Miss Agnes Beckwith, who undertook to swim from Westminster Bridge to Richmond, in fact as far as the tide would permit, and to swim a portion of the return journey so as to make a distance of twenty miles.

An immense number of spectators thronged the bridge and the Thames Embankment as the time approached for the start, and accompanied by the steamer *Matrimony*, gaily decorated with flags, under the command of Captain Bean, and attended on by her father and redoubtable brother William in a skiff, the youthful water sprite, dressed in a close-fitting amber suit, adorned with white lace, a jaunty little straw hat, and fluttering blue ribbons, parted the waters and commenced her tedious journey at twenty-six minutes past twelve o'clock. She reached Lambeth Bridge in 9 min., and Vauxhall, immensely cheered by a great crowd, in 17 min. 45 secs., and thus completed her first mile. Battersea Suspension Bridge brought her time to 34 min., and Chelsea Bridge to 48 min. She went under that obnoxious structure known as Old Battersea Bridge at 18 min. after one, having occupied 52 min. from the start. At Coates' boat-house she was fired at by way of encouragement, which, no doubt, was very comforting, and was certainly greatly appreciated by those on board the steamer, who cheered lustily, and probably took the compliment to themselves. […] At twelve minutes after three Miss Agnes received an ovation as she glided prettily under Barnes Bridge that must have been highly gratifying (9 miles ½ fur., in 2 hr.

46 min.) The half-distance, ten miles, was accomplished at half-past three, in 3 hr. 4 min., which was of course hailed with considerable applause. At five minutes to four the merry young siren shot under Old Kew Bridge, laughing and keeping up an animated conversation with her friends, in 3 hr. 21 mins. from the start, 11 miles and half a furlong having been covered. […]

Having reached the "Pigeons," and the tide having turned, Miss Beckwith, looking quite as fresh as when she started, went through numerous elegant evolutions in the water that were greatly applauded, and having disported herself in her almost native element as long as she thought desirable, retraced her way, and on arriving at Mortlake Reach, having accomplished rather more than she had undertaken to do, left the water at nine minutes to seven, the toilsome task having taken 6 hr. 25 mins. to swim over, and was greeted on landing with an amount of enthusiasm that this young water-queen so unquestionably deserved.

MR GEORGE CONQUEST will supply Provincial Managers with perfect reproductions of the Wonderful PROPERTY PARROT, as used by him at the New Grecian Theatre, Crystal Palace, and Surrey Theatres, in the Pantomime of "Roley-Poley," with Sole Right for each Town, for forthcoming Pantomimes. Apply to Mr H. SPRY, General Manager, Grecian Theatre, London.
21/7/1878

LOVELL V. WILLIAMS AND LUMSDEN. – This was an action heard on Wednesday before Mr Sergeant Wheeler and a Special Jury, in which James Lovell, cab proprietor and driver, of 5, Ashburnham Mews, Lot's Road, Cremorne, was the plaintiff, and the defendants, Messrs Charles William Howell, professionally known as Charley Williams, and A. Lumsden, both well-known Music Hall singers.

The case for the plaintiff, as stated by Mr Alsop, was that on June 12th, the plaintiff, standing with a hansom for hire near Evan's, Covent Garden, was hailed by the defendants at eleven o'clock a.m.

His Honour – I thought Evan's was a night house? Mr Alsop – Oh dear no, your Honour; that was a long time ago, when we were young.

The defendants were driven to the George Hotel, Lambeth Walk, to lunch, and afterwards to Croydon Races. They returned from Croydon at 5.30 p.m., taking up a friend, and calling at various public-houses on the way back. Williams struck and poked the horse improperly, and Lumsden wanted the driver to race with another cab, also poking and striking with Williams' stick, and finally, when the other cab got alongside, near Streatham Common, the horse, owing to the treatment of the defendants, swerved from side to side, and finally, resenting this treatment with a kick, got its feet on the splashboard and over the traces, and fell on an embankment. Williams told the cabman to repair the damage as well as he could, and it would be paid for; but Lumsden was abusive, and went on to London by another cab. The horse, previously valued at thirty guineas, and always very quiet, had, since the accident, turned out both a gibber and a kicker, and £15 was claimed for depreciation of its value; two days' loss of work were put down at £2, and repairs to the cab £1 9s. 6d., £18 7s. 6d. being altogether claimed.

The plaintiff's case was supported by Frederick Pickles, the rival cab driver, and an assistant of Mr Wright, veterinary surgeon, Bond Street.

At the suggestion of his Honour, the case was settled for £20.
28/7/1878

SEA SERPENT IN REALITY. – The Sea Serpent in Reality, a Monstrous Creature, measuring, it is said, 20ft. long, and as big round as a man's thigh. Also Two smaller, same species. Notice. – Not to be procured every day. A variety of other stock. Fresh arrivals daily. W. CROSS, Oldhall Street, Liverpool.
4/8/1878

MUSICAL ROCKS. WANTED, to Purchase a Set of the above; must be in tune. Address, stating all particulars, to MR C. RAYNER, 166, Stamford Street, S.E.
11/8/1878

THE new vocalist, Mdlle Alma Verdini, whose costume, almost hidden by floral decorations, attracted so much attention on the first night of the Promenade Concerts at Covent Garden, is not of American origin as has been stated. She is the daughter of a *parfumeuse* of great notoriety* in London and Paris, and was herself engaged in that occupation before adopting the vocal profession.
Madame Rachel (Sarah Rachel Russell or Levinson), a swindler who claimed the ability to make her clients "beautiful for ever". Another daughter, Helene Crossmond-Turner, had some success as an opera singer.

WANTED, PIERS, Lakes, or Enclosed Water, for MISS BECKWITH, the greatest Lady Swimmer in the World, in conjunction with her Brother Willie, the Champion Swimmer and Diver in England. Open for Engagements, for Fetes, Galas. Shares or salary, or will hire places. Splendid Posters, Opinions, &c. The greatest draw of any one in their line. Address, BECKWITH, King's Head, Westminster Bridge Road.

To Whom the Shoe Fits. The Individual that calls himself PONGO REDIVIVUS, who cautions Managers against Imitators, happens to be a Japanese. Pongo is an animal. I advertise PONGO REDIVIVUS SKETCH, in which I take the Character of PONGO, and as far as imitating, I should want far superior to a Japanese to copy from. We have met once last July in Manchester. He played it One Week at the Gaiety; I played it Three Weeks at the Peoples's. Talk is cheap, but it takes money to buy Whiskey. PEDRO STERLING.
18/8/1878

AT Judge's Chambers on Thursday afternoon, before Mr Justice Manisty, Messrs Collette and Collette, Solicitors, applied, on behalf of Mr Rousby, for a *habeus corpus* to bring up the child of himself and Mrs Rousby, the well-known actress. It was stated that the child, a daughter, about eight years old, had been absent from her father since 1874, in which year it was placed with Mrs Rousby's mother.

Mr Rousby stated that he was ignorant of the fact that Mrs Rousby's mother had died in 1876, and he found no trace of his child until Easter of this year, when he found that she had been placed in a convent in Exeter to be educated, both being Roman Catholics. Mrs Rousby some three weeks ago went down to the city and asked to be allowed to take the child out for a walk, but the Lady Superioress told her that Mr Rousby had given positive instructions that on no account should anyone be allowed to take the child out. The Lady Superioress having left the room for a few moments, Mrs Rousby, it was alleged, let the child out of the window. She herself also got quickly away, and the two were soon beyond reach. Hence the present application for a *habeus corpus* to bring up the child, who attended with her mother, Mrs Rousby being accompanied by Miss Dowse, Mrs Rousby's sister. It was alleged that Mrs Rousby was not a fit custodian for the child.

Mr Montagu Williams, who appeared on behalf of Mrs Rousby, denied that such was the case, and added that if time were allowed it could be shown that Mr Rousby was not a fit custodian for the child.

His Lordship said that before coming to any decision he would prefer to see the child and Miss Dowse alone.

The Court was cleared for the purpose, and after some time, on the readmission of the advocates, his Lordship said that, under all the circumstances, he thought that Miss Dowse had better have custody of child, with liberty to the mother to have access to it from time to time, and leave to apply to the Court if there were any idea that the child was being removed.
Eight months later Mrs Rousby died of consumption at the age of thirty.
25/8/1878

ON Wednesday information of the fatal result of a shocking gun accident at the Alexandra Palace was forwarded to the City Coroner by the authorities of St Bartholomew's Hospital.

It appears that on Monday, the 5th ult., being Bank Holiday, Mr Thomas, a master builder, of Milton Road, Brentford, with his wife and family (numbering five) went to the Alexandra Palace to spend the day. Having partaken of dinner, they left the main building to explore the grounds of the Palace. About 100 yards from the east end of the Palace were the "roundabouts" and swings, and to please the children Mrs Thomas went with them in that direction. From the route taken she had to pass the back of the rifle gallery, which, from its appearance, looked like the rear of a summer house, and no feeling of danger was experienced, because a stranger could not tell what the place was used for, and no notice of warning was put up. It appears that just as Mrs Thomas was passing the gallery someone fired, and instead of the bullet striking the butt at the end and then falling into a wooden box, it passed through two boards, and, missing the butt, entered the poor woman's head. It being the middle of the day and a large number of people being on the ground, there was a good deal of excitement. Mrs Thomas, in an unconscious state, was removed to Bartholomew's Hospital, and died early on Wednesday morning.
1/9/1878

ON Tuesday, during the performance of *Formosa* by Miss Annie Baldwin and company at Her Majesty's Opera House, Aberdeen, a most amusing incident occurred. It happened when, towards the middle of the first act of the drama, Bob Saunders, played by Mr Gomersal, the dog fancier, comes upon the stage with sundry fancy puppies stuffed, all except the head, into his coat pocket. Bob had just sallied from the right wing when, glancing towards the upper private box opposite, according to the custom of some experienced actors, his eye had probably caught that of one of the two male occupants. At that instant Bob had to speak the catch word of the part, "Buy a little dawg!" which, of course, was received with laughter by the audience generally; but the laughter was quickly turned to astonishment when one of the gentlemen in the box stood up, and with an excited look and in a very distinct Continental accent, protested that he did not want to buy one dog, and that he thought it a most unusual proceeding on the part of any actor to ask him "one so wonderful impertinent question!" "No; vat vould I vant a leetle dog for?" Mr Gomersal, judging it prudent to ignore the observation, uttered a few more lines of his part, but the stranger, in the tones of a man who wished to set himself right with somebody, again remarked, rather excitedly, that he did not want a "leetle" dog; and that he had visited the Theatre for amusement, and not for the purpose of purchasing a canine pet.

On Mr Weston (Miss Baldwin's Acting-Manager) visiting the box and endeavouring to explain the meaning of the offending speech, the foreigner became still more excited, and had to be ejected. Outside the Theatre he informed an admiring crowd that he did not think much of art "in dis country," and that where he came from Directors of Theatres did not sell "dawgs on dere stage." After the departure of the offending German the curtain was rung up, and each query of Bob's "Do you want to buy a leetle dawg?" was the signal for fresh merriment.

A Theatrical Company Drowned.
We last week announced to our readers the sad death by drowning, on their voyage from Calcutta to Melbourne, of Mr Cowdery and his wife, professionally known as Miss Bessie Edwards. Further particulars have come to hand, and will be perused by many with sorrowful interest.

News reached Melbourne on the 24th of July of the total loss of the barque *James Service*, belonging to that port, on her voyage from Calcutta to Melbourne with a cargo of castor oil and country produce. As all the crew and passengers have been lost, it will never be known how the wreck was caused, but from her position it is very evident that she must have been several hundred miles out of her proper course. The scene of the wreck is about forty miles to the south of Perth, Western Australia, on the Manderah Reef, which is about seven miles off the shore. The following are the passengers as far as known: – Mr and Mrs Cowdery (Miss Bessie Edwards), Mr and Miss Williams, Messrs P.B. Smith, W.F. Phillips, and J.W. Kelly. Miss Bessie Edwards was proceeding to Melbourne under engagement to the management of the Theatre Royal. Mr Cowdery was known as an "old man" actor. Mr Williams was for a long time principal violinist in Dave Carson's *troupe*, and was well known in India, while his daughter, Miss Williams, had gained laurels in the principal Indian cities as a soubrette actress.

One telegram is as follows: – "The body of Mrs Frank Towers has been found at the wreck of the *James Service*. The body was naked, with a band round the waist marked 'J. Towers.' On the finger was a wedding ring and a dress ring set with two brilliants and an emerald. The body was buried at Fremantle. Trunks and cases of luggage have been recovered marked 'Bessie Edwards,' 'C.A. Cowdery,' 'Williams,' 'J.W. Reddie,' and 'J.A. Steiber.' A later telegram is as follows: – "The identification of the body found as that of Mrs Towers is disputed, notwithstanding the waistband marked 'J. Towers,' and that the features are similar to those of Mrs Towers. A body came ashore on the 25th. It was that of Miss Bessie Edwards, ascertained by a photo in a trunk, which also contained a lot of gold tiger-clawed jewellery. A letter commencing 'July 20th. – Dear Willie,' has been picked up, and has been recognised as having been written by Miss Minnie Williams."
29/9/1878

A SHOCKING OCCURRENCE took place at the Alhambra Theatre in Leicester Square, on Tuesday evening, in the presence of a vast audience, while Offenbach's opera *Genevieve de Brabant* was being performed. A full chorus was on the stage at the time, it being the conclusion of the first act, and M. Jacobi's large orchestra was exerting itself to the utmost. Among the members of the orchestra was a man named Harry Johnson, aged thirty-four, who for the last nine years had been engaged there as a performer on the trombone. Having been in failing health lately he was advised to discontinue his performance, but he persisted, exerted himself too much, and fell down dead in the orchestra.
6/10/1878

AMATEURS IN PETTICOATS.
[…] The members of the St John's Dramatic Club had foolishly resolved to dispense with the services of ladies, and consequently their two essays in the way of dramatic representation* proved altogether beneath criticism, and worthy only of contempt. Mr Whiston, the Secretary and Treasurer of the Society, appeared in petticoats, and attempted to personate Alice Barlow, in Mr Byron's comedy *A Hundred Thousand Pounds*. He succeeded only in making himself ridiculous. His voice was as rough as a nutmeg grater, and in appearance he was about as comely as the heroine of a May Day "Jack-in-the-Green." His great feet sprawled out occasionally from beneath the skirts he should have been ashamed to don, and his great mouth reminded us of the individual who was described as being able to kiss three people at once. And then the great paws! A shiver of disgust ran through us when we saw them flung round the neck of Mr W. Kerridge, who personated Gerald Goodwin. This young gentleman had evidently escaped from Mr Spurgeon's College, where ambitious youth are taught to spout. His elocution was of the order usually heard at street corners, and supposed to be indulged in for the salvation of the hearer and the glorification of the speaker. We seriously hope that before this Kerridge makes another appearance he will curb his impetuosity and pay someone to cut his hair. […]

The comedy was preceded by the farce *Diamond Cut Diamond*. In this too we had to tolerate a man in petticoats, the sinner against good taste being Mr C.E. Watkins. Even the parson of the parish, who sat near us and who occasionally puts on a gown himself, looked shocked and beat a hasty retreat. Charlotte Doubtful – that is the character – was, if we are to credit Mr Watkins, a damsel with a partiality for plums, which she invariably kept in her mouth while speaking; and, moreover, she had a waist which was as thick and graceful as a cow in the middle. […]
**At the St John's Institute.*
13/10/1878

SUFFOCATION IN A TRAVELLING THEATRE.

On Saturday evening, the 26th ult., after the performance given by a strolling company of players at Newtown, Montgomeryshire, Mr Holloway, the proprietor, with his wife and three children, retired to rest in one of the caravans, leaving a coke fire burning. At about seven o'clock on Sunday morning the man awoke with the sense of suffocation, and called loudly for assistance, which was rendered by the occupants of the next van. On opening the door two of the children were found dead, and the other died soon afterwards.

An inquest was held on Monday, when Henry Holloway stated that he awoke about half-past seven in the morning and found himself very faint and parched, and on attempting to get up he fell on the floor. He, however, afterwards managed to stand upright, when he found one of the children lying near a patent American cooking stove. When he got assistance it was found that the three children were dead and a woman and a boy very ill. The woman was sent by Dr Pratt, who was called in, to the Monmouthshire Infirmary, and she is now recovering. It was stated that the amount of space for six people to sleep in was about 11ft. 6in. long, 6ft. 6in. wide, and 6ft. 6in. high, which was not enough for one person. It was also mentioned that a fire was made at about quarter to ten o'clock, and was thought to be out when the man went to bed at about eleven o'clock. The bed in which the three children lay was on the floor under that in which the parents lay, and only 2ft. 9in. space was between the two.

The Jury returned a verdict to the effect that the children died from overcrowding and the fumes arising from the coke fire, and they recommended that that attention of the sanitary authorities be called to such gross cases of overcrowding.

3/11/1878

THOSE who like to wonder and laugh at the same time would do well just now to visit the London Pavilion and see Wainratta, who, we believe, is known as "The King of the Lofty Wire." We have repeatedly alluded to that marvellous ability which he displays upon an almost invisible wire, and have told how he maintains his equilibrium while the said wire is made to oscillate violently; how he walks it with his feet encumbered by hoops; how he takes off his shoes and puts them on again, and how several other extraordinary feats are accomplished in mid-air, on a slender support, and without the aid of a balance pole.

Now Wainratta comes forward on the wire as a comedian determined to tickle the risibility of the spectators. When he mounts the wire he is attired in the ordinary evening dress of society. He strolls up and down with his hands in his pockets and with a cigarette in his mouth, like a veritable Regent Street dandy. The cigarette being finished, he divests himself of his coat and waistcoat, and – shall we tell it? – of his trousers. He for the moment presents quite a pitiable appearance. He seems to shiver in his shirt and to be ashamed. The make spectators roar and the female ones blush and giggle. But while they are giggling the shirt disappears, and Wainratta is seen in the ordinary costume of the gymnast and juggler. It can hardly be necessary to add that Wainratta is vociferously applauded.

10/11/1878

ON Sunday, the 10th inst., a shocking accident occurred in the Dumfries Theatre. Preparations were being made for the appearance of the Prince Charlie company, under Captain Gordon, on the following evening. A supernumerary, in the service of the Lessee, Mr Fryer, was engaged in adjusting a lime-light when the retort exploded, and a piece of metal struck him on the throat, making a large wound there, and completely severing the carotid arteries. Death was almost instantaneous.

MR EDITOR. Sir, – In your last impression, under the heading "Theatrical Gossip," a paragraph occurs, stating that a caterer for public amusement in Grimsby placed a large tank, containing a seal, upon the stage, and that one of his artists declined to proceed with his entertainment until the seal was removed,

which caused a riot amongst the audience, and the tank became a target for three-legged stools and ginger-beer bottles. In justice to myself, as Lessee of the Theatre Royal, Grimsby, I beg to say the disturbance in question does not refer to my establishment, where, for many years, I have held the management, and catered for the amusement of the inhabitants of Grimsby without publicly feeding seals upon the stage. Yours, &c., WILLIAM RAYMOND, Theatre Royal, Grimsby, November 13th, 1878.
17/11/1878

WANTED, Immediately, for Germany, a NEGRO GIRL, between Fourteen and Eighteen Years of Age, disposed to learn the Gymnastic Business. Apply, by letter only, to M. REBATTU, 49, Duke Street, St James's, London.
15/12/1878

CHARLES LAND, while Thanking an Author who has generously sent him a Glass and Gilt Pin as a return for the Libretto of Six Scenes of his Pantomime, will be glad if the "Prodigal Son" can call for the "Prop.," as the friction in Post would make it still more chafed, and it may yet do to hang on a Christmas Tree.
22/12/1878

10
1879
DON'T CHOKE THE BALLET

TO THE EDITOR OF THE ERA.
Sir, – Will you permit me through the medium of your powerful journal to ask if any of your readers will furnish me with the present address of Mr Van Eycken and Miss Eugenie Arheim, late of the Theatre Royal, Portsmouth, and of 20, Colebrooke Row, Islington. These people engaged me in London for their comedy company, and we duly opened at the Portland Hall, Portsmouth, on the 19th ult. All went merry as a marriage bell until the night preceding treasury, when Van Eycken and Arnheim, accompanied by their luggage, retired from their professional labours, having paid nobody. This little oversight may be attributed to the natural bashfulness of a retiring disposition, or they may, in pursuance of arrangements made, be piloting another company of trusting *artistes* round the country.

I, for one, was left fareless, with an angry landlady in the background, and eighty miles of snow-covered county in the foreground. It is said "There is a silver lining in every cloud." I shall be glad to see the "silver lining" of this one. Anyhow, I am sure you will agree with me that if actors are to be enticed away from home in deep winter, distributed on the sea coast, then deserted, and have no means of redress, it is a hardship of the worst kind.

I have used every endeavour to see Mr Van Eyken and Miss Eugenie Arnheim fruitlessly, and my letters have been returned to me; and as I can do nothing without their address, can you or any of your readers kindly assist me? Respectfully yours, CHARLES HINTON, 29 Leicester Square, 1st January 1879.
5/1/1879

JOHN DOBBIN and Alfred Ryan, two boys whose heads hardly reached the top of the dock, were brought before Mr Lushington on Thursday, at the Thames Police Court, charged with being in the Albion Theatre, High Street, Poplar, for an unlawful purpose, and attempting to steal £40. At nine o'clock on Wednesday night George Hichner, a constable, No. 415 K, received certain information which induced him to enter the Albion Theatre, and he saw the prisoner Dobbin halfway through the money-taker's box. Ryan was hoisting him up, but before he had time to steal the night's takings, amounting to over £40, the constable took him into custody. At the station the prisoners were searched, and on Dobbin was found a knife and five wax candles, while Ryan had a pipe, purse, and a bundle of superior cigars. Mr Lushington remanded the prisoners for a week, to enable the police to make further inquiries into their antecedents, and to find an industrial school for them.

MANAGERS, DON'T CHOKE THE BALLET, but send at once for WINDER'S RED, WHITE, or GREEN FIRE, without smoke or smell, warranted to burn twice the time of any offered by other makers. In

Pound Tins, 1s. 6d.; or 20lbs., 1s. 4d. London Agent, GEO. BRADFIELD, 98, BROOK STREET, KENNINGTON ROAD, S.E.
12/1/1879

"SMUT" AT THE MUSIC HALLS.
TO THE EDITOR OF THE ERA.
[…] During the past few days, Sir, I have visited two Music Halls – one situated at the West, the other at the East. I mention this because I wish to show that what I complain of is not fostered particularly by the poor pleasure-seekers, whose tastes are supposed to be low simply because they are not blessed with too large a share of this world's gifts.

At the West End house I have listened to two serio-comic vocalists, representatives of the fair sex, the one singing of the charms and fancies of her "Pussy" and the other dilating upon the joys of a certain article described as "Hokee-Pokee." At the other end of the town I have heard a gentleman singing of the state of affairs "When Adam Was Alive" and of the blessings of "Single Life," and a lady discoursing of her ginger-whiskered "young man." I have not the slightest hesitation in saying that in each of these instances indecency, or what I have ventured to call "smut," was present – and present by intention. As said above, there was no particular word which could *per se* be pronounced dirty, but the suggestion of dirt was there beyond a doubt.

Now, Sir, I want to point out that Managers who tolerate these things, and singers who are guilty of introducing them, are, metaphorically speaking, cutting their own throats. Increased prosperity may attend them for a time, but they will assuredly find that the injudicious laugh and the enhanced notoriety are dearly bought. Therefore I say to them – be wise in time. Rely on fun without filth. Thus the popularity of the Music Hall will rest on a firm basis, and none of us will fear to tolerate the presence within their walls of those females whom we respect and whose minds it is our duty to save from pollution. I am, Sir, your obedient servant, A MUSIC HALL PATRON.
(We give insertion to our correspondent's letter, but at the same time do not think that the evil of which he complains is very widespread. It lies with a few Managers to "reform it altogether.")

CHARLES PEACE*, the Notorious Blackheath Burglar. Life-size Models taken from Life and Coloured to Nature for SALE or HIRE. For terms apply this week to ALFRED MAZZONI, 7, HIGH STREET, BLOOMSBURY, LONDON.
**Peace was executed for murder on 25th February 1879.*
26/1/1879

WANTED, to Know Why the Tramway Company of Dublin wants to take an action out against Mr Norman for blocking up Capel Street. It is on account of Madame WALLIS, Sword Swallower, and the Great SCOTCH GIANT, showing at 42. Fresh Novelties Weekly. Tall People or Fat People Write. Brains and money sure.
9/2/1879

FOR SALE, about 100 BRASS HELMETS, lately worn by Her Majesty's 4th Dragoon Guards. Being very brilliant they are a valuable Stage Property. Can be worn as follows: – For English Dragoon, with Plume; German Dragoon, with Spike; French Dragoon, with Eagle; Turkish Dragoon, with Crescent; Russian Dragoon, with Double Eagle. Being a facsimile of those worn by 1st Dragoon Guards, now engaged on the Zulu Expedition. To Proprietors of Theatres, &c., who purpose giving descriptive Scenes of the Zulu War, they will be invaluable. Price 3s. 6d. each. A sample sent of receipt of order to THOMAS J. SANDS, Otley, Yorkshire.
2/3/1879

"H.M.S. PINAFORE" IN AMERICA.
TO THE EDITOR OF THE ERA.
Sir, – There are about 150 companies at the present time playing *H.M.S. Pinafore* in the United States, and only one Manager, whose letter I enclose, has made any acknowledgment to us – the authors. Of course, we have no claim to anything, as there is no International Copyright Act; the Americans, with quaint simplicity, preferring to get their books, music, plays, &c., for nothing rather than pay for them. But, one might fairly have expected a little conscientiousness, and even, perhaps, a little worldly wisdom amongst so many astute men. All honour, therefore, to Mr Ford, of Baltimore, who is not "one man in a hundred," but one of a hundred and fifty. Yours very truly, ARTHUR SULLIVAN. 9, Albert Mansions, S.W. 7th March, 1879.

"Ford's Grand Opera House, Baltimore, U.S.A. February 17th, 1879.
Messrs Sullivan and Gilbert, – I have produced your work *H.M.S. Pinafore* with some profit, and I trust in fair justice artistically to its merits. I desire to say that I will send you £100 sterling if you will advise me where I shall address you, as an acknowledgment of your authorship. Very respectfully, J.T. FORD."
9/3/1879

AT the Woolwich Police Court, on the 8th inst., Thomas Renson, aged thirty-one, who described himself as a "professional singer," of 8, Mill Lane, Deptford, and who was an exceedingly ragged and dirty specimen of the modern "wandering minstrel," was charged before Mr Slade with being drunk and disorderly, using bad language, and assaulting a policeman.

Constable Hearn, 364 R, said that the prisoner was in Church Lane, Charlton, at seven o'clock on the previous evening singing in a loud voice and making a disturbance of which the inhabitants complained.

Witness requested him to go away, when the prisoner, without a word of reply, struck him in the face, knocked him down, and kicked him. When he got up the prisoner knocked him down again, and he was obliged to call for assistance. Eventually the prisoner was put into a cab, and driven to the police-station.

Mr Slade asked the prisoner what he had to say, and the prisoner in a theatrical manner replied – It is only right, your Honour, that I should take this opportunity of saying that I have nothing to complain of individually with respect to that man (the constable). But I am an honest man, sir; poor as you see, but striving to get a virtuous livelihood. But the cruelty and indifference of my fellow men embitters my existence. For the last six months I have been singing about town some of the finest songs in the English language; I have sung for two hours at a time before the mansions of the rich and noble, and then perhaps they have given me two pence. Is is not brutal that people dwelling in style and elegance should listen to a vocalist for two hours, and then give him two coppers? There must be something wrong when a man like me who is capable of giving expression to the music of the best composers, should have his feelings agonised as mine have been by the coldness and contempt of the world. In the best streets and squares of London I have sung before the highest of the land as many as a hundred songs for eighteen-pence; but the people have no ear; the taste for music has degenerated, and I am the victim.

Mr Slade (who had listened patiently) asked him if he had finished his speech.

Prisoner (tragically) – I have no more to say.

Mr Slade – You will go to prison with hard labour for two months.
16/3/1879

TO THE EDITOR OF THE ERA.
Sir, – I should like to direct the attention of the Music Hall Managers who have addressed an appeal *ad misericordiam* to the Home Secretary* to the following glaring announcement which appears in the bills of the Gaiety Theatre, Barnsley, and is put forward as what is called a "monster attraction." Here it is: "Engagement for this night only of Willie Ward, Son of the Late Charles Peace, of Blackheath Celebrity. Who will appear on the Stage and Play Selections on the Concertina; also Exhibit the

Spectacles His Father Wore When Apprehended by P.C. Robinson. Willie Ward Will Also Be Prepared To Answer Any Questions Which May Be Put To Him By The Audience."

This announcement says much for the good taste of the Manager, who, I believe, rejoices in the name of Mr Ben Walker. Further comment is unnecessary. Your obedient servant, A COMIC SINGER.
They asked for the appointment of a Censor to prohibit indecent material in music halls.
30/3/1879

"JACK," the seal at the Polytechnic, met with his death on Friday morning. The water was on Thursday being let off, when, owing to the grating being out of repair, the rush of water carried the seal with it into the sewer. He dropped from the top into the lower sewer, a fall of fifty feet. A search was made, and this morning the seal was found in the sewer under the Euston Road, but he died while being conveyed in a cab to the Polytechnic.
6/4/1879

A SINGULAR excuse was tendered to the Brighton magistrates the other day by a young man of very respectable appearance, who had been given into custody for disturbing the congregation worshipping at St Paul's Church, West Street, a place of worship which has attained some notoriety as the scene of the Ritualistic practices of the Rev Arthur Wagner*. The prisoner, it was stated, continually interrupted the evening service by encouraging shouts of approval and laughter, and by frequently applauding, and, though two of his companions left the place when requested by the verger, he refused to give up his seat, and continued his disorderly conduct. In answer to the charge, the prisoner expressed his extreme regret, and attributing his behaviour to liquor, but he solemnly assured the Bench that he believed at the time that he was witnessing a performance by a troupe of Japanese now giving entertainments in the town. His novel apology excited considerable amusement, and the Bench merely fined him a small sum for being drunk.
Wagner is best remembered for his role in eliciting Constance Kent's confession that she had murdered her half-brother.
13/4/1879

DURING the performance of *Land Ahead* by Mr Wilson Barrett's company at the Old Theatre Royal, Bristol, on Saturday last (12th inst.), an unrehearsed scene created roars of merriment amongst the audience, and so upset the gravity of the performers that it threatened for a time to suspend the legitimate action of the drama.

In the first act Biddy Rooney, a merry-hearted Irish girl, admirably personated by Miss Lillian Lancaster, appears on the stage conveying to her cabin, by the orthodox plan of "a string to his leg," an obdurate pig. The grunter, whose yells had heralded his approach before the curtain was raised, slipped the string before Biddy had walked half down the stage. Terry Rooney, her husband (naturally portrayed by Mr J. Delaney, the Irish comedian), shouldering a shovel, came to the rescue, brandishing the weapon, and, improvising anathema, cajolery, and expostulation in the softest Irish, he tried to coax the erratic member of the company to enter a rustic sty, where straw and "wash" awaited him. Whether he suspected the stage commissariat, or had suddenly taken into his head the novel idea as to the reading of the part, we cannot say, but, pig-like, he obstinately refused to move an inch in the direction required. He would neither be wheedled nor threatened, and coming down to the footlights he held possession of the front of the stage with all the confidence of a leading actor. The gods cheered from the gallery, and the pig, responding with a bound forward, came so close to the footlights that he audibly manifested his disapprobation in notes that astonished the members of the orchestra. Terry Rooney "gave him one" with the shovel, which caused him to retire to the wings, but before he could be grabbed he was back again, and, amidst the roars of the audience, he once again held possession of the front of the stage, thought, like a "burnt child," he evidently had a respectful dread of the footlights, and there he remained till of his own sweet will he retired, when Biddy and Terry had got half through the first scene.

The real entertainment, to some of the audience, was the dexterity which Miss Lancaster and Mr Delaney, continuing the narrative of the drama, "minded the pig," and improvised additions to the text every now and then, as they both had to rush at the animal to save his nose from the footlights, both scarcely able to restrain their laughter; and it is saying a good deal for their natural acting throughout when we record the fact that it was difficult at times to distinguish between their natural laughter at the unexpected episode and that appropriate to the lively and animated text.
20/4/1879

WANTED, Fifty Pairs of NEGRO TIGHTS, Black or Brown. Apply, by letter or telegram, to COOKE'S Royal Circus, Aberdeen.
4/5/1879

AT the Cheltenham Theatre on Saturday evening (17th), during the performance of *Uncle Tom's Cabin*, an umbrella was dropped from the gallery on to the ceiling of the first floor underneath. A man named Higgs went for the umbrella, and fell through to the ground floor. As he did not return, his brother, who had accompanied him to the Theatre, went in search of him, and finally an acquaintance went in search of both. Eventually all three men were found on the ground floor of the house, where they had fallen on top of each other, the two brothers being in an insensible condition. The men were conveyed to the hospital, and one of them, James Higgs, still lies in a precarious condition, being, it is feared, seriously injured internally.
25/5/1879

A TRAPEZIST, known as Cee-Mee, proposed to perform at Stoodley's Circus, Ipswich, the dangerous feat of walking the ceiling head downwards, with his little daughter suspended from his teeth. Yielding, however, to the opinions of the Mayor and Borough Magistrates, the promoters have abandoned the idea.

AT a recent meeting of the Hackney Coach Committee in connection with the Manchester City Council the driver of No. --- coach was summoned before the Committee for "speccing" about the city, his stand being opposite the Town Hall, Albert Square. His defence was a novel and ingenious one. On being asked what he had to say for himself he said, "Mister Cheerman, all I've got to say is this – my hoss is musical, and he can't stand them kyrillions (Town Hall carillons). My guv'nor bought him off a Circus company, and he used to draw the band about. That's the way he got his musical eddication. He's all right with the chimes, till it comes to the hour; then he shivers. But when he hears the clock strike nine, or twelve, or three, Lor' bless you, he knows as well as any Christian them kyrillions comes on next, and he bolts. Lots of jobs I've lost through it. Same if he hears a German band. He'll bolt up any blooming street before he'll pass one, because they isn't musical. That's all I've got to say."

The Chairman *pro tem.*, (Mr Councillor Brierley) thought the case was one which deserved a little clemency, and expressed an opinion that a representation ought to be made to another Committee. If a nuisance existed in connection with the Town Hall, it was their duty to summon the Mayor before the Nuisance Committee for permitting it.
(The Councillor evidently could not see the justice of blaming a horse when a Mayor was at fault.) [ED]

HERE is a good story of the Moore and Burgess Minstrels. One day last week a young gentleman applied for tickets, but before buying them asked the ticket seller whether there would be any "coarse jokes" or "improper allusions" during the performance. He simply asked because "the Cliffords from Barnet were coming." (The name is fictitious but the story is true.) He was informed that "hardly ever" was there anything out of the way at the abode of the minstrelsy. The evening came; a large audience filled the house; the overture was played, and one of the "end men" approached his first joke. Suddenly up rose the rest of the band, and, motioning excitedly to "bones," murmered, "Hush, be careful; the Cliffords from Barnet are he-ah." At first the audience did not understand the joke, but when it was repeated, the annoyance of the party alluded to became so manifest that peals of laughter shook the house. At the third or fourth repetition "the Cliffords" could stand it no longer, and indignantly left the Hall.

WILL THE CH*NTR*L TROUPE explain why they did not fulfil their Engagement Whit Week at the Zoological Gardens, Clifton? A reply is requested by the Secretary without delay.
8/6/1879

HAMLET IN A FIX.
A dramatic performance "under the patronage of the nobility and gentry" was advertised to take place at the King's Cross Theatre on Wednesday evening last. It would hardly be correct to say a dramatic performance took place on the occasion, though certainly there was an exhibition, and of a very novel and peculiar kind; but what to call it and how to criticise it is a puzzle. [...]

The programme stated that at half-past seven precisely the laughable farce of *Chiselling* would be given by "talented amateurs of a well-known club," their names being studiously concealed. It was not, however, until a quarter past eight that the curtain drew up amidst considerable cheering. Evidently the rising of the curtain was looked upon as an event not to be quietly passed over, but as no one made an appearance the cheering was renewed, and this eventually encouraged a tall, melodramatic-looking gentleman – a Mr H. Rochford – to come forward and announce that in consequence of the gentlemen who were advertised to play *Chiselling* having been summoned to take part, as officers, in the Zulu War, the farce would not be given. This form of "chiselling," however, the audience took in good part, and Mr Rochford proceeded to favour them with a solo on the flute. We will not criticise his performance more than to note that his execution seemed somewhat hazy and uncertain, especially in the more florid passages; but is efforts were received with uproarious applause, and he was obliged to respond to the vigorous demands for an encore.

The stage was now left unoccupied that the audience might have time to recover. [...] As everything seemed so mysterious and unsatisfactory it occurred to us that the whole affair must be simply a hoax, but on inquiry we learnt that Mr Rochford was an artist's model with a mania for acting, and that a number of artists had hired the Theatre with the view of giving him a benefit; but whether it was to be a benefit of money, of vegetables, or of ridicule, did not seem quite clear; certain it is, however, they used him very badly.

After a long delay, which might have been agreeable enough to the artists themselves, though scarcely so to strangers, Madame Rochford sailed on to the stage and began to sing, but loud laughter so effectually disconcerted her that the song was altogether lost in the noise made by the appreciative artists; and she retired wildly gesticulating, and with a look which, if looks could kill, would have settled every artist on the spot. [...]

Selections from *Hamlet* were announced to conclude the, so far, most edifying entertainment, Mr H. Rochford being underlined for Hamlet. The curtain at last drew up, and a scene was discovered furnished with one chair. The audience having been allowed sufficient time to grasp every detail of this solitary chair, a billy-cock hat was gently rolled on to the stage from the prompt entrance, and settled itself mathematically in the centre. We were wondering what could be the object of this move, and what it could possibly have to do with a representation of *Hamlet*, when a walking-stick was thrown deftly to its side; and there the two articles lay undisturbed, until some inspired individual bethought him of throwing halfpence into the hat – an example followed by others, not a little to the satisfaction of the scene-shifters. If the empty hat was to signify the emptiness of the actors' heads, and the stick was intended as a symbol of their histrionic powers, the idea was not altogether bad.

This little excitement over, Hamlet (Mr H. Rochford) stalked on to the stage. He has a good stage presence, and his figure is undeniable; but from some cause or other, into which it would, perhaps, be indelicate to inquire, his articulation was decidedly thick, and his words were generally conspicuous by their absence; so that we have not a fair chance of forming an opinion as to his capacity. Finding he could not get on very well with his speech, Horatio (Mr E. Beauclere) and Marcellus (Mr T. Bradstock) came to keep him company; but their presence failed to do Mr Rochford much good, and the persistent way in which he repeated "Thrift, thrift, Horatio," at last resulted in a fine specimen of that favourite vegetable the leek being thrown at his head, and this fine specimen was followed by a good many others. Horatio, who had evidently studied his part, and meant "business," raised his eyes to the roof in so appealing a manner that we quite felt for him in his disappointment at being deprived of the opportunity of distinguishing himself; but, though he sedulously gave Hamlet "the word," Hamlet would have none of it, and, after the three had stood in silence for some time, staring helplessly at each other, a well-directed shower of cabbages, onions, radishes and other greenstuff soon transformed the scene in *Hamlet* into what looked very much like a kitchen garden. On this "situation" the curtain fell, amidst such a din as has seldom before been heard in a Theatre.

After a delay, Mr C. McBinnock appeared as the King, and began a speech, in the middle of which a gentleman in ordinary costume opened the folding-doors at the back of the stage and shook his umbrella at the King. After this episode, of course, any serious attempt to proceed with the scene was out of the question, and the King forthwith waltzed across the stage, hysterically moving his arms, fell on his knees, placed his crown at the back of his head, and finally, with the most hideous grimaces and leaping into the air, vanished from sight. There were loud calls for Hamlet, but Hamlet had evidently had enough of it. He was asked to give a song, but he was deaf to the appeal, and the curtain fell on a scene the like of which we are not very anxious to see again. Mr C. McBinnock's senseless buffoonery as the King was as disgraceful to himself as it was repulsive to witness; and if the youthful artists who got up this so-called performance, and made such a travestie of acting, have no more respect for their own art than they appear to have for one equally exalted, we should imagine their chances of Burlington House* must be remote. It was with intense relief and a splitting headache we left a scene of which ill-breeding and vulgar clamour were the most pronounced characteristics.

The venue for the Royal Academy's art exhibitions.
15/6/1879

ONE of the saddest accidents which it has been our lot to chronicle for some time occurred on Sunday evening last to a party of the members of *H.M.S. Pinafore* company, recently appearing at the Bath Theatre, whereby two of their number were unfortunately drowned. Many persons are in the habit of rowing to the neighbouring weirs at Batheaston, where numerous accidents have occurred. On account of the splendid scenery, the weir is very attractive, and more especially to visitors to Bath. Many such, although they may be adepts at boating, are not aware of the treacherous state of the water at this spot. The heavy rain of the past few days has, of course, swollen the river, and consequently persons visiting the weir were in more danger than if the Avon had been much lower, although when this is the case it is not safe for anyone unacquainted with it to approach too near it, for there is under the weir a sort of whirlpool which always exists.

It appears from particulars to hand, that a party, consisting of Mr R.C. Brooke, of Lyndhurst Terrace, Bath; Miss Hyde, who was a member of the company; Miss Wyse, actress, also a member of the company; Mr Townsend, photographer, Bath, and Mr Ives and Mr Leakey (who rowed in a skiff), decided to have a row up the river as far as Batheaston. They left Bath some time in the afternoon, reaching Batheaston all right, landed, and proceeded to the Waggon and Horses, where they had refreshments. A short time afterwards they re-entered the boat and proceeded to have a view of the weir.

Unfortunately, however, the boat got into the eddy and was overturned, and a most heartrending scene ensued. Miss Hyde, screaming, caught hold of Brooke immediately after the boat was upset, but he was unable to save her, and she was drowned. Brooke, by a most frantic effort, succeeded in saving his life by clinging to a tree.

The screams of the party were heard by some people, who obtained the drags from the Humane Society stations near the weir. Miss Hyde and Mr Ives had then sunk, and the boat floated past the Island before anyone could reach it. Mr Weaver (who was among the first on the spot), with others, then succeeded in getting Mr Brooke across from the Island, which is but a couple of yards from the bank, and he then was taken to the Waggon and Horses, where brandy was given him and his wet clothes taken off. The river was at once dragged, with the view of recovering the two bodies, but after two hours' fruitless endeavours further search was postponed. Shortly after seven o'clock on Monday morning P.C. Parfit and two other men dragged the river near the weirs and the Island. About a quarter to eleven their efforts were rewarded by the recovery of the body of Mr Ives, which was caught, it was thought, by the root of a tree on the Batheaston side, opposite the Island, and some sixty or seventy yards below the weir. It was brought over to the bank on the Batheaston side and there searched by P.C. Parfit, being subsequently carried on a hurdle to the Waggon and Horses, to await the inquest. On his shirt was marked "W.E. Glover," so that presumably "Ives" would be his professional name. His age is twenty-eight, and he is believed to be an American.

Mr Townsend must be commended for the amount of bravery and presence of mind which he showed on the occasion; for had it not been for this Miss Wyse would have been numbered among the dead. Fortunately, Mr Townsend caught hold of her, at the same time clinging to the boat, and in this way they floated nearly half a mile down the river as far as Cremorne, where they were happily rescued. Mr Leaky jumped out of his boat, and after much difficulty succeeded in rescuing Miss Walsh. Ives sank immediately after the boat capsized, and was seen no more, although efforts were made to save him. Those who were taken from the river were immediately conveyed either to the Waggon and Horses, Mr Candy's farm, or Cremorne. Miss Walsh was taken to her apartments in New King Street, Bath, but did not recover consciousness for a long time, and was then informed of the death of her friends. In order to keep an engagement the company left Bath on Monday morning for Exeter. [...]

The inquest on the unfortunate man Robert Ives was held on Tuesday afternoon, at the Waggon and Horses Inn, Batheaston, before Mr Biggs, Deputy-Coroner. [...] The Coroner in summing up the evidence referred to the great carelessness shown by Townsend and Brooke*, but said Townsend in some way made amends for his carelessness by the excellent manner in which he saved Miss Walsh. The evidence given would only warrant them in returning a verdict of accidental death, but he hoped they would append something to their verdict with respect to the letting out of boats without caution when the river was in such a dangerous state.

The room was then cleared, and after about a quarter of an hour the public were admitted, the Jury having come to the following verdict, viz.: – "That deceased was accidentally drowned by the upsetting of a boat near the Bathampton weirs; and we are unanimously of the opinion that any persons letting out boats should use caution in doing so, and in permitting apparently inexperienced persons to hire boats when the water is in a dangerous state as on the present occasion. The Jury would also recommend that the Humane Society or the parish authorities should place a large notice board in some prominent position near the weirs to caution boating parties from approaching too near them." [...]

The unfortunate Miss Florence Hyde, mentioned above, was the daughter of a well known and highly esteemed professor of music of Birmingham. Miss Hyde was in her nineteenth year, had been a member of Carl Rosa's opera company during the past two seasons, and, after playing in Durand's opera company, she recently joined the company organised by Mr D'Oyly Carte for performances in the southern counties.

The funeral of Mr Robert Ives took place at Bathampton on Thursday morning. Mr Herbert Brook (Acting-Manager of *H.M.S. Pinafore* company), Mr Penley, and Mr Le Hay, members of the *Pinafore*

company, travelled especially from Exeter for the purpose of being present. It was the wish of the company to have defrayed the expenses of the burial of their deceased *confrère*, but Mr D'Oyly Carte very generously insisted on himself bearing the costs.
The two men were responsible for letting the boat.
Miss Hyde's body was recovered by members of the Bath Rowing Club nine days after the accident.
6/7/1879

A GREAT NOVELTY. – MRS BLAND and her DAUGHTER will be at Liberty any time after this Notice. She is a yard high, two and a half yards round her naked shoulders, and weighs twenty stone. Would like to hear from any Friends. Address, Mrs BLAND, 28, Walker Street, Naylor Street, Oldham Road, Manchester.
13/7/1879

THERE was an amusing little incident, during the performance of *Drink*, at the Princess's Theatre on Thursday evening last. When Coupeau had opened the cupboard where the fatal bottle awaited him, the said bottle, insecurely placed, fell out and was smashed to pieces. Poor Coupeau was not to be deprived of his drink, for without it it was impossible for him either to induce "d.t." or to die. Moreover, it was necessary – absolutely necessary – to the actor's "business." Mr Charles Warner was equal to the occasion, and tottering first to one side of the stage and then to the other, coherency was mingled with incoherency, and among his mutterings were to be heard, by attentive listeners, the words "Bring another bottle, bring another bottle." Miss Fanny Leslie obeyed the behest, and the situation was saved.
14/9/1879

THE Hippodrome in Paris, a vast and well-ventilated building, which has this summer been the chief resort of amusement seekers, is now giving a really curious performance. There are four large omnibus horses of the Percheron breed, one of which is harnessed to a sledge, while a second sits inside it, and the two others go behind, their forefeet resting on the back seat, in the guise of lackeys. Nothing can be more comical. The seated horse has a humiliated air, and casts envious eyes on his comrades, as if anxious to change places with them.
21/9/1879

MR JOHN BENN, who made his first appearance in London at the Court Theatre in *Fernande*, writes to say that, in consequence of our somewhat hostile criticism of his miserable performance, he intends to withdraw his advertisement and to cease purchasing this paper. We mention this merely as a warning to newspapers that at any time may be tempted to express concerning this remarkably important person an opinion other than favourable. We thought we had let Mr Benn down very easily, for he was certainly the big blot on the opening act of the play.
28/9/1879

WANTED, a Coloured or White AGENT for the Original Wilmington Jubilee Singers – a Sober, Industrious Man; none other need apply. One that knows the country. Address, A.D. DAVIES, Manager of the Original Wilmington Jubilee Singers, 89, Brunswick Street, Ardwick, Manchester.
5/10/1879

WHILST the drama *Proof* was being played at the Exeter Theatre on Saturday evening, 4th inst., great alarm was caused by a man who was leaning over the iron rails of the gallery suddenly overbalancing himself and falling into the pit some fifty or sixty feet below. As he fell, his body first came in contact with a kind of cornice projecting from the upper circle, and from this he bounded on to the dress circle. In spite of these breaks, however, the man came into the pit with such force that he smashed the seat upon which he fell. Strange to say, his injuries were reported not very serious. He was conveyed to the hospital, where he is making progress towards recovery.

TO THE EDITOR OF THE ERA.
Sir, – Your issue of *The Era* of the 5th inst. contains *a False and a Most Malicious Libel on my Wife!* Miss Sarah Novara.

You are made the medium of publishing to the world that "the Lady's appearance was not much in her favour," *than which a more utter Falsehood was never printed!*

There is not a shadow of a shade of excuse for such a shameless allegation!

On the contrary, I (who was sitting in the stalls) heard the people in the Pit Draw in their Breaths, and say *is she not Beautiful!* And another said *She is just like an Angel!*

To do, as you have done, *is to injure Miss Novara's Prospects in her Profession, Most seriously*, and *entitles her to claim very Heavy Damages from you!*

I call upon you, therefore, to give up to me the name of this Most Cowardly and Most Malicious Slanderer, or on Wednesday I shall come to London and instruct my Solicitors, Ambrose Haynes and Sons, Grecian Chambers, Temple, to commence an action against you for Libel!

The Jury have only to look into the Face of Miss Novara in order to see – stamped in every line thereof – *Beauty of a Very High order, and Talent such had not been seen on the stage since the Days of Sarah Siddons!*

Ask Mr Wills, Dramatic Author, of 6, "The Avenue," 76, Fulham Road, *What he thinks of her Apperance?* and he will tell you that he told us in his studio he could get her on at the Royalty Theatre, "but that *she was* TOO BEAUTIFUL *for the Manageress (Miss Emily Fowler)* TO PERMIT OF IT."

As we walk in London – and as we do so here – Men AND WOMEN turn round and stare at Miss Novara! and a Painter here has asked permission *to paint her Portrait Gratuitously*, as she appeared in the last act of *Julia!*

She has eyes just like a Gazelle; and *a Natural Colour just like that of a* PEACH! – and I (who carried off the Prize for "Anatomy" in the University of Edinburgh) tell you that *I have never seen so splendidly proportioned a Figure!*

Ask Mr John Ryder *what he thinks?* and ask him, also, *whether he knows any one who will, less tamely, submit to an act of Injustice than will the Grand-nephew of the late Joseph Hume, M.P.*, who does himself the honour of signing himself, Yours faithfully, ROBERT MILLAR, M.D., Surgeon-Major on the Retired List of the Bombay Army, 18, Cliff Terrace, Margate, 6th October, 1879.
P.S. – I forward three newspapers – *not one of which dares to say what you do!!!*
P.S. – Since my wife's appearance "The Green eyed Monster" has been *Rampant here!!!*

[The above letter has been inspired by the following notice of the performance at the Theatre Royal, Margate, which appeared in our last: – "Miss Novara made her debut here on Friday evening (26th ult.), as Julia, in *The Hunchback*. The part, trying though it be, was played with great ability. The lady's appearance was not much in her favour, but this was fully compensated for by her refined elocution, her true conception of the character, and the taste with which she went through a somewhat difficult task. Taken as a whole, her first appearance was of a very satisfactory character, and such as might have been expected from one of Mr Ryder's pupils." It is evident that the Grand-nephew of the late Joseph Hume, M.P., is a gentleman who is not easily pleased.]
12/10/1879

WANTED, a Purchaser for a MAGIC DEMON DRUM, plays at command. Great novelty for Musical Clowns, &c. Cost over £6 when new; will take 30s. A. BRIERLEY, Star Music Hall, Wigan.
19/10/1879

A DISSIPATED looking individual, recently sentenced at the Northampton Petty Sessions to two months' imprisonment with hard labour for stealing a pair of slippers from Mr Stoodley's Circus, was heard to exclaim as he was removed from the dock, "Good luck! I have got a billet for the winter."
26/10/1879

MR HARRY YORKE, the popular *comique*, gave a meat tea on the stage of the Star at Hull to the poor little newsboys, supplementing this by presenting each boy with a cap and a warm pair of socks. It is almost needless to remark the people of Hull rewarded him by filling the house to overflowing.
9/11/1879

THE two small elephants at the Folies Bergère have been indulging in a little performance on their own account, having, through the bars of their cage, managed with their trunks to reach the piano, from which they have torn several keys, recognising in them, probably, the tusks of their ancestors. The piano now wants one A, two F's, three C's, and a G.
28/12/1879

11
1880
THROWN WITH GREAT VIOLENCE INTO A CHINA SHOP

NO ACTOR NEED FEAR SWALLOWING HIS MOUSTACHE or Whiskers coming off, if they use CLARKSON'S SPIRIT GUM. Sold only at his Repository, 45, WELLINGTON STREET, STRAND. Sixpence and One Shilling per Bottle; sent by Post, Two Stamps extra.
4/1/1880

THE other evening, at the Theatre Royal, Leeds, at present under the management of Mr Frank Emery, Lessee of the Prince of Wales' Theatre, Liverpool, an amusing incident occurred, which might, however, have ended seriously. In the pantomime of *Robinson Crusoe* there is a wonderful shipwreck scene. The ship, which is really the same that sails off the stage in a previous scene, is wrecked in sight of the audience, being worked by a wire rope from the roof of the Theatre, and suspended in the air some considerable distance from the stage, the waters rolling over the vessel in equal height, until the ship is lowered by the means above mentioned, when the waves close completely over the vessel and crew. On the night in question, however, when about five or six feet from the stage, the wire rope gave way, and the ship went with a fearful thud to the level of the stage, throwing the crew in all directions, and smashing the masts and vessel with such reality that the audience rose from their seats with enthusiasm, and the performers were unable to proceed until Mr T.H. Potter (Mr Emery's Stage-Manager), who was also one of the crew, came to the front to acknowledge the applause accorded to the scene. Fortunately, nobody was hurt beyond a severe shaking; and next morning the stage "shipcarpenters" were early at work to repair the vessel, which was ready for the following evening's voyage.
11/1/1880

AN incident occurred at the Theatre Royal, Manchester, on Monday, which shows to what wanton insults ladies of the Theatrical Profession are liable from blackguards with a little money in their pockets. In a scene where Miss Kate Lawlor and Miss Alice May are the only occupants of the stage, two contemptible snobs, who occupied one of the omnibus boxes, took the opportunity when Miss Lawlor was near of saying loud enough to be heard "Have a drink, Kitty." Miss Lawlor indignantly moved from the vicinity of the box, and cleverly altering the words of her part to suit the occasion, replied, "Ask those cads in that box." Of course, the management promptly and ignominiously ejected the fellows, and contemptuously returned their money. The audience showed their appreciation by loudly cheering the management, and hissing the cads as they disappeared.
18/1/1880

WANTED, PERSON who took Gong from Greenock on Fast Day, with Green Table-cloth, to return same at once, either by Daylight, Moonlight, or Lime-light, to prevent a new Light on case appearing in *The Era* next month.
25/1/1880

IN the Westminster County Court, on Wednesday last, Mr Judge Bayley and a Jury were occupied for a considerable time in trying the action "Chapman v. May," which was brought by a cooper's labourer at Crosse and Blackwell's, and said to be residing at 14, Lincoln's Inn Fields, where his wife was housekeeper, to recover from Mrs Samuel May, costumier, of Bow Street, the sum of £25 for personal injuries, loss of time, &c., alleged to have been caused through the negligence of the defendant's servants.

Alfred Chapman, the plaintiff, said that on October 28th he was passing down Castle Street, Long Acre, and, when opposite No. 36, where the defendant has a warehouse, he felt something fall on his head, and he was momentarily stunned and thrown against a gate. He was insensible for some time, and, on coming to his senses, he saw a box lying on the pavement, and a man in the defendant's employ took him to a tavern close by, and said, in the presence of the landlady, "I have let a box fall on this poor man's head, and I am afraid he is hurt." Witness was laid up for six weeks under the care of a doctor, and was still suffering from dizziness in the head, and also from the wounds in his head and knee. He was still out of work in consequence of the accident, and his average earnings were 35s. per week.

Dr John William Barnes said he attended the plaintiff for concussion of the brain and general shock to the system, and advised him to refrain from work for some time to come, and thought it possible that plaintiff might be suffering from the effects of the accident at that moment.

Robert Houghton, in defendant's employ, said that on the day in question he was lowering an "armour stand," or small empty box, into a truck which stood in the street in front of the warehouse. The "armour stand," so called, was simply a box with three sides, "crammed full of holes," after the fashion of the pedestals on which the men in armour stand in the great scene of *Les Cloches de Corneville*; and, seeing the plaintiff passing underneath, he pulled the rope with a "sudden jerk," and it broke. That caused the box to fall upon the plaintiff's head.

Seymour Stroud said he was engaged with the last witness in lowering the armour stands, and was on the pavement by the side of a hand-truck which was receiving the goods, when he saw the plaintiff approaching, and held up his hand to him and touched him on the shoulder to warn him, but he came on, and the box, which was about a foot or so above plaintiff's head, certainly slipped off the rope and struck the plaintiff.

His Honour having summed up the evidence to the Jury, they retired, and after an absence of about half-an-hour, returned with a verdict for plaintiff, damages £20, and his Honour allowed costs.
21/3/1880

EARLY visitors to the Globe Theatre on Saturday last must have been not a little astonished at the performance of the farce *Born to Good Luck*. "Born to bad luck" would have been more appropriate in this case as the title, for, although Mr Shiel Barry played with much humour as Paddy O'Raferty, not one of the other performers displayed either histrionic skill or even simple knowledge of their parts. So speedily did this become apparent to the audience that the performers were greeted with derision and the farce became a pantomime, the wildest confusion taking place. Even the scenery took part in the disorder, and, while one of the imperfect actors was painfully striving to collect his scattered wits, they were nearly driven out of his head by the sudden descent of a pole from the upper portion of the stage. It was a long pole, a strong pole, and a pole altogether, and it had to be broken in half in sight of the audience ere it could be removed, and then not without some damage to the wings. The laughter and jeering of the audience increased, until at length the curtain fell upon the most farcical performance of a farce we have ever seen. *4/4/1880*

AN accomplished orang-outan was lately exhibited at Munich which played the violin magnificently, and was particularly deft in executing "The Carnival of Venice." Its owner pocketed large profits at first, but one evening a doubtful spectator slyly gave the wonderful monkey a sharp cut with a penknife. The creature apparently did not feel the cut, so the visitor gave a vigorous pull at his tail, which suddenly came off, and brought with it part of the monkey's skin, displaying underneath a man, the father of the exhibitor of the animal prodigy, whose disguise had been so complete as to defy detection for a week.
11/4/1880

A NEW JULIET.
"Stalls Full, Boxes Full, Pit Full." Such were the announcements that met our gaze when we arrived at the Imperial Theatre on Thursday evening last. Sometimes such announcements are of a bogus character; but it was not so on this occasion. Every seat in the parts named seemed to have its occupant, and a little bit over. We had been favoured with two stalls, but desiring to fill one only we were not a little disconcerted to find ourselves packed between a stout lady with nerves and a middle-aged gentleman with elbows, both evidently determined to make us as uncomfortable as possible. And what came this vast crowd to see?

Well, the truth must be told. The rawest of raw amateurs, a young old lady, a pupil, we believe, of Mr Walter Lacy, inspired, we suppose, by her own vanity and by a belief in powers which did not exist, had refused to heed the kindly warnings of friends, and had undertaken to impersonate Juliet. The name of this daring damsel is Miss Ada Fellowes. Nature having blessed her with a good memory, she seems to have imagined that she was a born actress. Never was there a greater mistake. Barring the memory, Miss Fellowes possesses not even a microscopic bit of the stuff of which actresses are made, and, having said this, we suppose it is scarcely necessary to add that her qualifications for such a part as Juliet are absolutely *nil*. Juliet, like all her sex, is supposed to be beautiful; but there are degrees of beauty, and, as Miss Fellowes in this respect stands not very high in the scale, the fault is not her own, and it is one which we in all gallantry are disposed to pass over. Beauty does not rank, or rather ought not to rank, very high without brains; and, indeed, given the brains, we should not mind much if we had to dispense with beauty altogether. But who, we should like to know, can tolerate a Juliet who is without either commodity?

Far be it from us to say that Miss Fellowes has no brains at all. "Time was, that when the brains were out the man would die," says Shakespeare, and we suppose the same rule applied to women also. But then the possession of the proper quantity of the article is supposed to be productive of good sense and good judgement and good discretion, and where were these when Miss Fellowes determined to attempt a task in presence of which even genius might hesitate? Miss Fellowes has no genius; she has no soul; she has not even a voice. She invited ridicule, and she got it. A good deal of her Juliet was neither more nor less than dumb show.

This was more especially the case in the balcony scene. Even at the beginning of this she was, like the oft-quoted cow's tail – "all behind". It was whispered near us that, appalled by her own temerity, she had run away, so when Romeo was heard proclaiming that "Juliet is the sun," the sun had not risen, and was not visible. When it did show it did not shine. Miss Fellowes talked in whispers. Juliet was resolved that the Nurse should not hear her "goings on," and so both Romeo and the audience had great difficulty in knowing what she was talking about, and only the movement of her lips indicated that she was talking at all. Indeed Romeo – altogether well played by Mr Edgar – was so disconcerted by her want of ability that he was led to wish – not that he was a glove upon her hand, but upon her cheek. "Cheek" must have been running in his head as it was in the heads of everybody else – the "cheek" of the novice who was attempting a feat quite beyond her powers.

"Louder!" "Speak up!" "Turn it up!" were the cries which rose above the general titter prevailing during this scene. The friendly lady with the nerves – friendly, that is, to Miss Fellowes, but not to us –

thought she would really have to go out; she could not bear to look on, and to see rashness so ridiculed and vanity so condemned. The gentleman with the elbows laughed right out; and then, feeling a little ashamed of himself, seized his stout lady's opera-glass, and pretended to be very much interested in what was going on upon the stage. Approaching the famous bed-chamber scene, Miss Fellowes "played larks" with Juliet's dagger, upon which the holy friar – splendidly played by Mr John Ryder – had to keep a sharp eye in order to avoid personal injury. When the great scene was reached, there was more fun for the cruel audience, for Juliet certainly suggested a gaunt damsel afflicted with the toothache, and taking a dose of nasty physic before going to bed, with the hope of relief on the morrow.

But we are not disposed to pursue this subject further. We have been cruel only to be kind, for we are certain that it is kindness to tell Miss Fellowes, in terms that are unmistakable, that she is not fitted for the stage, and thus to attempt to dissuade her from courting derision. Mr F. Everill gave a very good rendering of the "saucy merchant" Mercutio, Mr Stephens made a satisfactory Paris, and Miss E. Miller was an excellent representative of the Nurse. The remainder engaged, like Juliet, were out of their element.
2/5/1880

AS two caravans of Sangers' new Circus entertainment, *Sea and Land*, were proceeding over Spon Lane railway bridge, West Bromwich, on Tuesday morning, the flag pole of the vessel in the last car caught the telegraph wires and started the horse off, causing the car to proceed down the incline at a terrific rate. Eventually it ran into the first caravan, which contained the band. This was overturned, and the seven occupants were thrown with great violence into a china shop. All are more or less injured, and three were taken to the hospital. Two are reported to be seriously hurt.
30/5/1880

ON Saturday evening, the 5th inst., an exciting and unrehearsed scene was enacted in the wooden building known as the Theatre of Varieties, Bolton. In consequence of the depression in trade the prices of admission have been reduced to the nominal charge of from one penny to fourpence, and, as there is a theatrical licence during the last few weeks, a dramatic company has been producing sensational pieces, the one selected for the Saturday referred to being *Robert Macaire; or, the French Jack Sheppard*. The penny seats having become uncomfortably crowded the occupants struggled to get into those reserved for the payers of twopence. The men in charge of the Theatre of course attempted to resist this intrusion. A youth name Foley, who was engaged on the staff, was called to assist in quelling the disturbance. Unfortunately he had in his possession a pistol loaded with powder and paper, which at the proper time he had to discharge in order to give suitable dramatic effect to the scene of *Robert Macaire*. Several of the roughs in the audience struck Foley, who, losing his temper, drew forth the "stage pistol" and threatened to shoot if they did not desist. This highly exasperated the audience, and a scene little short of a panic ensued, when a man named Atkinson struck the arm of Foley, and the pistol was discharged in the air without harming any one. Luckily at this moment the police arrived, and the disturbance was promptly quelled. The building is now closed.
13/6/1880

FROM a Dutch correspondent we learn a curious fact in connection with the famous Dutch company now playing in London. Some of the gentlemen belonging to the *troupe* appear to be amongst the most ardent of Holland's amateur bird fanciers. Hitherto, carriers have only been sent up by a Belgian club to London, and the birds have safely reached Antwerp; but the passage is considerably wider between London and Rotterdam. That passage has now been bravely accomplished by eight birds from the Rotterdam Telegraaf Pigeon Club; and the first prize, as well as the third, has fallen to Mr Keerwolf, the Dutch tragedian, who plays Govert, in *Anne-Mic*. The pigeons were let go on Westminster Bridge last Sunday at eight a.m., wind S.W. and sky clear. One of Mr Keerwolf's *doffers* (not a *duffer*, but a *male*

dove) reached Rotterdam at 2.47 p.m. Another of the competing birds got home by 3.51 p.m., as did Mr Keerwolf's female pigeon (*duif*).
20/6/1880

Novelty unequalled. World's greatest Wonder. ON HIRE, the Sacred Ox, RAJAH, born with an Arm, Hand, and Fingers. Full size and jointed to top of shoulder blade. Apply, J.R., West Bank, New Brighton.
27/6/1880

AMATEURS UNDER A CLOUD.
WHEN amateurs condescend to display their gifts to the vulgar crowd they in most cases give some reason for the act. Sometimes it is to introduce a new Juliet or a schoolboy Hamlet, but the general explanation of amateur performances is charity. Charity, that covers such a multitude of sins, is held accountable also for the sins and shortcomings of the host of novices cropping up from time to time, not merely at the outlying Halls and Concert Rooms of the suburbs, but even at our best Theatres. Consequently we felt little surprise at being invited on Wednesday afternoon to the Olympic Theatre to witness the efforts of as mild a *troupe* of amateurs as we have ever encountered in a London Theatre.

Why the amateurs played we could not discover. If for charity, the charity came badly off indeed; for when the curtain rose it was to an audience of forty-nine persons. True, one pretty little damsel in a private box was nursing a doll, but we suppose dolly does not count. Neither ought we, in compliment to the amateurs, to include an ancient tabby, who came to the steps of the stalls and looked round the empty – or nearly empty – house with the aspect of an ancient Manager speculating whether there would be people enough in the house to furnish Saturday's treasury. Nothing could be droller than the philosophical contentment of this long-tailed and four-footed spectator. Evidently puss was aware that the expenses of the house were already paid by the sanguine party just about to strut and fret their hour upon the stage. [...]

Since no other supposition is open to us, we can but come to the conclusion that the amateurs played because they had confidence in their own talents. We fear we must disabuse them, for, with a single exception, we have seldom seen worse acting. One of the aspirants, Mr Herbert Leonard, could not appear. He was, under the circumstances, to be congratulated; and, therefore, two of the characters had to be played by gentlemen who had not even rehearsed them. Oh! The belief of amateurs. Professional actors resign their parts rather than appear before the public without being fully prepared; but, of course, there is a royal road to the footlights known only to the amateur. "Acting is so easy, so simple. One has only to be natural, and speak a little louder than in the drawing room." [...]

The gentleman who played Mr Barker "without any rehearsal" was just what we expected he would be – thoroughly absurd and ridiculous. How could it be otherwise? He had not even the "gumption" to hold his tongue when memory failed him, but kept on, like a parrot, repeating the same word until, at last, in despair, he rushed to the prompter. Nothing more feeble could be imagined. Fortunately he played anonymously. [...] The gentleman who impersonated Mr Holloway "without even a rehearsal" trusted entirely to noise, ranting, stamping, and gesticulating instead of to acting, and a pretty mess he made of the whole affair. He had even put on his wig "without a rehearsal." In his anxiety to take time by the forelock he had left one of his own forelocks drooping over his manly brow, much in the style the caricaturists have depicted a certain Earl. But the appearance of this unknown actor was gentle and Arcadian compared with his extravagant demeanour. He was "out on the rampage" with a vengeance. When he had to throw himself upon the sofa he made a leap which overturned that homely article of domestic furniture, and there was the actor, heels in the air, kicking and struggling like a skater when the ice has broken amid the wreck of the sofa, which refused to stand upon its own legs any more after the rough treatment it had met with. The upholsterer will have to prescribe for that sofa, and it very likely that amputation of at least one leg will be necessary. Of tables, chairs, and other items of furniture we say nothing, but we hope the gentleman who played Joe Capsize, the cabman, feels no ill effects from the treatment he experienced on that terrible occasion. The "Unknown" clutched him by the throat, as Othello does Iago, and Mr Francis, the amateur, spoke thickly for some time after the grip he had received, and edged away when he saw his foe approaching again. Never did we see "a screaming farce" acted so thoroughly in keeping with that title. [...]

We have dealt at some length upon a performance quite worthless in itself, but showing what follies amateurs will commit when guided only by their vanity.
25/7/1880

AN extraordinary and terrible scene was witnessed in the Market Place, Leighton Buzzard, on Tuesday. A travelling Negro fire-eater was performing on a stand, licking red-hot iron, bending heated pokers with his naked foot, burning tow in his mouth, and the like, and at last filled his mouth with benzoline, saying that he would burn it as he allowed it to escape. He had no sooner applied a lighted match to his lips, however, than the whole mouthful of spirit took fire, and before it was consumed the man was burnt in a frightful manner, the fiery spirit running all over his face, neck, and chest. As he dashed from his stand and raced about like a madman among the assembled crowd, tearing his clothing from him and howling in most intense agony, a portion of the spirit was swallowed, and the inside of his mouth was also terribly burnt. He was taken into a chemist's shop, and oils were administered and applied; but afterwards in agonising frenzy he escaped in a state of nudity from a lodging-house, and was captured by the police and taken to the workhouse infirmary, where he remains in a dreadful condition.
15/8/1880

JAMES BILLINGS, aged eighteen, a waiter, was charged on Monday, at the Worship Street Police Court, with disorderly conduct and assaulting a beadle, in the Britannia Theatre, Hoxton, on Saturday, 28th ult. The defendant, who was in the gallery of the above Theatre, persisted in standing up, thus preventing persons who were seated behind him seeing the stage. On being remonstrated with he used obscene language, and offered to fight two young men near him. The beadle employed in the Theatre went up to the defendant and told him he would have to leave if he was not quiet, whereupon the defendant swore at him and struck him a violent blow in the face. He was with great difficulty got outside, disturbing a number of people as he was being removed. A constable who assisted in ejecting the defendant said his conduct was very violent. There had frequently been disturbances of this nature in the gallery of this Theatre of late. Mr Bushby said that visitors to places of public entertainment must be protected from this sort of disturbance. The defendant must pay a fine of 40s., or in default be imprisoned for fourteen days. The defendant, who had been laughing the whole time the evidence was given against him, said he would soon pay that.
5/9/1880

IT is really to be regretted that playgoers have not more consideration for *artistes* than to insist upon their repeating the same song or dance several times. In the new comic opera *Olivette*, on the night of its production, the lively dance called "The Farandole" was encored until the performers were compelled to resist the demand through sheer exhaustion. The voices and talents of *artistes* upon the stage are as much their capital and stock-in-trade as the goods kept by a tradesman, who would look rather blank if his customers demanded a double supply for a single payment.
26/9/1880

T. HOGINI Cautions Managers and Circus Proprietors not to encourage my APPRENTICE, run away July last from Southport. Two Years to serve. Would be sorry to put any Manager to any inconvenience. Must do so if they Engage him after this. T. HOGINI'S TROUPE still Performing with great Success at the ALEXANDRA PALACE, LONDON.
10/10/1880

WANTED, the Writer of the mean, scurrilous, and unsealed letter (dated from Sheffield), received by me at the Wear Music Hall, Sunderland, and who styles himself the Genuine Shot, to know that my Drama of "WINONA, THE SIOUX QUEEN" is the only Shooting Drama that has been Licensed since the Introduction into Parliament of the Dangerous Performances Bill. As the said Writer designates me a trickster, I hereby offer him or any other person a Reward of £100 who can prove upon good authority that I do not, or cannot, execute the following Backward Shots: –

Hitting a potato held by Miss Nevill lying upon my back and Shooting Backwards.
Cracking a small Hazel Nut with a Rifle Bullet Shooting Backwards.
Shooting an Apple from above the lady's head Shooting Backwards.
Shooting the Bowl off a Small Clay Pipe from above the lady's head, or from her mouth, by the Backward Shot.
Driving a Nail with a Rifle Bullet Shooting Backwards.

Breechloading Rifles, Ely's Bulletted Cartridges. N.B. – My reputation as a Rifle Expert rests solely upon my own skill and merit, and is not gained by ear-wigging Managers or Cackling to Audiences. At Liberty November 8th or 15th for Theatre or Music Hall. THEATRE ROYAL, SOUTH SHIELDS, November 1st, Six Nights. Birmingham, 22nd, Twelve Nights. Address, W.H. PATTERSON, T.R., South Shields.
31/10/1880

AN amusing end to a tragedy took place at the Music Hall, Lancaster, on Friday evening, October 29th. Mr E. Fletcher was playing Hamlet at the above Hall before a large and appreciative audience. The play went off in good style till the last scene, when Hamlet, who had to kill the King, stabbed that unfortunate monarch, and threw him back in his chair. But to the horror and surprise of the melancholy Dane, he saw the throne-chair on which lay the corpse of his guilty uncle slowly wheel to the edge of the platform on which it had been placed, and in an instant it toppled over, down went the King of Denmark on his head, up went the feet of the now struggling, living King, and vainly did the courtiers try to help him – he was wedged too fast in the chair. The audience roared with laughter, the actors chuckled, the musicians screamed. "Drop the curtain," said Hamlet. But the scene-shifter was far too much taken up with the joke to obey the summons, till at last the audience, breathless with laughter, saw the drop-scene fall on one of the most amusing episodes ever seen on the stage. After a short interval the curtain rose again, and Hamlet tried to regain the sympathy of the audience, but the ghost of the wicked King still cast his halo over the scene, and it was with a hard struggle Hamlet regained his composure, dying in the usual orthodox manner.
14/11/1880

INDEX

ACROBAT: dramatic suicide of in prison, 13

ACTOR: accidentally killed backstage at Covent Garden, 9; accused of twisting actresses' wrists, 50; almost drowns whilst on horseback, 68; declines to be hanged in reality, 40; dies during pantomime, 44; ejects drunken audience member in character as Hamlet, 15; impersonated by forger, 56; mauled by octopus, 25; neglects to learn lines, 69; over-enthusiastic as Romeo, 60; unable to remove stage handcuffs, 37; wedged in King's chair in *Hamlet*, 113

ACTORS: as pigeon fanciers, 110; attempt to save woman from police brutality, 42; force writer of insulting letter to apologise, 39; children of suffocated in travelling theatre, 94

ACTRESS: attempts to enter house by drawing-room window with fatal results, 87; commits suicide after row over luggage, 14; commits suicide under romantic circumstances, 65; defended by irate husband after mildly critical review, 105; dies after pantomime accident, 39; English claimed to be terribly defective, 31; fails as Fairy Queen *and* Juliet, 82; hit by falling timber, 25; injured by "vampire" trap, 31; kindness to old lady results in large inheritance, 23; nose misrepresented in cartoon, 6; sought by Mr Kettle, 4

ADVERTISING: new method delights Brummies, 16; photographs of lovely young men not useful as, 79

ALEXANDRA PALACE: fatal shooting accident, 92

AMATEUR ACTOR: accidentally breaks sofa on stage, 111; bizarre letter from hopeful Hamlet, 77; destroys fellow-amateur's eye, 31; invites ridicule and gets it, 109; wears spectacular moustache, 39

AMATEUR ACTORS: attempt to cadge free tickets, 8, 61; dismal performance of *Hamlet*, 74; in petticoats, 93; outraged by review, 28; prompted by audience, 36; targets of vegetable shower, 101

AUDIENCE MEMBER: behaviour results in fight on stage, 84; falls from gallery at York, 17; falls from gallery into pit via dress circle, 104; insists on smoking in theatre, 21; killed by falling pint pot, 17; leaps from gallery in suicide attempt, 38; smashes ginger-beer bottles, 26

AUDIENCE MEMBERS: eager to reach pub before closing time, 42; indulge in free-for-all fight in Plymouth theatre, 26

BALLET: need not be choked by coloured fire, 96; warmly appreciated by retired Major, 42

BALLET DANCER: half-starved in Amsterdam, 79

BALLET GIRLS: midnight rehearsals harmful to morals of, 80; must buy own shoes and dresses, 80

BALLOONIST: cannot be compared to huntsman, 52

BAND: accused of stealing baronet's wine, 24

BANDMANN, D.E. (actor): insulted by audience in Virginia, 13; lambasts critics who do not really attend performances, 24

BARNUM, P.T. (showman): has no interest in Welsh marionettes, 30; seeks lady chariot-drivers, 30

BECKWITH, Agnes (champion swimmer): swims twenty miles in the Thames, 89; seeks suitable venues, 91

BISMARCK, Count: should have used Rowland's Macassar Oil, 9

BOUQUET THROWER: professional, 85

CAMEL: mistaken for the Devil in Ireland, 17

CARPENTERS: almost crushed by own work, 12

CAT: held hostage by landlady, 79

CAT SHOW: attracts 20,000 visitors, 12

CHAMPAGNE: extortionate price of at theatre, 76

CHILD CLAIRVOYANTE: given obscene book, 77

CIRCUS GIRL: goes missing in Brighton, 84
CIRCUS PERFORMERS: thrown out of carriage into china shop, 110
CLOWN: assaults supernumerary after carrot fracas, 20; cuts off policeman's leg, 24; fractures man's skull in pub fight, 53; involved in dog-cart accident, 45
COLOURED FIRES: free from noxious ingredients, 44
COMEDIAN: provides poor newsboys with caps and socks, 106
CONJURER: causes anti-German commotion involving ducks, 10; impersonated by impostor, 75, 76
CRAB: played by Mr George Conquest in pantomime, 55
DANCER: burned by footlights, 5; objects to rival stealing arachnid theme, 11; suffers fatal burns in pantomime transformation scene, 58
DOG: interrupts own bath to save child from drowning, 22; killed by surfeit of rice pudding, 40; run over by train, 51
DWARF POLICEMAN: dies of apoplectic fit, 41
ELEPHANT: breaks into house, 67; life-size in india-rubber, 24; punishes tormentor, 43
ELEPHANTS: remove keys from piano, 106
EQUESTRIAN: fatally impaled by billiard cue, 73; goes insane in Birmingham, 88
FEMALE LOVELINESS: on the increase, 51
FAIRIES' WINGS: auctioned for a few pence each, 52
FAN: features helpful box plan of London theatres, 49
FANQUE, Pablo (circus proprietor): dies in Stockport, 12
FIRE-EATER: horribly burned at Leighton Buzzard, 112
FLAMBEAU: ignites actress' hair and actor's wig, 73
GAIETY THEATRE: has state-of-the-art telegraphic apparatus, 29
GAS SUPPLY: insufficient to illuminate *Antony and Cleopatra*, 28
GILBERT, W.S. (librettist): refuses to show railway season-ticket, 26; tormented by Italian organ-grinder, 55
GOATS: perform in opera, 88
GREAT VANCE: non-appearance of causes riot at Clonmel, 78
GUN: accidentally discharged in Covent Garden auditorium, 41
GYMNAST: effeminate-looking youth sought, 32; makes terrific leap at Hanley, 34
HATS: restrict view of stage, 50
HIGH-CHURCH CONGREGATION: mistaken for Japanese entertainers, 99
HORSE: dislikes Manchester Town Hall bells, 100
HORSES: take part in sledging scene, 104
INSANITY: effect of music upon, 85
LADY GODIVA: posters for burlesque version cause consternation in Gloucester, 38
LARD: stolen in sacks full of stale buns, 54
MECHANICAL MOUSTACHE: changes without using the hand, 22
MIMIC: fails to please in Bradford, 4
MONKEY: chases woman over fence, 23
MUSIC HALLS: accused of being "the parent of vice," 34; smutty songs at, 95
OFFENBACH, Jacques (composer): sculpted in ice cream, 64
OPERA COMPANY: subject of hoax at York, 10
ORAN-OUTANG: suspiciously proficient on violin, 109
ORGAN: vibration caused by smashes Dresden plate, 72
OXYHYDROGEN GAS: causes explosion at York theatre, 66
PANIC: at Bristol Theatre, 3
PANTOMIME: causes furore in Bradford, 9; elephant's back legs catch fire during performance, 71; free tickets given with one pound of tea, 73; may have "evil consequences" for pauper children, 45; shipwreck scene excessively realistic, 107
PARROTS: perform Bellini's opera *Norma*, 32
PEACE, Charles (criminal): son exhibits spectacles of and plays concertina on stage within weeks of father's execution, 98; waxwork representation of, 97
PIG: steals scene in Irish play, 99

POCKET SIMS REEVES: incapable of bilocation, 11
POTIPHAR (Old Testament character): smokes cigars in Jewish play, 46
PROPS: seized for non-payment of debt, 38
RAZOR: safe for the timid and nervous, 26
REINDEER: herd of for sale, 54
ROCK EAGLE: uninvited guest at actors' dinner, 51
ROPE CLIMBING: lady expert beats male challengers, 47
ROUSBY, Mrs (actress): kidnaps daughter from convent, 91; to burn or not to burn as Joan of Arc, 12
SANTLEY, Kate (actress): conspiracy to destroy career of, 32
SEAL: accidentally washed into drain, 99; presence of in on-stage tank resented by artistes in Grimsby, 94
SENSATION WIG: provokes roars of laughter, 15
SHEEP: highly-trained, 53; Royal children anxious about ultimate fate of panto performers, 30; stage career interrupted by birth of lamb, 45; use of in publicity stunt backfires, 58
SINGER: breaks bed in opera scene, 66; faulty diction leads to misheard lyrics, 78; has fatal fit in WC, 11; obliged to wear galoshes in *Il Barbiere di Siviglia*, 20; offended by indifference of audience, 98; suffers nosebleed on stage, 89
SINGERS: drowned in boating accident, 102; insistence on cab race ends up in court, 90
SIRES AND SONS FROM ALBION SPRUNG: startling new play, 75
SKATING (ice): at the Crystal Palace accompanied by fireworks, 44
SKATING (roller): 59, 60
SNAKES, escaped: terrorize inhabitants of Chelsea, 22
SNORING: causes nuisance at French play, 19
SNOW SCENES: have cooling effect in hot weather, 65
STARCH: fire-proof, 22
STUDENT: theft leads to untimely death of, 7
STUDENTS: riot in Glasgow theatre, 69
SULLIVAN, Barry (actor): admirers almost suffocate in Birmingham theatre, 14
THEATRE ROYAL, Stratford-upon-Avon: no longer an eyesore, 21
THEATRICAL AGENT: bogus, 71; tormented by bedbugs, 41
THEATRICAL COMPANY: drowned off Australia, 92
THEATRICAL REPORTER: assaulted by actress' husband, 36
TREATS: thrust upon pauper children, 18
TICKLING: leads to leg amputation and death, 27
TROTTERS (pig's feet): thrown at theatre's gas globes, 46
TURKISH GENTLEMEN: impersonated by members of Crichton Club, 86
UMBRELLA, dropped from gallery: causes three men to fall to ground floor, 100
VELOCIPEDE: ridden recklessly and furiously, 5
WAINRATTA (high-wire walker): removes trousers on wire, 94
WINONA, THE SIOUX QUEEN: indignantly defended by sharpshooter W.H. Patterson, 113

ABOUT THE AUTHOR

Julia D Atkinson was born in Bradford, West Yorkshire, in 1960. She was formerly a critic for the British Theatre Guide. Her ground-breaking article *A name not just now familiar to ears polite:* The Importance of Being Earnest *and* Lady Windermere's Fan *on tour, 1895-1900*, was published in the July 2015 issue of *The Wildean: a Journal of Oscar Wilde Studies.* She now lives in York.

Also available from the same author in this series:

Please Throw Two Carrots at Your Mother: Comic and Curious Clippings from the Legendary Theatrical Paper The Era, *1880-1890*
Fairies in Cabs: Comic and Curious Clippings from the Legendary Theatrical Paper The Era, *1890-1900*
Crocodiles in the Green Room: Comic and Curious Clippings from the Legendary Theatrical Paper The Era, *1900-1910*

A COMPLETE SOMERSAULT INTO THE ORCHESTRA

www.ingramcontent.com/pod-product-compliance
Lightning Source LLC
Chambersburg PA
CBHW081457070526
44586CB00019B/2404